AVERY DULLES

AVERY DULLES

Essential Writings from America Magazine

EDITED BY JAMES T. KEANE

Christian Classics ❖ *Notre Dame, Indiana*

© 2019 by America Media, Inc.

All rights reserved. No part of this book may be used or reproduced in any manner whatsoever except in the case of reprints in the context of reviews, without written permission from Christian Classics™, Ave Maria Press®, Inc., P.O. Box 428, Notre Dame, IN 46556, 1-800-282-1865.

Founded in 1865, Ave Maria Press is a ministry of the United States Province of Holy Cross.

www.christian-classics.com

Paperback: ISBN-13 978-0-87061-315-9

E-book: ISBN-13 978-0-87061-316-6

Cover image © Joseph Lawton.

Cover and text design by Andy Wagoner.

Printed and bound in the United States of America.

Library of Congress Cataloging-in-Publication Data

Names: Dulles, Avery, 1918-2008, author. ǀ Keane, James Thomas, editor. ǀ America Media (Firm : New York, N.Y.), compiler.

Title: Avery Dulles : essential writings from America magazine / Avery Dulles ; edited by James T. Keane.

Description: Notre Dame, Indiana : Christian Classics, [2019]. ǀ Summary: "Avery Dulles, published in partnership with America Media collects the essential writings of one of America's leading Catholic theologians of the twentieth century. This collection includes occasional and formal writings, book reviews, in memoriam pieces, reflections, and extended essays and highlights Dulles's wide-ranging interests in ecclesiology, salvation history, pastoral theology, and contemporary literature, as well as the Jesuit's warm personality and astute insights on the Church in an era of great change"-- Provided by publisher.

Identifiers: LCCN 2019022998 (print) ǀ LCCN 2019022999 (ebook) ǀ ISBN 9780870613159 (paperback) ǀ ISBN 9780870613166 (ebook)

Subjects: LCSH: Dulles, Avery, 1918-2008. ǀ Catholic Church--United States--History--20th century. ǀ Jesuits--United States--Biography. ǀ America (New York, N.Y. : 1909) ǀ Theology--United States--History--20th century.

Classification: LCC BX1406.3 .D85 2019 (print) ǀ LCC BX1406.3 (ebook) ǀ DDC 230/.2--dc23

LC record available at https://lccn.loc.gov/2019022998

LC ebook record available at https://lccn.loc.gov/2019022999

CONTENTS

LECTURES AND ADDRESSES

BOOK REVIEWS

APPRECIATIONS

AN INTERVIEW

EDITOR'S PREFACE

The first appearance of Avery Dulles, S.J., in the pages of *America* was not for a bylined article. Rather, he was named in the issue of September 28, 1946, in an advertisement from the publishing house Sheed & Ward:

> We have a good first word, too, from a young man—Avery Dulles—now in the Jesuit Novitiate. His was no long road home, but as he says "short and steep." He came to the Church from complete agnosticism while he was at Harvard, and his book is well-named: *A Testimonial to Grace* ($1.50). It is instructive, almost amusing, to see how patiently and firmly the Holy Ghost led him, and the good will and bewilderment with which he allowed himself to be led has something oddly touching about it. If anything can help us to know what to say to young and intelligent agnostics, we think it is this book.

The advertisement turned out to be prescient: twenty-two more books would flow from Avery's pen over the next six decades. Even more prolific was his writing for *America*, where his work appeared countless times in the form of theological essays, book reviews, explainers, reports, and more. For the first time in this volume, the best of those writings for *America* are gathered together in one place. The reader will see Avery Dulles, S.J., grapple with many of the same issues he addressed in his seminal books; over the course of this volume, one can also see his thoughts develop and gain nuance and depth on various theological and social issues. At the same time, many of the characteristics for which he was best known are present throughout: inquisitive and rigorous analysis, charitable treatments of opposing viewpoints, insightful synthesis, and careful parsing of complicated issues for the sake of the general reader.

We wrestled with how to present this material: sixty years of writings makes for a lot of text! Ultimately, instead of a chronological approach, we chose to present his writings by genre (though chronologically within each category). Those genres are "Reports and Reflections" (fourteen articles), "Lectures and Addresses" (fifteen articles), "Book Reviews" (seven articles), "Appreciations" (two articles), and finally one "Interview" (with Fr. James Martin, S.J., whose moving introduction to the life and work of Avery Dulles, S.J., follows this preface).

We have left all the scripture quotes in the various pieces intact: some are drawn from translations popular in the twentieth century, while others synthesize pieces of multiple translations—likely Dulles was quoting from memory.

Fr. Joseph A. O'Hare, S.J., former editor in chief of *America* and former president of Fordham University, gave the homily at Avery's funeral in St. Patrick's Cathedral in New York on December 17, 2008. His words on that day offer a succinct description not just of the theological work of Cardinal Avery Dulles, S.J., but also of what we hope this book offers to readers:

> Through his extraordinary gifts of insight and expression, he has left us a guide to his own personal pilgrimage that can enlighten the search of others, whether they are men and women of faith, seeking understanding, or citizens of the academy, where understanding is often searching for faith.

I am grateful for the assistance of Sean Connelly, who was of enormous help in gathering this material from *America*'s archives. We are also honored to collaborate on this volume with Ave Maria Press and are grateful for the hard work of everyone there, especially Catherine Owers. We hope and expect this book will continue to promulgate the enlightening wisdom of a profound theologian and a great soul.

James T. Keane
Senior editor, America Media

CARDINAL, JESUIT, PRIEST, THEOLOGIAN, TEACHER, WRITER, FRIEND:

An Introduction

by James Martin, S.J.

Cardinal Avery Dulles, S.J., was recognized in life and honored in death for many things. Scholars and intellectuals might point to his brilliant theological works, which, over many decades, helped the Catholic Church to navigate the sea changes in both teaching and practice that followed the Second Vatican Council. Bishops and pastors might point to his instinctive desire, so clear in his writings and lectures, always to seek consensus and synthesis rather than division, so that Jesus' words "that all may be one" might be fulfilled. Historians might point to the significance of the scion of one of America's most prominent Protestant establishment families not only converting to Catholicism but also joining perhaps its most prominent (some might say notorious) religious order and, at the end of his long and productive life, being named ("created" is the official term) a cardinal.

It's easy to see how someone could remember Cardinal Avery Dulles, S.J., in any or all of those ways: they are certainly all true. But I remember him more simply—as a humble, holy, and faithful brother in Christ. It was an honor to be a Jesuit with Avery and always a pleasure too. I am grateful for his scholarship, his leadership, and his inspiring example, but I am most grateful to have had him as a friend and a brother. We Jesuits knew him as undoubtedly learned and accomplished but also modest, hardworking, and, something that often surprises people, possessed of a martini-dry sense of humor.

One of my favorite of his jokes came when a fellow Jesuit mentioned a quote from St. John Berchmans, S.J., a seventeenth-century Jesuit who died in his twenties and was renowned for his holiness. Most Jesuits today know him best for his comment about his apparently long-suffering life in a Jesuit community: "Life in community is my greatest penance."

To which Avery responded, in his trademark growl, "Well, I wonder what the community thought about *him!*"

But before any further personal reminiscences, a brief biography of the great man.

Avery Dulles was born on August 24, 1918, and baptized a Presbyterian shortly thereafter. His family was prominent in politics and society, and would become more so in the following decades. His father, John Foster Dulles, later served as secretary of state under President Dwight D. Eisenhower (one of three members of the Dulles family to serve as secretary of state). Avery's uncle, Allen Dulles, was the director of the Central Intelligence Agency from 1952 until 1961. His aunt Eleanor Lansing Dulles oversaw the aid program to West Berlin and West Germany in the aftermath of World War II. Avery himself once wryly commented on the awkwardness of some of his visits to Washington, D.C., as a cardinal of the Catholic Church—perhaps the only one who ever flew into an airport named after his own father!

As an aside, Avery was often playfully teased by his Jesuit confreres about his famous name. Once, while visiting Georgetown University, in Washington, D.C., he had to ask a fellow Jesuit for a ride to that airport. But Avery, ever humble, studiously avoided saying the name.

"Which one?" said the Jesuit, trying to get him to utter the word. "National Airport?"

"The *other* one!" said Avery.

Avery attended the prestigious Choate School in Wallingford, Connecticut, before enrolling at Harvard University. In later years he would recall that he was once nearly expelled after he and two friends went joyriding in a cab near Harvard Square. Avery managed to convince Harvard's dons that he was a good enough student that there might be a chance at rehabilitation.

While at Choate, Avery had, in essence, lost his Christian faith and considered himself an agnostic during his early years at Harvard. However, his studies in literature and history soon forced him to confront serious questions about God and belief—not least because his studies included a heavy dose of medieval philosophy, a comprehensive system of intellectual thought in which theology, the study of God, was elevated as "the queen of the sciences."

During his junior year, he had a conversion experience of sorts, albeit of a bit more intellectual bent than most. He later wrote of an experience he had while on a study break, walking out of Harvard's library and along the Charles River:

> As I wandered aimlessly, something prompted me to look contemplatively at a young tree. On its frail, supple branches were young buds. . . . While my eye rested on them, the thought came to me suddenly, with all the strength and novelty of a revelation, that these little buds in their innocence and meekness followed a rule, a law of which I as yet knew nothing. . . . That night, for the first time in years, I prayed.

When I first read these lines in his moving memoir *A Testimonial to Grace*, I marveled that the conversion of a theologian whose work was often considered (unfairly) as dry and whose personality was often considered (unfairly) as the quintessence of rationality was initially influenced not only by the recognition of a "rule," but also by something as romantic as the sight of a young tree in bloom.

Soon after his graduation from Harvard in 1940, Avery Dulles was received into the Catholic Church. Many years later, a reporter wrote that he had described that moment as "the high point of my life." Ever precise, Avery corrected the record: "I don't believe I ever said that. I did say that the decision to become a Catholic was the best decision I ever made. But it was a beginning rather than a climax." He then enrolled in Harvard Law School, but a more momentous event took precedence: the entrance of the United States into World War II a year later. Avery served in the navy as a lieutenant and was awarded the *Croix de Guerre* by the French government. He planned to enter the Jesuits after his navy commission was completed.

Just before his service ended, however, Avery contracted polio at a naval base near Naples, Italy. Because the Society of Jesus had strict rules about accepting candidates with physical handicaps, acceptance was far from a sure thing. Avery later remembered that he arranged for part of his physical rehabilitation to be done at an outpatient center connected with the Boston Navy Yard. Why? So that the Jesuits wouldn't see that the return address on his application materials was a hospital.

It worked. He entered the Jesuit novitiate in the fall of 1946 and pronounced his "first vows" of poverty, chastity, and obedience two years later. After three years studying philosophy, two more teaching undergraduates at Fordham University in the Bronx, and three more years of theology study, he was ordained a Catholic priest at Fordham on June 16, 1956. One can assume Fordham had never seen such a proliferation of Presbyterians— or secret service agents—in its chapel before or since! He did one more year of theology studies after ordination and then was sent to West Germany in 1957 to do "tertianship," a year of spiritual formation that Jesuits undertake before taking "final vows" in the order.

Avery's intellectual acumen was already well known, and the Jesuits sent him to "the Greg," the Pontifical Gregorian University in Rome, for two more years of study in academic theology.

Finishing his studies in 1960 and returning to the United States, Avery no doubt expected to spend the next forty years or so teaching theology at one of the many Jesuit colleges and universities in the United States, or perhaps instructing young Jesuits in theology (all in Latin, naturally).

But Vatican II arrived, along with significant and often tumultuous changes in the Catholic Church and society as a whole. Avery served as a teacher of young Jesuits at Woodstock College, a seminary in Maryland, throughout Vatican II and the wild and woolly days after, but it became clear in the 1970s that he had been paying close attention to all the theological and philosophical developments of the time. In 1974, he moved from Woodstock to the Catholic University of America and at the same time published *Models of the Church*, a groundbreaking work of theology that is still used in many seminaries today.

In *Models of the Church*, Avery presented a number of different intellectual and theological frameworks for understanding what the Church is and isn't. Is the Catholic Church an "institution"? A "mystical communion"? A "sacrament"? A "herald"? A "servant"? The answer to all five questions (he later added a sixth, a "community of disciples") was both yes and no, because each model had its strengths and weaknesses.

What was going on theologically beneath the surface was perhaps more important than the assertions on the page, however. What Avery Dulles was suggesting in his presentation of these models was that none of them was a complete and accurate depiction of the Church. The Body of Christ, he was gently suggesting, is always more than any model and is not contained in any one schema, and many different ways of understanding the Church are valid and viable. As Patrick Ryan, S.J., a former student and longtime colleague of Avery Dulles, wrote in *America*, "Avery worked within Catholic circles and also ecumenically to reconcile opposing ideas and work out new syntheses, especially of theological thought." All of us, in Avery Dulles's way of thinking, have a lot to learn from each other.

In 1988, Avery left Catholic University to become the Laurence J. McGinley Professor of Religion and Society at Fordham
University, a post he would hold until his death in 2008. In the
coming years, he wrote a number of other significant theological works, including twenty-one other books. Most well-known
are *Models of Revelation* in 1983 and *The Assurance of Things Hoped
For: A Theology of Christian Faith* in 1994. He also published more
than seven hundred theological reflections for other journals,
most often in *America* and *First Things*. He regularly stressed the
importance of finding multiple convergences among theological viewpoints and the necessity of giving different theological
points of view a fair hearing, making him a voice of moderation
and reconciliation in the world of academic theology, one sometimes riven by ideological and intellectual strife.

In an interview for *America* at the time of Avery's being
named a cardinal in 2001, I asked him about the role of the theologian in today's increasingly secular world. In response, Avery
subtly answered the common observation that he had developed
a more "traditional" outlook in his later years:

> The theologian is always trying to see how the tradition of the
> church can be adapted to speak to contemporary culture. But
> speaking to the culture does not necessarily mean embracing
> the dominant presumptions of the culture. These presump-
> tions have to be scrutinized, accepting what is good and reject-
> ing what is bad. . . .
>
> From my own knowledge of church history, I would judge
> that the principal errors occurred when the church has adapted
> too much to the culture, reflecting the prevailing values of the
> culture and tending to obscure the distinctiveness of the Gos-
> pel. So the task of the theologian is to be very critical, to use
> in some cases what St. Ignatius would call *agere contra*. Where
> one sees a tendency to move in a certain direction that is con-
> trary to the Gospel, Ignatius would say, move in the opposite
> direction. Throughout my career I have tended to be critical of

what I saw as the principal dangers of the day. Sometimes the danger was to be insufficiently open and to adhere too strongly to past traditions, forms, and ways of behaving. The opposite danger confronts us today in thinking that everything is up for grabs. We have to be careful to insist on what is permanently and universally true. That is what I have been trying to accent in my recent work.

In addition to his academic and intellectual work, Avery Dulles also offered his services to academia in other ways. He was president of the Catholic Theological Society of America as well as the American Theological Society, and he also served on the International Theological Commission.

In 2001, Pope John Paul II announced that Dulles would be made a cardinal of the Church. Because cardinals were traditionally also ordained bishops, there was a slight problem. Jesuits make a promise when they take their final vows never to "strive for or ambition" for high offices in the Church, and they are expected to decline ordination to the episcopacy. (St. Ignatius Loyola, the founder of the Jesuits, took a dim view of what is called "ambitioning.") But no one suspected Avery of ambitioning. The problem was more practical: Avery was advanced in years, and the prospect of perhaps the country's most well-known Catholic theologian, whose schedule would already tax someone half his age, now being called upon to preside at ordinations and confirmations around the country seemed daunting.

Therefore, the pope granted Dulles a dispensation: he would be named a cardinal but could remain a priest.

He came home from the ceremony in Rome the same old Avery, staying in community at Spellman Hall with other Jesuits and living the life of a spare academic. His ecclesiastical honors never, ever went to his head, and he was just "one of Ours," as we say, in chapel, at table, in the rec room, and in the classroom. His Jesuit brothers did discreetly arrange for one honor, but it was for the safety of Fordham's students and the residents of the Bronx: they tried whenever possible to provide him with a driver. (Avery was, for all his experience and acumen, probably the worst driver in U.S. Jesuit history.)

Throughout, Avery also continued to teach. Though he was modest about his own teaching abilities (in recognition of his own somewhat deadpan teaching style, he once described himself as "Dull, Duller, Dulles"), nearly all of his students remember his classes with fondness and deep appreciation. "Avery had no special techniques as a teacher in a classroom. He simply stood at the podium and talked. To be frank, he sometimes droned, occasionally writing a word or two on the blackboard," Fr. Patrick Ryan, S.J., noted in *America*. "His only gestures were made with his left hand, pulling at a non-existent beard or gesturing downwards in the general direction of hell. Somehow I found it mesmerizing. He had so much to say, so many thoughts to provoke."

Avery also told me that he felt an increased responsibility to accept invitations to lecture, no matter how inconvenient. It was part of being a cardinal, he felt. Another prominent Catholic writer told me how he had once turned down an invitation to a student group in a small college in a far-flung town, only to open a newspaper months later and see a photo of his replacement: Avery Cardinal Dulles, who was seated amid a group of smiling undergraduates.

On a personal level, I was also always grateful to Avery for his willingness to offer sage advice. In his later years he was often identified, at least within Catholic theological circles, with a certain traditionalist element in the Catholic Church, but in my experience he always remained a great synthesizer, a great listener who remained open to new ideas and perspectives.

Of course every Jesuit knew of him and admired him. Though Jesuits are supposed to pray for humility, we were all very, very proud of Avery.

I first came to know him when I wrote a book called *In Good Company*, about my entrance into the Society of Jesus. My publisher suggested my sending it to Avery for an endorsement, which I did, sheepishly. In response to my letter (in pre-email days), I received not only a generous "blurb" but also a neatly typed, two-page summary of the typos and errors (theological and otherwise) in my manuscript. Avery noted, for example, that in describing the stained-glass windows at Campion Renewal Center, a Jesuit retreat house outside of Boston, I had mistakenly characterized them as depicting the traditional "gifts of the Holy Spirit." No, wrote Avery, they are the "fruits of the Holy Spirit."

I confessed to a fellow Jesuit that I felt like an idiot for missing something so basic.

"That's pretty expensive theological advice you're receiving," he said.

Nonetheless, Avery reviewed almost every one of my books for theological soundness from then on until his death. I was exceedingly grateful.

A few years later, when my book *My Life with the Saints* raised a thorny theological point, I didn't want simply to forge ahead, so I asked my boss at the time, the editor in chief of *America*, Fr. Thomas Reese, S.J., what he thought.

"Why don't you send it to Avery?" he suggested. "He'll give it a fair read."

He did a lot more than that; I got back not just Avery's unofficial imprimatur but also, in a long meeting in his office, some wise counsel about the theological issue at hand.

In 2001, a few months after Avery was named a cardinal, the New England Province of the Society of Jesus (of which I was a member) decided to give Avery its highest accolade: the *Ad Majorem Dei Gloriam* Award ("For the Greater Glory of God," a phrase taken from St. Ignatius's writings). My interview with Avery had appeared not long before, and my Jesuit superiors in Boston, under the misapprehension that I was Avery's close friend, asked me to ask him if he would receive it.

When I called him the next day, Avery said, "Do I have to give a long speech?" I said no, not as far as I knew.

He laughed. "Then I accept!"

And he rang off with his traditional farewell, doubtless learned during his navy days: "Over and out!"

When I called my provincial to tell him the good news, he asked if I might accompany Avery to Boston. I said that I would.

So one day in October I showed up at Spellman Hall, the Jesuit community in which Avery lived on Fordham's campus. The most famous—and decidedly not apocryphal—story among Jesuits about Avery came after he moved into Spellman and concerns laundry. And it must first be said that the tale is not surprising for someone who had lived in "institutional communities" from his time in the navy to his time as a Jesuit, where hundreds of men with only a few items of clothing to their name threw them in a bin for "Brother Launderer" when they needed cleaning. In any event, one day Avery knocked on someone's door at Spellman Hall and asked for help with his laundry. The Jesuit followed Avery down the hallway, down the staircase, and then, puzzlingly, into the kitchen. Avery opened the dishwasher, pulled out the rack, and asked where the clothes went. No one laughed harder at that story than Avery.

We had a brief but hair-raising car ride from Spellman Hall to the Fordham train station, where he deposited his car, and made our way to Penn Station and boarded the train to Boston, where the talk was scheduled. Avery worked the entire train ride up, marking a manuscript of a new book, at one point asking me to look it over. "Avery," I said, "I'm not a theologian."

"But you're a writer. See what you think."

Before the awards dinner, he asked me to help him on with his (still-new) cardinal's cassock, cape and cap (technically *ferraiolo* and *zucchetto*), and pectoral cross. I had to kneel down to reach the bottom buttons on his cassock. Then he said, "Is this cross facing the right way?" I admitted that I had no idea.

He said, "Well, I have no idea either."

Then he spread his arms, smiled, and said, "How do I look?" Looking at his tall frame and lined but distinguished face, I wanted to say what many people often remarked: "You look like Cardinal Abraham Lincoln."

Instead I said, "As my mother would say, 'You look very handsome.'"

The dinner was only a few weeks after the September 11 attacks and so Avery was asked to offer some words on hope. His clear and direct words brought the audience to a hush:

> Our hopes tend to fade whenever we cease to be in control. For the moment we Americans seem to have lost control of our destiny. We are afraid because our future does not rest in our own hands. On September 11 two great symbols of our security collapsed, or at least suffered grave damage. The World Trade Center towers looked very solid, as did the walls of the Pentagon, but both proved to be paper thin. The growing likelihood of biological warfare raises our anxiety yet further. Not only our wealth and military power, but also our health is at risk.
>
> It will be for others to address the economic, military, and medical problems. As a theologian, I have to recognize that Christian hope never rests on material things. As individuals we try to follow the teaching of Jesus, who reminds us that rust corrodes, moths consume, and thieves break in and steal. Jesus instructs us to build treasure in heaven, the one bank that can never fail. The only thing that counts in the end is whether or not we hear the greeting of the Lord, "Well done, you good and faithful servant."
>
> Jesus Christ is not only the personal hope for each one of us. He is also the hope of the world. If the world turns away from Him, it goes terribly astray. The pursuit of riches produces massive poverty; the pursuit of freedom begets slavery; and the pursuit of peace ends in destructive violence. But with the strength and generosity that comes from the Lord we can take part in building here on earth what the liturgy calls

"a kingdom of truth and life, of holiness and grace, of justice, love, and peace."

As I reflect on the past half century and more, I am immensely grateful for my vocation to share in the apostolate of the Society of Jesus. As Jesuits, we are dedicated to the gospel of hope. We seek to place our own hope in God alone and to help others to focus their hopes on Him. This apostolate of hope is immensely relevant today, when many people are on the brink of discouragement and despair. But you, at least, are not. Seeing so many of you at this dinner, I am reminded that we Jesuits could achieve nothing without friends such as yourselves, who support our work and do it with us. You are as important to our work as any Jesuit is. Whatever the future holds, we can only be assured of this: that nothing we do together in the service of the Lord will be done in vain.

Afterward, Avery asked what time we should leave for New York the following day. Not wanting to tire him out, I suggested we leave around 10:00 a.m. I had forgotten about his famous Protestant work ethic. A look of surprise registered on his patrician face, and he said, "Ten a.m.? That's a waste of a morning. Let's leave as early as we can." We boarded an 8:00 a.m. train, and he worked the entire way to New York.

The symptoms of the poliomyelitis Avery Dulles had contracted six decades before began to return in the final years of his life, eventually limiting his movements and finally his speech. One of the most moving moments of my Jesuit life was Avery's final McGinley lecture, delivered at Fordham University's Rose Hill campus in the Bronx on April 1, 2008. Rendered almost mute by that point, Avery had asked Fr. Joseph O'Hare, S.J., the former president of Fordham University and a longtime friend, to read his final lecture aloud. We all—Joe O'Hare included—choked up at these words:

> Suffering and diminishment are not the greatest of evils, but are normal ingredients in life, especially in old age. They are to be accepted as elements of a full human existence. Well into my ninetieth year I have been able to work productively. As I become increasingly paralyzed and unable to speak, I can identify with the many paralytic and mute persons in the Gospels, grateful for the loving and skillful care I receive and for the hope of everlasting life in Christ. If the Lord now calls me to a period of weakness, I know well that his power can be made perfect in infirmity.

When Avery went to offer the audience his blessing, he couldn't raise his right arm by itself. Undaunted, he reached across his body with his left hand, picked up his right hand, and made the Sign of the Cross that way. Not a dry eye in that house.

After Avery died that December, his funeral mass was celebrated in St. Patrick's Cathedral—a beautiful and moving liturgy presided over by Cardinal Edward Egan, archbishop of New York, which featured many prelates of the Church and public dignitaries as well as thousands of the faithful who came to pay their respects to the deceased cardinal. When his coffin was carried out onto Fifth Avenue, the crowd burst into applause.

Not long afterward, Avery was buried with his Jesuit brothers at the cemetery in Auriesville, New York.

A week later at Fordham in the Bronx, Joseph O'Hare, S.J., former president of the university, gave the homily at another Mass for the repose of Avery's soul. His inspired words that day included this apt mention of an important part of Avery's own faith life:

> I have often reflected on the motto Avery chose for his coat of arms when he became a Cardinal: *Scio cui credidi*. I know in whom I believed. Avery's fidelity to the truth of Catholic tradition, what he believed, was rooted in his deep and confident trust in the one in whom he believed, the ultimate source of

that tradition, Our Lord and Savior Jesus Christ, who now has welcomed him to everlasting life.

Those words are perhaps the most appropriate ones with which to end this brief introduction and invite you, the reader, to begin to appreciate Avery's remarkable works and deeds in the rest of this book.

Rest in peace, Avery, with the One in whom you always believed.

REPORTS
AND
REFLECTIONS

1. THE COUNCIL AND THE SOURCES OF REVELATION

December 1, 1962

There are few decisions more delicate or fraught with consequences for the Christian life than those pertaining to the nature of revelation and the sources of Christian doctrine. Now that the Second Vatican Council turns its attention to these issues, Catholics the world over should intensify their prayers that the Spirit of Truth may so guide the assembled Fathers that their determinations will not merely be free from error—this we can presume—but will positively serve the needs of the apostolate in our time.

One question which had inevitably to come before the Fathers concerns the relationship between scripture and tradition. According to the Council of Trent, the Christian revelation is "contained in written books and in unwritten traditions which . . . have come down to us." This decree unquestionably settled the divine authority of both the inspired scriptures and of nonscriptural tradition. But it is highly doubtful that the council meant to define the relationship between these two authoritative sources. Many Catholic theologians today hold that Trent deliberately refrained from pronouncing on the further question whether there are any dogmas of faith contained, not in the Bible, but only in tradition.

The modern Catholic, thinking of certain doctrines such as the Immaculate Conception and the assumption of the Blessed Virgin, is normally inclined to imagine that they must have been handed down from the earliest times by oral tradition alone. But this assumption, on reflection, appears rather naive. Is it historically probable that any Christian of the first three centuries, if asked about the matter, would have been able to form a clear idea of what is meant by the Immaculate Conception? The doctrine depends for its intelligibility on various points concerning original sin and redemption which were not clarified until much later. And even if we allow the hypothesis that the early popes and bishops explicitly believed in these doctrines, their views can hardly be regarded as the true source for the Church's recent dogmatic affirmations. For this to be the case there would have to be reliable historical testimonies from the earliest period, which are in fact lacking.

For reasons such as these, some Catholic theologians hold that many modern dogmas, while truly belonging to the primitive Christian tradition, were originally held only in a global and implicit form. In this view, it is quite probable that these truths were no more explicitly affirmed in apostolic tradition than they are in the Bible itself. Some would say that these doctrines are in scripture, not according to its obvious literal meaning, but in some deeper or fuller sense—a sense gradually discerned by the Church as it prayerfully ponders on the word committed to it. If this be true, there is no cogent reason for contending that there are "more truths" contained in apostolic tradition than in the inspired scriptures.

Some would object at this point. There is at least one defined doctrine evidently not found in the Bible itself, namely, the canon or authoritative catalog of the inspired books. But even this is not so obvious. As we study the history of the canon, it becomes apparent that the Church, in drawing up the catalog of sacred books, does not seem to have relied primarily on explicit testimonies to their inspiration handed down from apostolic times. To a great extent, the question of canonicity appears to have been settled by the Church's sense of the quality of the books themselves. This was perhaps the decisive factor in overcoming hesitations that had lasted in some cases (e.g., for Hebrews, James, and 2 Peter) for several centuries. Thus Catholics need not totally reject the view, widely held among the Protestants in our time, that the Holy Scriptures manifested themselves to the Church as inspired.

Questions such as these are highly involved. There is much to be said on both sides, and no one can presently predict what, if anything, the council is likely to say. Very likely, the Fathers will settle only what is most essential, not going appreciably beyond what has been said by earlier councils, but leaving Catholic theologians the liberty and responsibility to work out the finer technicalities. A decree that undertook to decide more than has presently become clear to the consciousness of the Church would not in fact advance matters. It would provide only an apparent solution.

A second great problem which the council may take up has to do with the application of modern tools of scholarship to the study of the Holy Scriptures. Many popes since Leo XIII have lent their support to this endeavor; they have encouraged Catholic biblicists to take full advantage of all the techniques afforded by present-day archeology, linguistics, and literary analysis. But in recent years there has been a rather outspoken minority who feel that this approach is dangerous and unsound. Fear is expressed that such scrutiny of the holy books may end up by casting doubt upon their historical accuracy.

This apprehension is rarely if ever felt by Catholic scripture scholars who have become accustomed to the new approach. On the contrary, they quite unanimously declare that their scientific formation makes them better able to appreciate the degree and kind of historicity with which God evidently wished to endow his inspired Word. They are convinced that the type of historical truth contained in the Bible cannot be adequately judged by modern and Western norms without reference to ancient Hebrew literary conventions. The encyclical *Divino Afflante Spiritu* (1943) encouraged Catholic exegetes to go about their task without fear of molestation from those whose piety was less sophisticated.

The biblical scholars as a group are hopeful that the Second Vatican Council will ratify and underscore the charter already given, in less solemn form, by the encyclical of 1943. It is urgent, they feel, for the Church to state in clear terms that it wishes to make use of all the light which human learning can supply for the better understanding of the Word of God.

Each of the issues mentioned in this note is intimately related to the goals for which Pope John XXIII convened the present council. He did not want the council to smother any new tendencies in the Church that are sound and healthy; he had no desire to consecrate the conservatism of an older generation. On the contrary, his professed aim was to renew the Church and to adapt its thinking and practices to the needs of the contemporary world. He further expressed the hope that the council, instead of erecting new barriers between Catholics and other Christians, would in every way facilitate friendly conversation between believers of different communions.

The more recent theological opinion on the relation between scripture and tradition, which would regard them as two aspects of a single source, rather than as two separate deposits, has made it possible for Catholics to find a meeting ground with Protestants. They can agree with Protestants that in some genuine sense all revelation is contained in scripture, while insisting at the same time that scripture never discloses its full meaning unless read in the atmosphere of authentic tradition. In a similar way, the new tendency to apply the tools of scholarly research to the Bible has fostered lively and fruitful contacts with non-Catholic scholars. It has provided a common basis for discussion with men of learning who do not share the Church's exegetical tradition. If the Second Vatican Council finds a way of encouraging these twin tendencies, it will discharge an important part of its mission. Such action will make it easier for the Church to renew itself according to the Gospel and pave the way for more cordial conversation with our separated brethren.

2. FAITH AND DOUBT

March 11, 1967

Many sincere Christians in our time are tormented by the feeling that they ought to be perfectly certain about matters of faith, while in fact they are not. They are gnawed by doubts that strike at the roots of their religious life and cause inner anxiety of spirit. To what extent, they ask, can and must the believer be certain about his faith?

Faith is by its nature a commitment, and without firmness there is no commitment. The biblical idea of faith is clearly opposed to doubt, as appears from the story of Zachary (Lk 1:18–20) and the words of the risen Jesus to his bewildered disciples (Lk 24:38; Jn 20:27). As a decision arising from the very center of the person, faith engages a man totally to the One who can command his full devotion. It therefore surpasses in existential weight those relatively superficial assents to general, abstract, or inconsequential truths in which one is not personally involved. In this sense faith requires certitude.

The Catholic is committed by his faith not simply, as all Christians are, to God's self-giving in Christ, but to a Church that claims power to pronounce decisively on doctrinal questions. Adherence to the Church implies acceptance of all its dogmas. While regarding the Church as their spiritual home, they feel authorized to take a somewhat critical attitude toward it, as a good citizen does toward his government or a loyal son toward his parents. Can their doubts be reconciled with their remaining in the Church?

In many cases, the questioning is confined to particular doctrines. Clearly accepting God, Christ, and the Church, the believer hesitates with regard to certain teachings, often of a technical or peripheral character. He may wonder about the "two natures" in Christ, about certain Marian privileges, or about some miraculous events of biblical history. So long as these doubts are not willful or arrogant, but honest and humble, there is no cause for alarm. In many instances, the questioner misunderstands the formula he is attacking. At other times, what he is rejecting is not a dogma but a reformable Church teaching, or even a mere popular belief. Or perhaps he is not rejecting anything, but simply saying that he can make no sense of what he hears; he cannot see its value or relevance. Or he might even assent on the level of deliberate commitment, without being able to suppress hesitations that trouble his mind and heart.

In all such cases it is important to move slowly. The priest or counselor should not be too hasty in demanding a full and enthusiastic commitment to doctrines that are scarcely understood. If we keep the emphasis on the saving mysteries at the heart of Christian faith, which grip us with their inner power, other teachings will gradually fall into place. With the growing stress on religious freedom and pluralism—within the Church as well as beyond its borders—we shall have to be more patient than in the past. We must expect individual believers to build their lives primarily upon those affirmations that they find religiously important. Provided a man does not deny the teaching authority of the Church, he may be permitted to pay less attention to peripheral doctrines that he cannot presently assimilate. At most, he can give such truths what Newman would call a "notional" (rather than "real") assent. Only after prolonged and prayerful study does the full relevance of certain doctrines come into view.

More serious are those doubts that seem to call into question the stance of faith itself. Many believers in our day are attacked by the suspicion that faith, as such, may be unwarranted. They are tempted to reject Christianity altogether and base their lives on what seems obvious and clear from experience. If a person has such feelings, he should not be distressed, as though his faith ought not to be threatened. By its nature, faith is suspended over the abyss of unbelief, and hence is liable to be questioned at any time. Caught in the grip of involuntary doubt, the believer must continually turn to God with fresh humility. "I do believe; help my unbelief" (Mk 9:23).

When taken too much for granted, faith degenerates into superstition or fanaticism. When seared by doubt, it comes into its own as faith; it proves itself as steadfast adherence to the unseen God. The man of faith, like Abraham, ventures boldly into the unknown and hopes against hope (Heb 11:8; Rom 4:8). Relying on God's Word alone, faith grounds man's existence in its true source and gives solidity to his whole life. "Unless your faith is firm," said Isaiah to King Ahaz, "you shall not be firm" (Is 7:9).

3. FAITH AND DOGMATIC PLURALISM

May 13, 1967

Faith is not in the first place an assent to dogmas, but an adherence to God as he discloses himself in Jesus Christ. Vatican Council II calls it "an obedience by which man entrusts his whole self freely to God" (*Constitution on Divine Revelation* 5). Dogmas are official statements that accurately express certain limited aspects of the faith, but the Gospel itself is too rich and dynamic to be fitted into even the most carefully chiseled formula.

In the early generations, Christianity existed with few if any statements of that precise and authoritative kind which we today call dogmas. Since the fourth century, however, dogmatic pronouncements have increased in number and subtlety to the point where they are today felt to be a burden. The multiplicity of dogmas can make us lose sight of the unity of the faith. Must the believer feel obliged to find his way to God by accepting each and every dogma?

Once a dogma is enacted, it cannot be simply reversed—not, at least, according to the Catholic view. But this does not mean that it must be imposed upon every individual as an explicit object of his assent. Quite evidently, the Papuan aborigine cannot be held to confess that the Father and the Son are not two principles but one co-principle of the Holy Spirit! With respect to certain dogmas, many of our contemporaries feel not unlike the Papuan aborigine. The Hellenistic and scholastic thought world in which most dogmas took shape is no longer our world. Hence

Pope John called upon Vatican Council II to restate the faith in the "literary forms of modern thought."

As a pastoral council, Vatican II generally avoided technical expressions. A recent investigation apparently failed to detect in the eight-hundred-odd pages of the council documents any statement that Christ had "two natures." While this venerable doctrine is true enough if rightly understood, it can be misleading. It may make people think of Christ as a divine-human centaur—as one who went through life on two levels, with his two intellects and wills separated from each other like passengers on different decks of the same bus. So interpreted, the dogma strikes many as incredible and repugnant. We must squarely face the question whether, in clinging to the ancient formula, we are not preventing men from looking on Christ as the contemporary Christian should.

Recognizing that dogmatic formulations are culturally conditioned, the Church can accept a certain dogmatic pluralism. At the Council of Florence, in 1439, it was agreed that the Greeks who came into union with Rome should not be required to confess in their creeds that the Holy Spirit proceeds from the Father and the Son; they could continue to say, as they previously had, that he proceeds from the Father through the Son. The two formulas sound quite different, but the Church recognized that the mystery was too deep to be encompassed by either of them.

The *Decree on Ecumenism* teaches (17–18) that many of the theological formulations that have been disputed East and West are complementary rather than conflicting. "In order to restore communion and unity or preserve them, one must 'impose no burden beyond what is indispensable' (Acts 15:28)." The unity of faith that holds the Church together need not consist in the acceptance of the same formulas by all; its basis is Christ, who can bind together men who speak about him in different ways.

This does not mean that every manner of speaking in the Church is legitimate. The confessional writings of different groups must be carefully appraised in the light of the Gospel.

No doubt corrections will be needed before some of them can be accepted. But it may prove unnecessary to require, as a precondition of unity, that all should accept exactly the same dogmatic formulations. With certain explanations, the Protestant may properly say that man is justified by "faith alone" and that "the Bible alone" is the source of saving truth. These slogans do not exclude the necessity of "good works" and of "tradition" as many Catholics today interpret them. Ecumenical progress calls for great toleration with respect to the ways in which the faith is conceptualized and formulated.

According to what we may call the "law of incarnation," the Gospel should be expressed in every age and geographical region according to men's natural genius and cultural endowments. The catholicity of the Church shines forth most splendidly when the Word of God is refracted according to the diverse gifts of various peoples. Their legitimate differences, according to Vatican II (*Constitution on the Church* 13), "do not hinder unity but rather contribute to it."

4. FAITH COMES OF AGE

August 5, 1967

Typically, the faith of the individual passes through certain radical transformations corresponding to the stages of life. In a curious way, these stages seem to be reflected on a larger scale in the historical career of the Church as it grows toward maturity.

The faith of the child is spontaneous and unreflective. Naturally religious, the child seeks a protective environment in which he is surrounded by benign powers. He responds readily to the idea of heavenly forces that take him in their care. In the absence of serious challenges from without, the child is not compelled to think critically. He confuses myth with reality, illusion with genuine insight, and easily falls prey to superstition.

At the stage of adolescence, the critical faculties awaken. Prone to assert themselves as individuals, the young are often antagonistic to authority. On the other hand, their exuberant vitality, harnessed to a vigorous faith and fired by zeal to transform the world according to a high idealism, can inspire great feats for God. But the adolescent's faith has its defects. It is too often egotistical, assertive, more critical of others than of self. It needs the humiliation of experience in order to discover the value of suffering, sacrifice, submission. It has to lose some of its self-confidence before it can be properly receptive to the values others have to communicate.

A mature faith is one that has overcome the superficial enthusiasm of youth as well as the naive credulity of the child. Through harsh experience it has learned that evil persists and will persist, that man's ideals and labors, even when well intended, are

short-sighted and ambiguous. Focused on the God of mystery
rather than on tangible values, such a faith is equipped to face
tragedy, diminishment, suffering, and death.

In the past generation, the Catholic Church in this country
has passed rapidly from childhood to adolescence, and is now
being called to full maturity. Thirty years ago, American Catholicism was passive and uncritical; it was the hereditary faith of
isolated ethnic groups in ghetto situations. About the end of the
1930s, the Church began to emerge from its shell and enter into
vital contact with its environment. The dislocations of World
War II, with the draft and military service, thrust the mass of
American Catholics into the mainstream of American life. The
intelligentsia sponsored the Thomistic revival. Catholic higher
education expanded enormously; there were many conversions
and abundant vocations to the priestly and religious life. Catholics were convinced that their Church had an answer to every
problem.

With the 1960s we seem to have entered a new era. John F.
Kennedy and John XXIII, each in his own way, summoned Catholics to abandon the alienation of a pretended superiority and
take upon themselves the hopes and joys, fears and anxieties,
of their contemporaries. Instead of standing in judgment on the
world, Catholics now began to study their own deficiencies. They
felt obliged to expose and overcome everything childish, obscurantist, anachronistic, and corrupt in their own heritage. While
seeking to change the world according to Christ, they saw the
need to refashion their image of Christ according to the most exi-
gent standards of modern critical thought.

To reconcile traditional Catholicism with modern secularity is proving difficult indeed. Traditional Catholicism demands
that we should be submissive to authority, that we should find
the fullness of truth in a limited number of sacred sources, that
we should adhere to a deposit of faith completed centuries ago.
Modernity demands that we think critically, that we should be
ready to change and to correct our ideas, that we make ourselves

receptive to the contributions of every group of men. Can these two mentalities be combined in the same individual? Can a man accept the authoritative claims of the Church and still enter sincerely into dialogue with other religious groups and secular quasi-religions? Psychologically, the two attitudes are hard to combine.

Many people are tempted to choose between faith and reason, Church and world, tradition and modernity. But God is summoning us to bring these polar opposites into a new synthesis. As men of faith, we must allow no fragment of the Gospel to perish. As modern men, we must disengage the Gospel from every antiquated worldview and culturally conditioned ideology. The contemporary Christian need not look on the world with the eyes of an ancient Israelite or a medieval Aristotelian. A mature faith is humble enough to criticize its own presuppositions and learn from the science of its day. By continually dying to its own previous formulations, faith plunges ever deeper into the mystery of God.

5. FAITH AND NEW OPINIONS

October 28, 1967

M any priests and bishops in our time are disturbed by the new opinions being circulated in the Church— opinions in some cases contrary to what has hitherto been considered defined doctrine. A few years ago, hardly any Catholic would have felt free to deny that original sin was inherited by all men from Adam, or that Jesus was conceived without the co-operation of a human father, or that he is present in the Eucharist by "transubstantiation." Quite understandably, therefore, Catholics are shaken when they are abruptly told that some reputable theologians call such doctrines into question.

Are these new opinions a bad thing? If the Church's prime function is to afford intellectual security to its members, they are. Or if one takes it for granted that the previous understanding of the doctrines in question was accurate, one may deplore the new tendencies. But if the previous views may have been mistaken, and if mistakes should be corrected, then it is good that questions are being asked.

The view that received interpretations of the faith should not be challenged stems from a mentality that has done great harm to the Church. Many of us can remember the painful efforts we made, only a few years ago, to suppress our own doubts about whether Eve had been fashioned from one of Adam's ribs, whether the Flood had covered the whole earth, or whether Jonah had really lived three days and nights in the belly of the great fish. Now that a more liberal understanding of the Bible has prevailed, thanks to the courageous insistence of scripture scholars, we smile at the naïveté of our former difficulties. But we should not forget that in the meanwhile many sincere and intelligent men have left the Church because it seemed to require them to accept myths and legends as facts; and many more, who by rights should have found their spiritual home in the Church, were kept out.

The theologian should not be content to defend officially accepted views. He must also keep the inherited body of doctrine under constant review, questioning what is really questionable and denying what he believes to be false. Only if theologians are honest is there any hope of keeping Catholic doctrine abreast of the times. A Church in which candid questioning was forbidden would rapidly stagnate and become obsolete.

Much of what passed for Catholic doctrine some ten or twenty years ago was inadequate for our times. John XXIII, calling for an "updating" of the Church, remarked that the substance of an ancient doctrine is one thing, and the way in which it has been formulated, quite another. And John Courtney Murray, in what was perhaps his last public statement before his death in August, added that Pope John's statement should not be simplistically interpreted as if only words were at stake. What is demanded is a creative reinterpretation of the ancient deposit of faith.

As Fr. Murray also observed, mistakes are bound to be made, even by men of intelligence and goodwill. When bold rethinking is the order of the day, we must be more than usually patient with those who, in our opinion, have fallen into error. It will not do to cut them off with a curt anathema sit. As long as they are seeking to achieve a better understanding of the Christian faith, and not to undermine or renounce it, they belong with us. We should be grateful for their efforts to grasp more accurately what God intends us to believe.

One who writes on theological subjects is faced with a difficult pastoral problem. If he mentions the new opinions without denouncing them, he runs the risk of scandalizing some readers.

Should he then maintain a discreet silence, hoping that his readers may never find out what radical questions are being asked? Before long they will discover the new opinions through popular news media, which stand to gain from sensational presentations.

When the faithful are scandalized, part of the blame usually falls on popularizers who allude to new tendencies without explaining how they are compatible with the substance of the faith. But a greater responsibility, in many cases, rests on those who exaggerate the fixity of Catholic doctrine. If a person is taught, for example, that "transubstantiation" is the only orthodox interpretation of what happens in the consecration at Mass, he will be upset when he reads that some theologians today feel authorized to dispense with both the term and the concepts behind it.

Pastoral wisdom consists not so much in protecting people from new ideas as in helping them to see why innovations are necessary and desirable. In every age, the faith is projected in terms of currently accepted views about man and the universe. When man's assumptions and forms of thinking change, the faith must be restated in new ways to prevent misunderstandings. In loyalty to the ancient tradition, the theologian must seek concepts and formulas suited to his own time. This does not mean that nothing is certain. The entire history of doctrine shows that the Church never simply negates what has once been taught with full authority. Yet the manner of presentation can vary surprisingly, so that old beliefs take on new and unexpected shapes. We cannot predict the limits of future change. But to fear and resist change itself would betray a lack of confidence in the Holy Spirit, who continues today, as in the past, to fulfill Christ's promise (Jn 16:13): "He will guide you into all truth."

6. FAITH AND MEANING

January 13, 1968

I n the affluent West, many persons are tormented by what Viktor Frankl calls the "existential vacuum." More delinquency and psychological problems are caused, he maintains, by the feeling that life is meaningless than by any other form of anguish. As an inmate of Hitler's death camps, Frankl discovered that prisoners could put up with extraordinary hardships and humiliations without losing their serenity and regard for others, provided they were convinced that their life, and hence their sufferings, had some ultimate meaning.

What Frankl says about "man's search for meaning" has important implications for the life of faith. In his heart, everyone yearns for living contact with something beyond himself that gives meaning and value to his own existence. Man's idealism may take many different forms, such as dedication to truth, to peace, to justice, or to the true good of his fellow men. When a person has found something that gives transcendent meaning to his existence, new energies are awakened within him. He sees more and performs better. In short, he becomes a man of faith.

Every man of faith has some sort of God, something to which he is ultimately committed. But unless that object is perfectly and unconditionally good, he is in effect an idolater; he is serving a false god. Is there, beyond all finite goods, some absolute good to which one can give unconditional allegiance? Many philosophers, after devoting long years to this question, have ended in uncertainty. Others who have come to believe, as philosophers, in some Absolute, have found it too remote and hypothetical to kindle their enthusiasm.

Those whom we call men of faith, in the strong sense, are not mere philosophers. They are persons who have experienced, at some privileged moment, an overpowering sense that the divine has manifested itself to them. A common feature in the Old Testament prophets, the apostles, and the great Christian saints is their intense realization that God is personal and that he comes in love to call men into union with himself. The Christian mystics, as Bergson observed, are a very diverse and original lot, but they show a remarkable agreement in their views on the deepest meaning of life. The world, they tell us, is ultimately ruled by God; God is active and creative love; he gives himself most fully to us when he catches us up in his divine generosity. Christ was not in the ordinary sense of the word a mystic. But his life and teaching exemplified in the highest measure what human life, energized by the divine generosity, can become. Totally in possession of himself because totally given to others. He proved by example that man can best find himself when he is ready to lose himself for the Love that gives meaning to his life. Christ awakens faith by inviting men to let go of all the supports that an unworthy selfishness would cling to. The faith of Christians has always focused on the saving mystery of life through death as shown forth in Christ's Cross and Resurrection.

The man of faith does not know the answer to all speculative questions, but he has a few firm convictions that have burned themselves deep into his soul. The aura of light may be small, but it must be intense. So it was for the great Swedish statesman Dag Hammarskjöld, who on Pentecost 1961, just four months before his death, jotted down this entry in his spiritual diary:

> I don't know who—or what—put the question, I don't even know when it was put. I don't even remember answering. But at some moment I did answer yes to Someone—or Something— and from that hour I was certain that existence is meaningful and that, therefore, my life, in self-surrender, had a goal. From

that moment I have known what it means "not to look back" and "to take no thought for the morrow."

In the present Year of Faith many churchmen are taking the occasion to insist on perfect doctrinal orthodoxy. Surely we ought not to neglect even the smallest items of revealed truth. But there are weightier matters (cf. Mt 23:23). It is possible to be fully orthodox and still not be, in the sense of the present article, a man of faith. Unlike Hammarskjöld, many of the timid, anxious believers and untroubled "practicing Catholics" who crowd into the pews on Sunday seem never to have experienced the joy of staking everything on the following of Christ. The man who has heard Christ's call to sacrifice, and has answered a humble and wholehearted yes to him, is a true man of faith. His life cannot be a failure, because he has found a meaning that lies beyond all the transitoriness of this world. "This is the victory that overcomes the world, our faith" (1 Jn 5:4).

7. FAITH AND ITS CONTENTS

April 13, 1968

An Irish pastor is supposed to have told his congregation that the doctrines of the faith are conundrums devised by God to keep us humble. Some insufficiently instructed Catholics seem to accept this view. They believe in the Trinity, the pope, the seven sacraments, indulgences, and possibly guardian angels, for the good, but insufficient, reason that all these tenets seem to be imposed by ecclesiastical authority.

This authoritarian, extrinsicist view of faith can easily breed a sense of emptiness and indifference. Some imagine that it makes little difference what God has revealed so long as we believe it. Devout Christians sometimes say, unconscious of the implied blasphemy, "I'd be just as glad to believe that there are five or ten persons in God as that there are three." Such an attitude reflects a dangerous failure to appreciate the intimate connection between the act of faith and its doctrinal content.

The content of faith, especially in central matters such as the Trinity and the Incarnation, cannot be divorced from faith itself. Faith is not an empty sack that can equally well be filled by anything God chooses to say. The doctrines are articulations of what faith, in its inner reality, already is. They illuminate the inherent structure of any act of faith.

Faith is inherently Trinitarian because of the way God comes to man. Before man can respond in faith, God must first manifest himself. This he does by his Word, and especially by Christ, the Word Incarnate, who is God's perfect self-realization in created form. But we could not recognize Christ as the Father's Word to us unless our hearts were attuned to him by the Holy Spirit. Thanks to the inward anointing of the Spirit we can say, "In your light we see light" (Ps 35:10). Because faith is an active reception of God as he communicates himself under the twofold form of Word and Spirit, faith is Trinitarian in structure.

From another point of view, the structure of faith is Christological. The dialogue of God's self-communication and man's acceptance reaches its highest point in the event of Jesus Christ. Every other divine gift or human acceptance is only a reflection of what God intended to accomplish, and did accomplish, in Christ. For this reason the New Testament can describe Christ as the "author and finisher of faith" (Heb 12:1). All faith comes from, and tends to, him.

The total Christ-event may be broken down into three steps. First, in the Incarnation, God shows his loving initiative: he comes in the Spirit and empowers Mary to conceive the Word made flesh. Second, Christ as man responds with total generosity, especially in his passion and death.

The obedience of the Cross might appear to be a victory for evil, but it is the greatest triumph of grace and brings Christ's human existence to its supreme fulfillment. Thus the Cross ushers in the third phase, the Resurrection, which expresses the mystery of life through death.

The central doctrines of the Incarnation, the Cross, and the Resurrection embody what the Christian community, over the centuries, has found most meaningful in the Christ-event. They also articulate, in the highest degree, the movement of our own inner life of faith as we enter into dialogue with God.

In revelation—corresponding to Incarnation—God enlightens us by his Spirit, thus enabling us to conceive and utter his Word. Then in our act of faith we freely respond, adhering to God's Word with fidelity. As we surrender ourselves in love, we already begin to experience the peace that only God can give. Since the life of grace on earth gives an anticipation of the glory that is to come, it corresponds in some way to Christ's risen life. Thus our experience in faith mirrors on a smaller scale the form of Christ's own life, which is its source and exemplar.

What we have said about the Trinity and Christology could be extended, with some distinctions, to the whole range of revealed truth. Theology in our day cannot be content to make up lists of truths that have to be believed, even though they may seem irrelevant or meaningless. Since theology is the study of God as he gives himself in friendship, the theologian cannot speak about God without also speaking of man. Good theology enriches human life by focusing attention on its heights, its depths, its total meaning and direction. By faithfully performing this task, theology can dispel the illusion that faith is a mere matter of passive conformity with Church decisions. Faith is a living communion with the God of love.

8. KARL RAHNER ON *HUMAN LIFE*

September 28, 1968

A s every thinking Catholic is aware, the present polarization of opinion regarding the encyclical *Human Life* has created a dangerous situation in the Church. Enthusiastic proponents of the papal position, using repressive measures in order to enforce a consensus, might unwittingly detonate a widespread revolt among intellectual Catholics, both clerical and lay. On the other hand, opponents of the encyclical, by speaking in an intemperate way, might undermine the respect that ought to be given to the teaching office in the Church. In the long run, both these courses of action would produce harmful effects.

In the September 1968 issue of *Stimmen der Zeit*, Karl Rahner, probably the most prestigious Catholic theologian of our day, has published some reflections that may well point a way out of the present impasse. Instead of taking a position for or against the substantive doctrine of *Human Life*, he addressed himself to the question of how the various groups within the Church should conduct themselves in view of the present undeniable diversity of opinion. In a brief and selective summary such as this, one can only suggest a few of Rahner's incisive observations. In the first place, Rahner points out that *Human Life* cannot reasonably be considered irreformable doctrine. But this does not mean that it may be ignored. Since Catholics believe that the magisterium ordinarily operates under the guidance of the Holy Spirit, the presumption should be in favor of the pope's declaration. Any such presumption, however, must also allow of the possibility that a Catholic can arrive at a carefully formed and critically tested conviction that in a given case the infallible magisterium has in fact erred. Nobody today denies that there are cases in which official, reformable teaching of the Holy See has in fact been erroneous. As examples, Rahner cites the views of Gregory XVI and Pius IX on liberal democracy, and various statements about the Bible issued in the aftermath of the Modernist crisis. It cannot therefore be assumed that a Catholic who conscientiously opposes the non-infallible doctrine of the magisterium, as it stands at a given moment, is necessarily disloyal. (In this connection an American Catholic might think of the long struggle of John Courtney Murray to obtain a revision of certain papal pronouncements on Church-state relations.)

In the present case, Rahner continues, the complexity of the issue is such that no one opposed to the encyclical can claim absolute certainty for his own stand. But it is normal and inevitable that some should be unable to accept the pope's doctrine. The encyclical, although it claims to be an interpretation of the natural law, does not in fact give very persuasive intrinsic arguments. The encyclical seems to look on human nature as something static and closed—not open to modification by free and responsible human decision. But for some time, many moral theologians have been teaching that what is distinctive to human nature, as distinct from plant and animal life, is precisely man's power to modify his own nature according to the demands of a higher good. The pope, in fact, seems to allow for a measure of rational manipulation of human fertility in permitting the practice of rhythm and the use of the "pill" to regularize the menstrual cycle. Undoubtedly this differs somewhat from the use of the pill for directly contraceptive purposes, but in some instances the distinction is so subtle that many will regard it as hairsplitting. Since a notable majority of the papal commission is known to have come out against the position later taken in the encyclical, one can hardly expect the majority of Catholics to find the reasoning of *Human Life* convincing.

On the basis of these general observations, Rahner then discusses what conduct is proper for various classes of persons within the Church—bishops, priests, moral theologians, and married couples.

Bishops, Rahner says, should surely instruct the faithful about the meaning and weight of the pope's decision, and warn the faithful to take it seriously. They should caution against emotional reactions based on a kind of allergy toward doctrinal authority. On the other hand, bishops should not act as though the encyclical were irreformable or as though everyone who dissented were guilty of contempt of authority or were separating himself from the Church. They should refrain from imposing canonical penalties on persons who respectfully and discreetly propose another view.

Priests in their preaching and confessional practice, according to Rahner, should emphasize central points of undisputed Catholic doctrine, such as that the use of marriage is not an egoism *á deux* or a mere exercise of hedonism. Married life should in principle be open to the begetting of children, and any restriction of fecundity must be done within the limits of the moral law. Stressing these fundamental points, priests can avoid getting backed into the position of feeling and acting as though the only important question were the "pill."

In his pastoral guidance, the priest, in Rahner's opinion, should not take it on himself to "correct" the views of those who are disposed to follow *Human Life*. But when he discerns that the penitent in good faith is strongly committed to a different view, the priest need not consider himself obliged to try to upset the penitent's good faith.

Turning then to moral theologians, Rahner holds that they should not feel faced with a choice between falling totally silent or defending the encyclical as absolutely certain. In fact, neither of these attitudes is warranted. In order to speak loyally and credibly, the moral theologian must present the arguments on both sides. If he personally dissents from *Human Life*, he cannot be expected or required to keep his position secret. While he could easily be silent on some question where there is a wide consensus among Catholics, rendering his dissent a merely personal one, the situation is quite different when the question is universally recognized as controverted. If no one could voice his opposition to reformable doctrines, the development and correction of the Church's official teaching would be seriously hampered.

Finally, Rahner lays down some principles for married persons. If after mature deliberation they find themselves unable to accept the current teaching, they should not feel subjectively guilty or accuse themselves of formal disobedience to the Church. Indeed, Rahner adds, they may in practice follow their critically tested, conscientious decision without feeling obliged to submit their decision to the approval of a confessor.

In conclusion, Rahner points out that the Church, as a society involved in the total history of mankind, moves forward slowly in working toward a definitive position. The ecclesiastical magisterium is an indispensable element, but still only one element, in the total interplay of forces that work together to achieve clarity of doctrine. Many other factors, such as the "sense" of the faithful, new acquisitions of knowledge by individual Christians and theologians, and the "signs of the times," which present ever new and varying questions, all have a contribution to make. It would therefore be unrealistic to demand total clarity from the outset. In the conduct of married life, as in many other important questions, the individual Christian, relying on principles such as those outlined in the preceding paragraphs, must seek to reach a conscientious personal decision that does justice to all the factors. He must assume responsibility for his own decision before God.

Since Rahner's article makes many important points and qualifications not indicated in these pages, his article should not be judged on the basis of this summary. But even these remarks should suffice to show that there is a large possibility of agreement among Catholics who may be divided as to whether the pope's doctrine on the individual marital act is objectively correct. Nothing that Rahner says in his article depends on the presupposition that the decision of *Human Life* is either right or wrong. For this reason his remarks are particularly helpful in meeting the present crisis within the Church. While we cannot presently achieve full agreement among Catholics regarding the morality of contraception, we can and must achieve a tolerable *modus vivendi* between Catholics who accept the encyclical and those who, for serious and conscientious reasons, feel they must dissent.

The tension between the values of authority and liberty, almost universally felt since Vatican II, is especially acute in the American Church today. On the one hand, Catholicism in this country has a long tradition of unswerving loyalty to the Holy See, and on the other hand, the American heritage makes us sensitive to the values of pluralism and dissent. Rahner, while writing out of a European background, speaks to both these sets of values. He combines a sincere respect for the Church's teaching office with a human and Christian appreciation for the rights of personal conscience and free expression.

As is clearly proved by the statements recently issued by the hierarchies of several European nations, the American bishops need not exact wooden conformity to the letter of *Human Life* on the part of every Catholic regardless of his conscientious convictions. In view of the American tradition of freedom and pluralism, it would be a serious mistake to use the encyclical as a kind of Catholic loyalty test. Nothing could so quickly snuff out the spirit of personal responsibility, which has done so much to invigorate American Catholicism in the past few years. Nothing could be more discouraging to young people and intellectuals, upon whom the future of our Church so greatly depends. Nothing could be more destructive of the necessary autonomy of Catholic universities and journals, which have begun to prosper so well. Nothing, finally, could be more harmful to the mutual relations of trust and cordiality that have recently been established between bishops and theologians.

If the present crisis is prudently handled, it can become an occasion of growth. The American Church stands only to gain from a fuller discussion of the issues raised by Rahner's article and by other similar statements. It will take time before the desired consensus is achieved. And by what means is this to be fostered? There is every reason to think that freedom and moderation, rather than force and intimidation, will eventually prevail. But meanwhile much unnecessary suffering could be caused by undisciplined protest on the one hand and by bureaucratic overkill on the other.

9. INFALLIBILITY REVISITED

August 4, 1973

Rome's latest declaration, though it has set forth advanced views on certain points, in others lags behind today's best theology. It also rejects Küng's position without meeting his exegetical and historical arguments.

On July 5, 1973, the newswires across the world were buzzing with reports that the Holy See had come out with a new document on infallibility, condemning, it was suspected, the positions of Hans Küng. The document, popularly referred to by its opening words as *Mysterium Ecclesiae* (The Mystery of the Church), is a declaration of the Congregation of the Doctrine of the Faith (formerly known as the Holy Office), signed by Cardinal Franjo Šeper as prefect and Archbishop Jerome Hamer as secretary. (The document is officially described as a "Declaration in Defense of the Catholic Doctrine on the Church against Certain Errors of the Present Day.") The declaration, having been ratified and confirmed by Pope Paul VI in a private audience, was signed on June 24. In entitling this document a "declaration," the congregation wished to indicate, according to a Vatican press release, that it "does not teach new doctrines, but it recalls and summarizes the Catholic doctrine that has been defined or taught in former documents of the magisterium of the Church; it gives the right interpretation of this Catholic doctrine and indicates its limits and scope."

The major points in this statement are a reformation of what has become common teaching over the past century. All sixty footnotes refer to official Catholic documents. There are some forty references to Vatican II, some ten references to Vatican I, and several references each to Trent, to the Synod of Bishops of 1971, and to various utterances of Paul VI. As this documentation suggests, the declaration does not offer any new exegetical or historical evidence for the positions it adopts. It relies almost solely on earlier Church documents as authorities. For this reason, the declaration will not satisfy the objections of some scholars; nor is it intended to do so.

"The Mystery of the Church" falls into six sections that are concerned with four main topics. Section I deals with the unity of the Church; sections II to IV, with infallibility; section V, with the historical conditioning and reinterpretation of dogma; and section VI, with the priesthood. There is no evident unifying theme except that everything in the declaration has some reference to the Church. It has been suggested that the common denominator might be that Hans Küng has written on all the points touched in this declaration—but so have many other authors. Fr. Küng has not taught anything resembling some of the positions here condemned—for example, those relating to the unity of the Church. Thus it is probably better not to presume that there is any particular thematic unity. The declaration is a kind of syllabus of recent errors concerning the Church. No adversaries are named, but it seems quite evident that Fr. Küng is alluded to in section IV, and the Vatican press office, in a release accompanying the declaration, referred to "some ideas of Professor Hans Küng."

The various sections of the declaration call for separate study. The first section is an effort to establish a very close, or even absolute, identity between the Church of Christ and the Roman Catholic Church. This represents a subtle but important change from Vatican II, which took pains to distinguish between the Church of Christ and the Catholic Church, stating that the former "subsists in," but is not exclusively identified with, the latter. The present declaration blurs over this distinction by stating that Catholics are bound to profess that "they belong to that Church which Christ founded and which is governed by the successors of Peter and the other apostles." In this sentence, the first "which" refers to the Church of Christ, the second to the Roman Catholic Church. The phrasing seems to imply what Vatican II refused to assert, that Jesus Christ founded the Roman Catholic Church. Section I insists rather unilaterally on the institutional perfection of the Catholic Church. It presents the Church not primarily as a communion or community of persons assembled under the lordship of Christ and the invocation of the Holy Spirit but as a "general means of salvation." The Church is said to bring its members to salvation because it is "endowed with all divinely revealed truth and with all the means of grace with which Christ wished to enhance his messianic community." Peter and the other apostles are described as "the depositaries of the original apostolic tradition, living and intact, which is the permanent heritage of doctrine and holiness of that same Church"—that is, of the Catholic Church.

By concentrating on what Fr. Yves Congar, O.P., once called the "hierarchical machinery of mediation," the declaration, in my opinion, unduly narrows the very concept of the Church. Vatican II, more adequately, depicted the Church primarily as a mystery of grace, a wonderful gathering of men brought into union by the Spirit of Christ. The declaration, by considering only the "means of grace" entrusted by Christ to his apostles and their successors, gives the impression that the Catholic Church lacks nothing and that other Christian communities can have nothing positive to contribute to the ecumenical dialogue. Whatever good things they have, the Catholic Church has in even greater measure. Without using these precise words, the declaration conveys this impression.

Section I closes with a condemnation of two errors. The first is the idea that "Christ's Church is nothing more than a collection (divided, but still possessing a certain unity) of Churches and ecclesial communities"; the second, that "Christ's Church nowhere really exists today, and that it is to be considered only as an end which all Churches and ecclesial communities must strive to reach." I am not aware of anyone who holds either of these positions in the crude form here stated. Many theologians, both Catholic and Protestant, believe that something of the Church of Christ is to be found in the various Churches and ecclesial communities, and that the perfection of the Church is an eschatological reality toward which all existing communities should aspire. These moderate positions, however, are clearly endorsed by Vatican II. It would be unfortunate if the present condemnation were to cast suspicion on these sound and ecumenically fruitful initiatives of Vatican II. Sections II and III of the declaration deal respectively with the infallibility of the universal Church and of the magisterium. With regard to the infallibility of the faithful as a whole, the declaration combines, but does not advance beyond, the teaching of the *Constitution on the Church* (12) and the *Constitution on Divine Revelation* (8). On the infallibility of the magisterium, the doctrine of Vatican II, as found in these two constitutions, is presented with several significant nuances.

For example, it is asserted that the charism of infallibility does not dispense the pope and the other bishops from studying with appropriate means the treasure of divine revelation contained in scripture and tradition. This concession raises (but does not answer) the question whether a definition would be infallible if, in a given instance, insufficient study were given to the sources. Some Christians answer that divine providence would never allow such a catastrophe to happen, but I suspect that theology can do better than to invoke such a *deus ex machina*. More attention must be given to the necessary conditions for an infallible declaration.

Also, in section III, the declaration asserts that the Church has from the beginning always believed that the magisterium possesses infallibility in expounding the deposit of faith. As a historical assertion, this statement raises serious problems, if only because the term "infallibility" was not applied to the magisterium until late in the Middle Ages. Whether some equivalent claim may be said to have been made from the beginning is far from clear. A great deal depends upon how one understands infallibility. The interpretation given to infallibility in the present document is not something that can plausibly be ascribed to churchmen of the early centuries.

Similar objections will be raised regarding the statement at the end of section III that the dogmas, as "the objects of Catholic faith, have always been the unalterable norm both for faith and for theological science." The term "dogma" is here used in a sense given to it only since the eighteenth century. There is nothing precisely corresponding to this notion in the theology of the patristic or medieval periods. In our own time, many theologians would say that the object of faith is God as he comes to us in Jesus Christ, rather than dogmas, which are human formulations of certain aspects of the mystery of our redemption.

Section IV contains the passage most evidently directed against Hans Küng. It states that the faithful are in no way permitted to see in the Church merely a fundamental permanence in the truth that could be compatible with occasional errors even in the definitive teaching of the magisterium. In proposing his theory of the Church's "indefectibility" in the truth, Küng has quite consciously set himself against the doctrine of magisterial infallibility as commonly understood in the Church since Vatican I. The present declaration tells us, not surprisingly, that the Holy See is not presently prepared to accept Fr. Küng's thesis. No effort is here made to meet the exegetical, historical, and systematic arguments Küng has presented.

Personally, I believe that a purely juridical understanding of infallibility, such as the declaration here seems to favor, is not theologically viable. I would hold that the entire Church has a kind of permanence in the truth of Christ that may appropriately be called "infallibility." Going beyond Fr. Küng (as I understand him), I would add that the Church's infallibility may at times come to determinate verbal expression through the pronouncements of popes, bishops, or councils, when it is given to them to see clearly how a controversy should be resolved. On such occasions, the Church at large may react somewhat as did the Fathers at Chalcedon when they exclaimed, "Peter has spoken through Leo."

Recognizing the necessity for "reception," Vatican II asserted that when the magisterium teaches infallibly, the assent of the Church can never be wanting, because the same Holy Spirit directs both the magisterium and the body of the faithful. The assent of the Church, to be sure, is not the source of the magisterium's infallibility (God is the source), but it is a sign that the magisterium, in a specific pronouncement, has not acted without the help of the Spirit. Section IV concludes with a brief discussion of the so-called hierarchy of truths which, according to the *Decree on Ecumenism* (11), exists among the Church's doctrines. The declaration interprets this hierarchy with reference to the order of derivation: "Some dogmas are founded upon other dogmas which are the principal ones, and are illuminated by these latter." Then occurs the statement that all the dogmas, since they are revealed, must be believed with the same divine faith. The declaration here goes beyond Vatican II, which was content to say in the *Constitution on the Church* (25) that the definitions of popes and councils must be believed "with the submission of faith." In insisting that the dogmas themselves must be believed on a motive of divine faith, the declaration here minimizes the human element in the formulation of dogma.

Most interpreters would understand the doctrine of the hierarchy of truths, in the *Decree on Ecumenism*, as implying that not all dogmas are equally important. It is more necessary to believe the central mystery of Christ than to accept some peripheral connected truth, such as the Immaculate Conception. The declaration, in basing the assent of faith solely on the fact of divine attestation, seems to put all dogmas on the same level, and thus to undermine the clear intention of the *Decree on Ecumenism*.

Section V, which deals with the human conditioning of doctrinal affirmations, was perhaps written by a different hand than the paragraphs just considered. At any event, it shows a much more sophisticated theology, hardly reconcilable with some of the statements in Section IV. The first paragraph declares that the hidden mysteries of God, which we accept in faith, by their nature far transcend the human intellect. This seems to imply that no human formulation, even though it is a defined dogma, can adequately express the mystery to which we assent. The assent, therefore, can hardly be to the dogma in isolation.

Then, in a remarkably deep and concise paragraph, the declaration points out that statements of revelation are conditioned in four ways by the historicity of the human subject. The meaning is affected, in the first place, by the expressive power of human language at a given time and place. Second, dogmatic truths are sometimes expressed in reference to a limited human context, so that a formulation well suited to its original context may be found inadequate in the framework of a later context. Third, official Church pronouncements are commonly directed to the solution of particular questions or the refutation of particular errors, and this purpose must be borne in mind by future interpreters. Fourth, it can sometimes happen that doctrines are enunciated by the magisterium in terms that bear traces of changeable human conceptions.

This fourth concession is particularly remarkable in view of the fact that two encyclicals—*Humani Generis* (1950) and *Mysterium Fidei* (1965)—rejected the idea that the concepts employed in dogmatic formulations are time-conditioned. In the second of these encyclicals, Paul VI taught that transubstantiation, and the other formulas used by councils to propose the dogmas of the faith, "express concepts which are not tied to a certain definite form of human culture, or to a certain stage of scientific progress, but exhibit that which the human mind, in its universal and necessary experience of reality, perceives. . . . Hence they are suited to men of all times and places." Vatican II, especially in the *Decree on Ecumenism* and in the *Constitution on the Church in the Modern World*, pointed out that revelation is and should be understood in different ways according to the temperament and culture of different peoples. That this important theme of Vatican

II should now be taken up again and stated even more explicitly by the Congregation of the Doctrine of the Faith is surely cause for rejoicing.

The remainder of Section V deals with the problem of the reinterpretation of dogma. It explains that the formulas that were at one time suitable for expressing divine revelation may subsequently be in need of clarification. In fact, it may even happen that some older dogmatic formulas might give way to new expressions that present the meaning more clearly and completely in a new context of understanding. All of this might well seem applicable to a technical term such as "transubstantiation."

These concessions are then reviewed in the light of the Vatican I teaching that the meaning (*sensus*) of the dogmas remains constant. At this point, the declaration, taking up Pope John XXIII's famous distinction between the deposit of faith and the manner of presentation, asserts that the former remains identical while the latter varies. This seems to me to be an oversimplification, in view of what the declaration itself acknowledges regarding the reconceptualization and reinterpretation of dogma in new human contexts. The Church's understanding of revelation, and not simply its exposition of it, changes and develops over the centuries.

The sixth and last section of the declaration has no organic relationship with what precedes. It deals with priesthood. After some passing mention of the priesthood of Christ and the common priesthood of the faithful, the congregation turns to the ministerial priesthood, the main point of concern. The English translation gives the impression of saying that priestly ordination can come only through the laying on of hands by a bishop whose lineage goes back to the apostles. This would imply that Christian communities that have lost the apostolic succession of bishops cannot have a true Christian ministry or a genuine Eucharist. An attentive reading of the Latin text, however, shows that the congregation has carefully measured its words. It states that the rite of ordination comes down from apostolic times and that, because the early bishops ordained presbyters, there arose in the Church the ministerial priesthood. The document does not deny that priestly ministry could be received in some other way than through the laying on of hands by a bishop who stands in the apostolic succession.

Priestly ordination, according to the declaration, confers an indelible character to which special powers are attached. The Synod of 1971 is quoted as an authority for holding that "only the priest can act in the person of Christ and preside over and perform the sacrificial banquet." Hence follows the conclusion: "The faithful who have not received priestly ordination and who take upon themselves the office of performing the Eucharist attempt to do so not only in a completely illicit way but also invalidly."

This sentence, at first reading, appears to say more than, on careful scrutiny, it clearly teaches. Does it mean that no sacramental event takes place when an unordained minister presides at the Lord's Supper? Perhaps not. For one thing, the declaration is speaking of those who "take upon themselves" the function (*qui proprio ausu munus sibi sumant*) of offering the Eucharist. This leaves open the possibility that one who is, in extraordinary circumstances, designated by the community for this function might be competent to officiate. Second, the term "invalidity" has various meanings in modern theological literature. Some would understand it as signifying that the Church cannot or does not guarantee the efficacy of the rite; others, as signifying that the rite is inefficacious. If the first of these meanings is here intended, the declaration may be teaching simply that the Church does not officially recognize a Eucharist in which an unordained person arrogates to himself the role of celebrant. The fact that the declaration leaves open the possibility of such an interpretation is of considerable ecumenical significance.

What is notable in the whole treatment of the priesthood is an intense preoccupation with powers, especially sacramental powers. This represents a movement away from the thrust of Vatican II, which attempted to focus more on priestly service and to set the sacramental activity of the priest in the wider context of his functions as minister of the word and builder of community. It is to be hoped that the present declaration, in its change of emphasis, does not represent a general trend; for in that case one would have to admit that the theology of ministry is regressing to a preconciliar stage.

Since the Second Vatican Council, Rome has produced a number of encouraging and progressive documents, especially those bearing on communications and the social apostolate. The present declaration, unfortunately, does not rank among these positive achievements. It is defensive in tenor, reactionary rather than forward-looking. Although it contains some excellent observations on particular points, such as the historicity of dogmatic formulations, the document as a whole lags behind the best theology of the day. On the other hand, it is not a repressive statement. It is moderate in tone and is worded with great circumspection.

"The Mystery of the Church" does not live up to the promise of its own title. To judge from its contents, it might better have been named "The Power of the Hierarchical Church." In reading it, one wonders what became of the biblical and ecumenical renewals that were so recently under way, not least in Rome. The pluralism and openness to dialogue so warmly recommended by the late council seem to have been eclipsed. The philosophy behind this declaration is still predominantly juridical, clerical, authoritarian, and objectivistic—somewhat outdated.

Claims of authority may at times be necessary, but they do not normally increase the prestige of the claimant. Generally speaking, Rome teaches most credibly, not when it asserts its own prerogatives, but when it manifests its confidence in the Lord and its concern for the interests of the Gospel.

10. HERESY TODAY?

March 1, 1980

Heresy is frequently defined as the denial of a revealed truth taught as such by the universal magisterium of the Church. This definition is itself not unproblematic. Can we unequivocally identify statements made by popes, councils, and other church officials as truths revealed by God? Recent explorations in the epistemology of revelation and in the theory of religious language give grounds for caution. And even if this difficulty is solved, one has to face the problem of determining whether revelation is being contradicted. Usually those accused of contradicting the Church's dogmas perceive themselves as interpreting the dogmas in a new and appropriate way.

If Church teaching were perfectly static, judgments about orthodoxy and heresy would be much simpler than they are. But doctrine develops and shifts as the Church meditates on the implications of revelation and reformulates its faith in the context of a changing world. Only a living community of faith can teach the Gospel in a manner that is both faithful to the original revelation and attuned to the current situation. As the Church strives to meet this twofold demand, it relies heavily on theologians to explore new doctrinal options. But their proposals will be subject to further discussion. In some cases they will be viewed by conservatives as dangerously novel and by progressives as excessively cautious.

Doctrinal crises normally arise when a new mode of feeling and thinking begins to assert itself among Christians. One such shift occurred in the patristic era, when theology adopted Hellenistic philosophical categories, thereby sparking controversies such as those attendant on Arianism. Another major shift occurred when Thomas Aquinas and other thirteenth-century scholastics restated Christian doctrine in predominantly Aristotelian categories. Since the Middle Ages, several other major category shifts have occurred. Whenever this happens, some thinkers transpose the Christian message inadequately into the new categories, and others who make the transition rather successfully are misunderstood and accused of heresy.

An original restatement of the Christian message, if genuinely innovative, cannot be adequately judged from within the previous framework, for the adequacy of that framework is precisely what is being challenged. One cannot adjudicate the validity of Nicaea by simply quoting biblical texts, nor can one assess the legitimacy of Thomism by the principles of Augustinianism. In our own day, the theological systems of a Karl Rahner or an Edward Schillebeeckx cannot be finally appraised by the extent to which they conform to neo-scholastic criteria. In every major shift, a delicate process of discernment is necessary. The Church relies not simply on the letter of biblical, creedal, and dogmatic texts, but on living persons gifted with spiritual discernment.

So demanding is the task of discernment that one is tempted to defer judgment. In some cases it may indeed be advisable to apply the principle of Gamaliel (Acts 5:38–39). An authentic development, it is claimed, is irrepressible, and false teaching, like a rotten tree, frequently collapses of its own weight. But since false doctrine corrupts, and since specious errors often endure for centuries, the Church may not have the right to remain silent. To preserve itself as a community of faith and witness, the Church must foster unity of belief within its own membership and must forthrightly condemn what it recognizes as proceeding from an alien spirit. Special care must be taken to keep the preaching and catechesis of the Church from being contaminated by the intellectual and ethical standards of an unbelieving world.

If it be conceded that the discernment must at times be made, further problems arise with respect to the organs by which the Church discerns. Who has a right to speak for the Church? Should judgments of heresy and orthodoxy be made by the Holy See, by individual bishops, by groups of bishops, by the theological community, or by the general consensus of believers?

Normally there will be considerable harmony among all these organs, but in the event of disagreement one may have to choose among them. Let us therefore briefly consider each of these organs, beginning with the last. As a criterion of orthodoxy, the "sense of the faithful" is very difficult to apply. Although the Holy Spirit is surely at work sustaining the faith among God's people, the opinions of Christians are also heavily influenced by the secular atmosphere. Thus a public opinion poll of persons who consider themselves Christians or Catholics cannot necessarily be taken as representing the "mind of the Church." It must also be asked whether the average lay person has sufficient background to assess new theological options. Theologians normally make use of technical terminology. In many instances, they write with self-imposed methodological restrictions and thus propose their conclusions hypothetically. Not surprisingly, therefore, persons without specialized theological training will often disqualify themselves as judges of orthodoxy.

Can the theological community be relied on to police itself? In the late Middle Ages, the theology faculties of the great universities, especially Paris, played an important role in issuing judgments of orthodoxy and heresy. Notwithstanding the close union between the *sacerdotium* and the *studium* that then existed, the system did not work particularly well. The magisterium of the Church became overinvolved in academic disputes between rival theological factions. The vesting of judgmental powers in the theological community would be even less likely to work well today, when that community is far less homogeneous than it usually has been.

From my own experience of the field, I would be inclined to say that theologians, by training and temperament, are better equipped to propose theories and arguments than to render judgments about what may be prudently believed and preached in the Church. Some doctrinaire theologians are over-inclined to denounce their adversaries as heretics. Others, deeply committed to the value of freedom in scholarly speculation, are reluctant to decide definitively against any theory that may present itself. Within the profession, it is disputed whether the theologian must be a believing Christian or whether, as some now hold, unbelievers can practice the art of Christian theology. It is likewise disputed whether the theologian's primary allegiance is to the community of faith or, as some are now holding, to the academic community. Because of the internal controversies about the Church-relatedness of theology itself, it is particularly difficult to recommend that theologians be set up as judges of orthodoxy.

We turn, then, to the other option indicated above: that popes and bishops should have the primary responsibility for determining questions of orthodoxy and heresy. This option is in accordance with the traditional Catholic understanding of the pastoral office. Popes and bishops, as pastors, may generally be counted on to have a sufficient comprehension of the issues at stake and a balanced grasp of the faith to be preached in the Church. As heads of communities they are able to call on expert advice when it is needed. The local bishop, by himself, will rarely be in a position to give more than a preliminary judgment, but if this does not suffice to settle the problem, conferences and synods of bishops, aided by theological consultants, can give confirmatory judgments. In more serious cases, the local or regional episcopate will enter into communication with the Holy See, which is equipped with its own Congregation for Doctrine. In serious crises, a general council may be needed in order to clarify the teaching of the Church.

Generally speaking, the Catholic Church has been well served by its papal, episcopal, and conciliar structures. It has successfully escaped both narrow sectarianism and vapid latitudinarianism. While providing for a variety of theological schools and encouraging earnest scholarly debate, the Church has kept its theologians within the bounds of Christian orthodoxy. Catholic preachers and teachers, by and large, can be counted on to transmit not simply their personal opinions but the faith of the Church. If I had not perceived this to be the case, I, for one, would not be a Catholic.

If any legitimate complaint may be made about the past conduct of the ecclesiastical magisterium, it is perhaps that popes and bishops have been excessively defensive. When they feared that the patrimony of faith was in danger, they have acted with a severity verging on harshness. This has been notably true in times of doctrinal crisis such as the Counter-Reformation and the Modernist upheaval. In the early 1950s, when I was a theological student, the Church was beginning to emerge from the anti-Modernist repression, and the surfacing of new ideas occasioned painful conflicts. Catholic biblical scholars had to struggle long and hard before their right to use modern scholarly methods of investigation was publicly acknowledged in the Church. Under Pope Pius XII, several distinguished Jesuit professors of theology in France were suspended because of their efforts to discuss the problems of nature and grace in categories other than those of baroque scholasticism. The Dominican Yves Congar was removed from teaching and was impeded from publishing some of his works on ecumenism. The Jesuit Pierre Teilhard de Chardin was not permitted to teach in Paris or to publish any of his books in his own lifetime. John Courtney Murray was for several years forbidden to write on questions of Church and state. Even Karl Rahner was in difficulties for his view on eucharistic concelebration, among other points. This list could obviously be prolonged. In retrospect, the restrictions may be judged to have been excessive, especially in the light of the dramatic reversals of the Second Vatican Council. But the stern measures were taken out of deep and laudable concern for the integrity of the faith, and in time the validity of many of the new proposals was in fact recognized.

Encouraged by Vatican II, theologians have recently been searching for new ways of making the faith accessible to the modern mind. They have understood the council as commissioning them to draw on new resources and to reevaluate traditional positions. They have questioned and hypothesized, not frivolously or ostentatiously but, in most cases, with scholarly seriousness and deep pastoral concern. While their efforts were dismissed in some quarters as irresponsible or disloyal, they were prepared to accept a measure of unpopularity as a hazard inseparable from their vocation. In certain cases, no doubt, individual theologians overstepped the limits of discretion and espoused opinions which, on mature consideration, will be found incompatible with Christian and Catholic faith.

The recent surge of investigative activity on the part of the Roman Congregation for Doctrine, which has come to a head in the present pontificate, is not necessarily an ominous sign. Theologians should be in dialogue with the official Church, through its doctrinal commissions. It is to be hoped, however, that the congregation will seek to establish generally positive rather than hostile relations with the wider theological community, and that theologians who have tried to serve, even occasionally by questioning certain official positions, may be encouraged rather than threatened. An atmosphere of fear and recrimination could be detrimental to the whole apostolate of the Church.

I am still hopeful that positive and cordial relations can be established between the theological community and the ecclesiastical magisterium. New procedures and modes of consultation have gradually been evolving. The International Theological Commission, as it achieves its own distinctive character, will perhaps come to serve as a mediating structure. National and regional conferences of bishops are seeking ways of regular contact with theologians, so as to prevent misunderstandings, ruptures, and mutual denunciations. The Doctrinal Commission of the Holy See has revised its investigative procedures within the past decade, and further procedural improvements are probably to be expected. But future conflicts cannot be ruled out. One has the feeling that so long as a negative judgment on any theologian remains a real possibility, a certain constituency will remain dissatisfied.

In the perspectives of history, the theological community has reasons for deep gratitude to Rome. Not only has Rome been the great defender of orthodoxy (a benefit never to be forgotten), but it has frequently vindicated the freedom of theology against unjust suspicions and condemnations. In the thirteenth century, Rome protected Thomas Aquinas and his associates against the jealousy of traditional theologians and the hostility of local Church officials. Again, in the seventeenth century, Rome prevented the theologians involved in the disputes about actual grace from recklessly branding their opponents as heretics. Under Pius XII and John XXIII, the Biblical Commission repeatedly defended scholarly exegetes against unfair harassment, partly from other Roman agencies, but also from critics in their home countries. Although there are times when Rome must denounce and condemn, these are not its sole or primary doctrinal functions. Esteeming the life of the mind, popes and bishops have generally supported the difficult and demanding tasks of theological inquiry. As the Council Fathers at Vatican II declared in their "Message to Men of Thought and Science," "Your road is ours. Your paths are never foreign to ours. We are the friends of your vocation as searchers, companions in your fatigues, admirers of your successes and, if necessary, consolers in your discouragement and your failures."

11. THE TEACHING AUTHORITY OF BISHOPS' CONFERENCES

June 11, 1983

homas J. Reese, S.J., at the end of his article "The Bishops' 'Challenge of Peace'" (May 21, 1983), mentions the statement of Cardinal Joseph Ratzinger to the effect that the bishops' conference does not have a mandate to teach (*mandatum docendi*). In the commissioned report of the consultation on peace and disarmament held in Rome on January 18–19, 1983, Cardinal Ratzinger is summarized as having argued that the *mandatum docendi* belongs only to individual bishops in their dioceses or to the college of bishops with the pope.

Since we do not have the full text of the cardinal's remarks, it is difficult to know exactly what he had in mind. His statement, however, should presumably be interpreted in a way compatible with canon 753 of the newly promulgated Code of Canon Law. This canon states, in part: "Bishops who are in communion with the head and members of the college, either individually or gathered together, whether in episcopal conferences or particular councils, although they do not have infallibility in teaching, are authentic teachers and masters of the faith for the Christians (*christifideles*) committed to their care." The code thus seems to accord to episcopal conferences a certain doctrinal authority.

In an article for the first issue of *Concilium* (1965), Cardinal Ratzinger himself touched on the present question. Bishops' conferences, he maintained, are a legitimate form of the collegial structure of the Church. They are the modern successors of the synodal activity of the regionally different "colleges" of the ancient Church. Building on an earlier article by Jerome Hamer, O.P., Cardinal Ratzinger stated that episcopal conferences on the national or regional level are genuine, though partial, realizations of collegiality with a view to the totality of the Church. The true notion of collegiality, therefore, should not be restricted to the relations of all the bishops of the world under the presidency of the pope.

Reinterpreting the meaning of episcopal ordination in the light of the doctrine of collegiality, Cardinal Ratzinger asserted that by this sacrament the individual is incorporated into a fraternal association of bishops, each representing the local Church to which he is assigned. The bishop, then, is not a little pope, monarchically governing a single diocese. "There can be no room for egotism in dioceses or communities that are concerned only with themselves, leaving all the rest to the care of God and the Holy See. There must be a common responsibility for one another. Being catholic means, then, being united with others."

It can, of course, be asked whether the collegial union of bishops on the national or regional level includes doctrinal as well as merely pastoral concerns. I do not see how the pastoral can be defined in a way that excludes the doctrinal, for within the Church of Christ all pastoral activity has, or should have, a doctrinal basis. Indeed, the first task of the pastor is to feed the people with the Word of God. Reaffirming the position of the Council of Trent, Vatican II, in its *Decree on the Bishops' Pastoral Office*, insisted that the ministry of teaching and preaching is "eminent among the chief duties of bishops" (12).

The National Conference of Catholic Bishops (NCCB) in the United States has regularly issued statements having a broadly doctrinal character. In an important address on the mission of the conference, the then archbishop Joseph L. Bernardin, as president, stated on May 4, 1976: "We have made a number of significant doctrinal statements which have had an impact on our teaching efforts. Consider, for example, the pastoral letters or statements on 'The Church in Our Day' (1967), 'Human Life in Our Day' (1969), 'Basic Teachings for Catholic Religious Education' (1972) and 'Behold Your Mother' (1974)." He also called attention to a number of other doctrinal initiatives, including the work then in preparation, "To Live in Christ Jesus" (1976), a pastoral reflection on the moral life. If he were speaking today, he would have to add the "Pastoral Letter on Marxist Communism" (1980).

Far from implying that the NCCB had exceeded its mandate in these documents, Pope John Paul II, in his address to the bishops of the United States on October 5, 1979, congratulated them on their exercise of the ministry of truth in their collective statements and pastoral letters, especially "To Live in Christ Jesus."

"The General Catechetical Directory," prepared by the Sacred Congregation for the Clergy in 1971, urged bishops' conferences to prepare national directories applying its principles and guidelines. Accordingly, the NCCB prepared and in 1977 approved its "National Catechetical Directory," a thoroughly doctrinal piece of work, subsequently approved by the Congregation for the Clergy in 1978.

Several Roman congregations, including the one now headed by Cardinal Ratzinger, have expressed approval of the doctrinal activity of bishops' conferences. The Congregation for Doctrine, in its 1976 *Declaration on Sexual Ethics*, felicitated those episcopal conferences that have issued "important documents" conveying "wholesome moral teaching, especially on sexual matters."

The very fact that the NCCB, like the other national conferences, has a Committee on Doctrine would seem to imply that the conference itself has doctrinal responsibilities. The NCCB Committee on Doctrine has periodically issued theological evaluations of ecumenical statements. It has engaged in dialogue with theologians on the doctrine of ministry and on the relations between bishops and theologians. At times it has appraised the doctrinal soundness of theological works, notably the controversial report on human sexuality published in 1977.

The United States Bishops' Conference is by no means singular in making doctrinal pronouncements. Many other conferences do likewise. For example, the Latin American Bishops' Conference, in its meetings at Medellín (1968) and Puebla (1979), sought to lay down doctrinal reflections as well as pastoral guidelines on the various questions they addressed. The German bishops, for their part, have, as a conference, been heavily involved in doctrinal teaching. As an instance one may cite their "Letter on the Priestly Office—a Biblical and Doctrinal Aid," released in 1969. The German episcopal conference composed a theological critique of an ecumenical study on ministry in 1973. More recently, it has been active in assessing the orthodoxy of theologians such as Hans Küng. On April 29, 1983, the German bishops' conference issued its own statement on war, peace, and nuclear arms.

In raising the question of the *mandatum docendi* in January 1983, Cardinal Ratzinger was perhaps concerned that the various bishops' conferences, involving themselves in controversial issues of an international character, might issue mutually conflicting statements, thus dividing the Catholic community. There are in fact significant differences of approach between the German and American statements on nuclear arms. The Holy See is justified in wishing to exert a moderating influence so as to prevent dissension among Catholics who follow the teaching of different groups of bishops. On the other hand, national conferences feel a legitimate responsibility to address the specific pastoral problems arising in their own countries. If, in so doing, they seem to disagree with the hierarchies of other countries, they may call attention to one another's shortcomings and imbalances. The issuance of diverse statements by different hierarchies may be an excellent way to initiate dialogue with a view to reaching an ultimate consensus.

In the 1965 article previously referred to, Cardinal Ratzinger himself clearly favored open dialogue among different bishops' conferences. In the course of his argument for the collegial character of such conferences, he remarked:

> These reflections applied to the whole church would mean that there should also be initiatives from the various parts of the church; initiatives that indeed would have to be coordinated, clarified and supervised by the center, but should not be simply substituted by uniform directions. Why is it that today there are no such things as the letters [written in their day] of St. Ignatius of Antioch, of St. Polycarp, of St. Dionysius of Corinth? Why should it not be possible that bishops' conferences address themselves to each other in words of thanks or encouragement or even correction of false ways if such have been followed? (*Concilium*, vol. 1 [1965], 63)

In making his theological argument on the basis of episcopal ordination and collegiality, Cardinal Ratzinger discountenanced a purely juridical view of authority as descending from the papacy. Bishops as individuals or in conference, he concluded, may laudably exhort, console, and correct persons over whom they do not have jurisdiction. By implication he was saying that for such instruction episcopal orders and communion with the Church suffice. No additional *mandatum docendi* is required.

In "The Challenge of Peace," the United States bishops acknowledge that the various statements in the letter have different doctrinal weight. Some statements repeat and interpret what has been taught by Vatican II or by recent popes. Other statements reiterate settled principles of Catholic moral theology, such as the principles of proportionality and discrimination. Still others are the bishops' own prudential applications of moral principles to the complex situations of the day. With regard to this last category, the bishops do not impose any obligation to assent, but they require that their teaching should be seriously considered by all Catholics in forming their own consciences. Archbishop Philip M. Hannan of New Orleans is therefore not out of order in holding that Catholics are free in conscience to disagree with the particulars of the recent pastoral letter.

Although an impressive case for the doctrinal authority of conference statements can be made both canonically on the basis of the code and theologically on the basis of episcopal ordination and collegiality, with or without a *mandatum docendi*, these theoretical points may not be decisive. In actual practice the influence of such statements and the assent that they elicit depend chiefly on the intrinsic qualities of the documents and on the reception accorded to them by discerning critics and by the general public. Once a document is published, it shapes its own destiny. It makes an impact if, and only if, it speaks powerfully and appropriately to the felt concerns of the readers. Some papal documents issued with high credentials (such as the apostolic constitution, *Veterum Sapientia*, issued by Pope John XXIII in 1960) have been ignored and forgotten. Some statements of local bishops, such as the pastoral letters of Cardinal Suhard of Paris and Cardinal Montini of Milan, have been translated into many languages and have given light and inspiration to believers all over the world.

Episcopal charisms, whether individual or collegial, can greatly contribute to the quality of episcopal statements, but they cannot be invoked to supply for the lack of such quality. When these charisms are put to work in a careful process of study, consultation, and revision, the result may be a statement having an influence far greater than the juridical status of the document or the official mandate of its authors would have the grounds to anticipate. In the final analysis, the authority of the letter "The Challenge of Peace" will depend on the way it is received. If the discussion it engenders leads to greater wisdom than is to be found in the text itself, the bishops will, I assume, be more than satisfied.

12. THE MANDATE
TO TEACH

March 19, 1988

One may be grateful that the Congregation of Bishops has circulated what is obviously a rather tentative working paper (*instrumentum laboris*) for the eventual document on the theological and juridical status of episcopal conferences. The English text sent to Archbishop John L. May in his capacity as president of the National Conference of Catholic Bishops (NCCB) reads like a bad translation. Marred by numerous misprints and by some erroneous references, it is in parts unintelligible. All this is regrettable, but the very roughness of the present draft may be taken as an indication that the congregation is open to criticism and is prepared to make extensive revisions. The bishops' conferences of the world need not hesitate, therefore, to make criticisms and counterproposals.

The main theses of the document, as I read it, are two: that episcopal conferences are not in the true and proper sense collegial and that they have, as such, no mandate to teach. Although many readers, like myself, will find the arguments given for these positions unpersuasive, the positions themselves need to be taken seriously, since they are supported by theologians and churchmen of stature, such as Cardinal Henri de Lubac, Cardinal Jerome Hamer, and Cardinal Joseph Ratzinger. To quibble with the format and logic of the present text will not necessarily bring about any change in the conclusions of the document; it is quite possible that, if the original authors are in charge of the revisions, the same positions will be presented more cogently than they now are. Everything depends on who will control the final version.

The questions of collegiality and teaching authority are intertwined, since to deny the first is to call the second into doubt. Whether bishops' conferences are properly collegial organs has long been disputed. The Second Vatican Council, while giving a clear ecclesial status to the conferences, avoided explicitly saying that they were or were not properly collegial entities. During the council Karl Rahner, Jerome Hamer, and Joseph Ratzinger contended that the conferences had a dogmatic foundation in the collegiality of the body of bishops and that the conferences were consequently partial actualizations of collegiality.

Pope John Paul II, in various addresses to conferences of bishops, has lent support to this view. For instance, he told the Brazilian hierarchy in 1980 that episcopal conferences are a "particularly appropriate organ of collegiality" and referred to conference statements as reflections of collegiality as concretely incarnated in a particular group of bishops. This view resonates with the self-understanding of many conferences. Cardinal Joseph Bernardin, in his presidential address to the NCCB in 1976, maintained that the conference is far more than a service agency designed to help the member bishops minister more effectively to their individual churches. "In the perspectives of theology," he asserted, "the conference is a concrete embodiment and implementation of the collegiality of the bishops of the United States" and thus indirectly an embodiment of the communion linking the local churches to one another in mutual solicitude and charity.

In their more recent statements, theologians such as Hamer and Ratzinger seem to have changed their position. They now speak of the conferences as having only "affective" as opposed to "effective" collegiality, and as being collegial only in an analogous and improper sense of the word. This position, I suspect, rests on a fear that the conferences might overstep their proper limits. Anyone who wishes to defend the collegiality of the episcopal conferences will have to show that the conferences do not infringe on the prerogatives of the total college, with the pope as its head, and do not override the pastoral responsibilities of the local bishops. This brings us to the question of teaching authority.

The competence to frame dogmas and other infallible teachings cannot be exercised by the bishops except through the full college in union with the pope as its head. But every bishop participates in this collegial authority. Individual bishops who are in communion with the college can preach and teach the Word of God authoritatively to their people. From early times, bishops have frequently exercised their teaching authority in particular councils, which have contributed in important ways to the development of the doctrine of the Church as a whole. Any argument against the teaching authority of bishops' conferences will have to be carefully framed so as not to impugn the acknowledged authority of particular councils, which was reaffirmed by Vatican II (*Decree on the Bishops' Pastoral Office in the Church* 36).

The working paper (*instrumentum laboris*) takes the position that the episcopal conferences do not, properly speaking, as such, possess any teaching office (*munus magisterii*). This position, though vigorously asserted, does not seem to follow logically from the authorities cited, such as the council's *Decree on the Bishops' Pastoral Office in the Church* and the revised Code of Canon Law. The *Decree on Bishops*, as I read it, strongly suggests that the conferences do have teaching authority, for it states that they are organs in which the bishops of a particular region jointly exercise their pastoral office (38); earlier the same document describes the pastoral office as including the three offices (*munera*) of teaching, sanctifying, and governing (11).

The new code, in canon 753 (quoted in the working paper), states explicitly that the bishops gathered in conferences are authentic teachers and instructors in the faith for the people entrusted to their care and that the faithful are obliged to adhere to the authoritative teaching issued by such gatherings. In other canons, episcopal conferences are given various doctrinal responsibilities, such as issuing catechetical materials (775), regulating the catechumenate (788), overseeing the doctrinal content of university teaching (809, 810), authorizing editions of holy scripture (825), and establishing procedures for the censorship of books (830). Many episcopal conferences, in their efforts to fulfill these and like prescriptions, have set up doctrinal committees.

The U.S. bishops' conference has taken on considerable doctrinal responsibilities, as have the conferences of other countries. The National Conference of Catholic Bishops (NCCB) has, for example, published a pastoral on moral values (1976), a National Catechetical Directory (1977), and a number of other doctrinal statements. The Vatican Congregation for the Doctrine of the Faith in 1976 felicitated the NCCB on its "wholesome moral teachings, especially on sexual matters," and Pope John Paul II, in his address to the U.S. hierarchy at Chicago in 1979, did likewise. In his apostolic exhortation *Reconciliation and Penance* (1984), the pope wrote at some length on the "social magisterium" exercised by the different episcopates in the circumstances of their own countries. I take these papal statements as confirmations of the teaching authority of bishops' conferences.

From January 2 to January 9, 1988, an International Colloquium on the Nature of Episcopal Conferences meeting at the University of Salamanca specifically addressed the question of teaching authority. According to the published accounts (Ladislas Orsy in *America*, February 6, 1988; and J. A. Komonchak and J. H. Provost in *Commonweal*, February 26, 1988), the participants reached general agreement that the conferences as such—and not simply the individual bishops who are present at the conference meeting—do have true teaching authority, although this authority is subject to many limitations.

If these limitations can be more clearly spelled out, there may prove to be a viable alternative to the position of the working paper that episcopal conferences do not "properly speaking" and "as such" possess a teaching function or office (*munus magisterii*).

All parties acknowledge that the conferences must teach in communion with the whole episcopate and especially with the Holy See. The exercise of a totally independent magisterium by the conferences could lead to divisions in the Church and to a species of ecclesiastical nationalism detrimental to catholicity. More clarity is needed on the juridical force of conference documents and on the cases in which review by the Holy See is a requirement. The present working paper has some brief but helpful comments on the moral authority of the conference and on the qualified right of bishops to dissent respectfully from certain conference statements. It also warns against the danger that the conferences might coerce the spiritual freedom of individual bishops or paralyze them in the exercise of their personal responsibility to teach.

Other problems must likewise be faced. As the working paper points out, there is a certain risk of bureaucratization. Consensus statements tend to be riddled with compromises. The conference staff, while indispensable for the process of drawing up documents, can sometimes usurp the initiative that should remain in the hands of the bishops. A further problem has to do with the authority of boards and committees that occasionally act on behalf of the conference, as did the administrative board of the U.S. Catholic Conference (USCC) in the December 1987 statement "The Many Faces of AIDS." Can statements of conference boards and committees claim any magisterial authority? Still further questions relate to the sphere of competence of bishops' conferences. For example, one often hears complaints that the NCCB and its staff have overreached themselves, speaking on highly technical questions of a socioeconomic character foreign to the proper mission of the Church. Finally, it is objected that the NCCB, at its regular meetings, has insufficient opportunity for the kind of serious dialogue that would be needed to arrive at a genuine consensus. The meetings are too large, the agenda too heavy, and the time too short.

The working paper, for all the immaturity of the present draft, quite properly raises questions of the type just listed.

Similar questions, indeed, plague practically all bureaucracies, not excluding the Vatican itself. Because of the importance and complexity of these questions, the working paper should not be cavalierly dismissed. It provides a welcome occasion for reflection and discussion.

13. THE TEACHING MISSION OF THE CHURCH AND ACADEMIC FREEDOM

April 21, 1990

The problem of academic freedom in Catholic universities has been much discussed in recent years, but as yet we seem to be far from achieving a consensus even among Catholic specialists. I shall try to cast some light on the question by considering the role of the university and its religious education programs in relation to the magisterium, or teaching authority of the Church. What does it mean to say that the Church teaches? Is the teaching of the Church a synonym for that of the hierarchical magisterium? If so, what place remains for the teaching of parents, catechists, and theologians? Can university theologians, in the name of academic freedom, claim the right to teach in opposition to the pope and the bishops? And if not, can they be said to have academic freedom at all? In view of the complexity of these questions, I shall consider myself successful if I can manage to avoid further confusing an already confused discussion.

The Teaching Mission of the Church. What does it mean to speak of the teaching mission of the Church? What does the Church teach, and how? According to a widely prevalent theological convention, endorsed by the documents of Vatican II, Jesus Christ had a threefold office as prophet, priest, and king. In his prophetic office he spoke to the world in the name of God. The term "prophet" in this context means one who speaks in the name of another—that is, God. In Greek the verb *prophemi* means to speak on behalf of; a *prophetes* is a spokesperson. As a prophet of God, Jesus announced the advent of the eschatological kingdom. But he did more than deliver a bare announcement. He also instructed his disciples in the mysteries of the kingdom. This authoritative instruction constitutes what we may call the prophetic teaching of Jesus. It is prophetic in the technical sense that Jesus spoke authoritatively as one sent by the Father.

The Church as a whole participates in the threefold office of Christ. As explained in Vatican II's *Dogmatic Constitution on the Church*, the Church, as prophet, has the task of announcing the good news, or of evangelizing. As an authoritative witness, it continues to proclaim the good news given in Christ. But it does more than proclaim. It has the task of offering precise and progressive instruction to its faithful so that they may to some extent understand the message they have received. This instruction may be called teaching.

Teaching may be attributed to the Church as a whole, but it is actually carried out by particular persons. The popes and bishops have an indispensable role in the total process, but they are not the sole educators of the faithful in matters of religion. Parents, according to Vatican II, are the first educators of their children. Every Christian believer, by virtue of baptism and confirmation, has a vocation to be a witness to the Gospel, and those who are reflective and educated in their faith have the capacity and the responsibility to instruct others.

The Church as a corporate body has the obligation to see to it that the faith is not corrupted or distorted in the process of transmission. For this reason certain controls are established. The entire process of transmission takes place under the supervision of the pope and the bishops, who are divinely appointed successors of the apostles in maintaining the correct understanding of the Christian message. The bishops have among their principal duties those of personally preaching the faith and instructing their people by sermons and pastoral letters. Their most effective teaching is often done when they associate others with themselves in the teaching apostolate. Priests and deacons, who are ordained to preach and to teach, are closely associated with the bishops. So also are a multitude of religious educators and catechists, some of whom function in Catholic schools, others in parishes and nonacademic situations.

It is helpful, therefore, to distinguish two ways in which the Church teaches—the official and the unofficial. It teaches officially through the pope and the bishops, who are by divine institution empowered to teach in the name of Christ. These officeholders speak in the name of the Church, in the sense that their official positions are those of the Church as a public institution. They have the right and duty to establish the doctrine of the Church as such. Without an official teaching organ, the Church would not be able to maintain a coherent body of teaching, and it would to that extent be deficient in carrying on the prophetic ministry of Christ. But the hierarchical officeholders are not the sole agents by whom the Church teaches. It teaches unofficially by means of those of its faithful who have sufficient knowledge to be able to bring others to a certain understanding of the faith. Religious instruction on the elementary level is called catechesis; on higher levels, it takes the form of advanced courses in Christian doctrine and theology. The entire process of Christian education takes place under the supervision of the hierarchical magisterium. To ensure the proper continuity between official magisterial teaching and day-to-day religious education, some teachers of religion are given an office or commission from the hierarchy.

Theologians as Teachers in the Church. All education in Christian doctrine involves a measure of reflective understanding of the Christian message and thus may be called, in some sense, theology. Theology has been defined in many ways, but it is difficult to improve on the phrase of Anselm, who spoke of "faith seeking understanding." Every believer who seeks to acquire or impart an understanding of the faith may be called, at least in a rudimentary way, a theologian or a teacher of theology.

In modern times the term "theology" is usually restricted to scholarly reflection upon the faith by persons who have attained a high degree of competence, normally certified by advanced degrees or noteworthy publications. In their pondering of the faith, theologians normally deal with questions such as these: What is the precise meaning of the accepted statements of faith? What is the basis of such statements in the source of revealed knowledge? How can the credibility of such statements be shown? What is their inner coherence and intelligibility in relation to the total Christian message? What relevance do they have for the human quest? What are the theoretical and practical consequences of the things that Christians believe, or should believe? The theologian seeks to answer such questions by drawing on all the sources of knowledge that might prove helpful, but the most basic reference point for theology is the faith itself, authoritatively set forth in normative documents.

In recent years there has been some debate about whether the theologian has to be a believer. Normally theologians are believers, for there would be little point in attempting to explore the implications of a faith one did not accept. Furthermore, it may be doubted whether a nonbeliever could be a really competent theologian. One who simply looks at a religion from outside without sharing its beliefs will rarely be a good interpreter of the tenets and implications of that religion. We may conclude, then, that theology is a reflection upon faith from within the commitment of faith. Those who attempt a purely detached analysis may be engaged in some legitimate type of religious studies, but they generally remain at the surface level and fail to achieve the kind of penetration that is expected in theology.

What, then, must the theologian accept? To do Christian theology at all one has to acknowledge the existence of God, the fact of revelation, the centrality of Christ in God's saving plan, and the reliable transmission of the Gospel through scripture and the Church. In addition, Catholic theology is predicated upon the validity of the Catholic tradition and upon the guidance offered by the hierarchical magisterium. The Catholic theologian who wishes to remain a Catholic is bound to accept the definitive or irreformable doctrine of the magisterium and must be favorably disposed to accepting whatever the magisterium puts forth as obligatory doctrine.

There are limits, therefore, to the freedom of theology. Under pain of self-destruction, it is prevented from denying its own foundations. This kind of limitation is by no means peculiar to theology. Every discipline is bound to admit the reality of its own object and the conditions of accessibility of that object. No geologist, while remaining a geologist, can take the position that the earth does not exist or that it is unknowable. Astronomy cannot deny the heavens, optics cannot deny light, and medicine cannot deny the fact of disease. As a human being, the theologian remains free to become an unbeliever, even an atheist, if so prompted by conscience. But in so doing one automatically ceases to be a theologian. Let it not be said, therefore, that the theologian, as theologian, can reject revelation or that the Catholic theologian can reject the canonical scriptures and dogmas of the Church. To accept these things is not a limitation on theology, but rather the charter of its existence and freedom to be itself. The more firmly theology is grounded in faith, the more capable, generally speaking, will it be of understanding the nature and contents of faith.

Although Catholic theology must, as I have just said, submit to the Word of God as it comes through scripture, tradition, and the hierarchical magisterium, theology does not simply repeat what is in its sources. It reflects on the sources with a view to answering contemporary questions, questions not explicitly answered in the sources themselves. It seeks the intelligibility of the revelation in all the ways I have just indicated—through positive theology, which probes the sources; through apologetics, which seeks to establish credibility; through systematics, which concerns itself with the inner coherence of the whole scheme of revelation; and through practical theology, which ponders the implications of the revealed message for human conduct. Within its particular sphere of competence, theology is free to reach whatever conclusions are indicated by a proper application of its own method. Popes and bishops have no mandate to tell the theologian how to do theology, beyond the negative mandate of seeing to it that theology does not undermine the life of faith itself. Theology, therefore, possesses a certain freedom over against even the hierarchical magisterium. Without that freedom it could not be theology, and hence it could not be of service to the Church. The medieval axiom *non ancilla nisi libera* ("of no help unless free") holds for theology.

While emphasizing the fidelity of theology to the teaching of the hierarchical magisterium, I have not ruled out the possibility of dissent. I recognize that in certain cases, which I would take to be rare in view of the overall reliability of the magisterium, a given theologian may find the official doctrine unconvincing. A proper docility will move the theologian to seek reasons in favor of the teaching in question, but there comes a point where the will cannot compel the intellect to assent, and where the possibility of an error in non-infallible magisterial teaching must be reckoned with. The approved theological manuals have for many years taken account of this eventuality, and since Vatican II, the United States bishops have put out guidelines for the public expression of dissenting positions in the Church.

Dissent should be neither glorified nor vilified. It is not necessarily an act of greater probity and courage to dissent than to assent. Whenever dissent is expressed, it tends to weaken the Church as a sign of unity. Nevertheless dissent cannot be totally eliminated. It may be subjectively and even objectively justified. To deny its existence or to seek to suppress it would be more harmful than to acknowledge it and deal with it honestly.

Theology always stands under correction. The hierarchical magisterium has the power and the responsibility to approve or disapprove of theological teaching from the standpoint of orthodoxy. By approving of the works of the Fathers and Doctors of the Church, including saints such as Augustine and Thomas Aquinas, the Church has given them a quasi-official status, so that the faithful may be confident that the works of these authors will lead them to a better grasp of the faith. But the magisterium never has canonized, and, I think, never could canonize, the theology of any school or individual. Just as faith differs from any systematization of faith, so the doctrine of the magisterium differs in its object from theology. Even when popes and bishops approvingly quote the works of theologians, they do not make the theology of these authors binding on the faithful.

The magisterium can associate certain theologians very closely with itself. Some, for example, are members of, or consultors to, the Congregation for the Doctrine of the Faith. Some are asked to draft papal encyclicals or other official documents. Some are given a canonical mission by their bishops to teach in seminaries or other ecclesiastical faculties. According to the apostolic constitution *Sapientia Christiana*, published by Pope John Paul II in 1979, those who teach with canonical mission "do not teach by their own authority but on the strength of a mission received from the church" (27.1).

Occasionally one hears it said that professors who have a canonical mission teach "in the name of the church." Although a proper interpretation can be given to this phrase, I prefer to avoid it, since it tends to obscure the distinction between the role of bishops, who can by their teaching publicly commit the Church, and that of theologians, who cannot. Theology is by its very nature a private enterprise. A theologian who has a *nihil obstat* from the Holy See or a canonical mission or mandate from the competent authority is able to exercise his or her functions with the added prestige that comes from these tokens of official trust. But the theologian is not thereby dispensed from having to proceed according to the proper methods of the theological disciplines and from being subject to criticism from peers for any failures of scholarship or reasoning.

Academic Freedom. Up to this point, I have been attempting to clarify what is meant by the teaching of the Church. I have found it helpful to distinguish between the teaching of the Church, which is that of the hierarchy, and teaching in the Church, which is nonhierarchical. Both bishops and theologians teach, but they do so in different ways. Bishops teach with authority to bind in the name of Christ; theologians teach in an academic, non-authoritative way. I have spoken of the sense in which theology is bound to the doctrine of the official magisterium and of the senses in which it is free. It will now be possible for me to turn, in what follows, to the issue of academic freedom. Such freedom applies most obviously to teachers in the academy, that is to say, in institutions of higher learning that are committed to exacting standards of scholarship. Is the theologian or the professor of other sacred disciplines, such as biblical studies and canon law, entitled to academic freedom, and if so, in what sense?

There is no official or uncontested definition of academic freedom. In current usage, at least in the United States, the term generally denotes the freedom of professionally qualified teachers, first, to pursue their scholarly investigations without interference; second, to publish the results of their research and reflection; and, third, to teach according to their own convictions, provided that they remain in the area of their competence and present the alternative positions with sufficient attention and fairness. Many statements on academic freedom add that in cases of dispute, the competence and professional conduct of the teacher should be assessed by experts chosen from among academic colleagues or peers.

In the United States there is a strong tendency to maintain that academic freedom is essential to the very concept of a college or university. The American Association of University Professors (AAUP), in a series of statements since its inception in 1915, has promoted this position. Limitations on academic freedom are considered injurious to the academic standing of the institution and likely to imperil the accreditation of its degrees by professional associations.

As the AAUP has recognized on several occasions, the concept of academic freedom raises delicate questions for Church-related institutions. A Catholic college or university is not purely and simply an academy in the secular meaning of the term. It seeks to discharge a service toward the Church and toward the religious development of its students, especially those who are Catholics.

It could be objected, of course, that any such practical orientation to goals that lie beyond the cultivation of rationally acquired knowledge is extraneous to the nature of the university. If so, theology, as I have explained it in this paper, would have no place in the university curriculum. This solution, as drastic as it is simple, is unrealistic. It rests upon a purist concept of the university that neglects the relation of education to the world as it is and to human beings as they are. The Church and the Catholic people legitimately expect that some universities will provide an intellectual environment in which the meaning and implications of the faith can be studied in relation to the whole realm of human knowledge. Without Catholic university theology, the Church would be less able to relate to the culture of the day and to reflect on its faith with the instruments of contemporary knowledge. Catholic parents and students often choose Church-related colleges and universities because such institutions provide a favorable situation in which to gain a mature, reflective understanding of the faith.

If theology were expelled from the university, Catholic parents and students would be deprived of a fundamental educational right. The Church would be deprived of an important resource for its mission. The university too would suffer because, as Cardinal Newman pointed out, other disciplines would occupy, without adequate warrant or competence, the territory vacated by the departure of theology. The larger society would stand to lose because in our pluralistic culture Catholic theological faculties provide valuable input from one of the major religious traditions of the nation.

It would be ironic indeed if university education, which arose in many parts of Europe under the sponsorship of the Church and which frequently looked upon theology as its crowning discipline, were now to be defined in a way that excluded theology. It is an undeniable fact that many of the leading universities of the world, both in the past and in our own day, have flourished under ecclesiastical sponsorship and direction. It would be sheer ignorance to deny the quality of scholarship that emanates from some of the major Catholic universities and theological faculties in the United States and in many other countries. To define university education so as to exclude such institutions and faculties is evidence of a narrow parochialism that is, in its own way, sectarian. If religious sectarianism is to be rejected—as indeed it should be—secular sectarianism should not be established in its place.

Supposing, then, that theology as a systematic reflection upon faith does have a right to exist, at least in some universities, we must inquire what kind of academic freedom is desirable to protect this discipline. It does need protection. History provides abundant cases in which civil and religious authorities have unjustly intervened to prevent theologians from publishing and teaching according to the canon of their own discipline. Several years after the death of Thomas Aquinas, a number of his positions in philosophy and theology were condemned by the bishop of Paris and the archbishop of Canterbury.

Some of his faithful followers were severely punished for heresy. Before long the condemnations were withdrawn, but the very occurrence of the error illustrates the likelihood that local episcopal authorities will be overzealous in seeking to enforce orthodoxy. In modern times the authority of the state has been even more oppressive than that of the Church in attempting to control theology. Consider, for example, the actions of the Parlement of Paris and of the Emperor Joseph II of Austria, not to mention the excesses of German National Socialism. Clearly, then, theology stands to gain, as do other disciplines, from the protection of academic freedom. But academic freedom must be rightly understood.

The prevalent secular theories of academic freedom are not fully satisfactory. They give rise to several difficulties. First, they raise the question whether academic freedom absolves the Christian or Catholic theologian from the obligation to teach in accordance with the Christian or Catholic faith. Some theorists contend that no professor can be required to adhere to any substantive teaching. To set limits to scholarly conclusions, it is argued, is to violate a basic principle of academic freedom.

This view of the matter, in my opinion, embodies some confusions. No one can be coerced into personally holding the faith. Faith is by its very nature free. But a rejection of Catholic faith, even if merely private, would be detrimental to theology as a reflection upon faith. A nonbelieving professor would be ill suited to present the tradition of the Church from the point of view of faith or to assist the student to reflect upon the implications of faith. In teaching according to his or her own convictions, such a professor could not be teaching Catholic theology. Thus a person hired for the purpose of teaching Catholic theology might well be disqualified by a failure to hold and profess the Catholic faith.

Further difficulties arise from the contention, frequently made, that academic freedom implies that alleged violations of the norms of Catholic theology should be judged only by colleagues, or "peers" as they are commonly called. It is not entirely clear who the peers of a Catholic theologian in a Catholic institution would be. Would they all be Catholics? Would they be theologians? If the question under dispute is whether a Catholic theologian has exceeded the bounds of orthodoxy, non-Catholics or non-theologians could hardly be qualified to reach a verdict. I would even doubt whether a group of Catholic theologians could be expected to render a truly objective judgment. Peer pressure would be too strong. According to a long-standing Catholic tradition, pastoral judgments concerning purity of doctrine are, in the last instance, the prerogative of the ecclesiastical magisterium.

I deliberately insert the words "in the last instance." For reasons already indicated, when I spoke of the condemnations of Thomistic doctrine in France and England, I am apprehensive that bishops or their curial assistants, possibly aroused by one-sided letters of complaint, might pronounce over hastily upon technical questions in which they were not fully competent. They should make sure that they have correctly understood exactly what the theologian is saying and why. This will often require a familiarity with the state of the discipline and with the special meaning that certain terms have acquired in the literature of the field. Theologians need scope in which to develop tentative positions and to make hypothetical statements that could easily be misunderstood by non-specialists. They are entitled to raise some legitimate questions about the current non-infallible teaching of the magisterium. They must, of course, be held to prudence in the ways in which they publicize their theories and hypotheses, but they cannot always be responsible for the uses that others make of statements quite proper in themselves. To avoid perpetrating injustice, bishops may sometimes have the duty to enter into a dialogue process something like that suggested in the guidelines adopted by the United States bishops at their Seton Hall meeting in June 1989. According to that document, "In cases of dispute, the theologian has the right to expect access to a fair process, protecting both substantive and procedural rights." In a university, due process for its professors will normally be provided for by the statutes and the faculty manual.

Every theologian should enjoy academic freedom, in the sense of a right to inquire, publish, and teach according to the norms of the discipline. But because "theology" is an essentially ecclesial discipline, the freedom of the theologian must not be absolutized over and against other elements in the community of faith. While the freedom of the professor as an individual scholar should be respected, it should be seen in the context of other values. One such value is the integrity of Catholic theology as a meditation on the shared faith of the whole Church. Whoever substitutes a purely individual or deviant faith forfeits any title to be called a Catholic theologian. Another such value is the maintenance of sound doctrine. Although sound doctrine is a particular responsibility of the hierarchical magisterium, it is of foundational importance for theology itself. In the interests of their own profession, theologians should support the magisterium as it seeks to safeguard the apostolic heritage, whether by way of positively encouraging sound developments or by way of administering, on occasion, a word of caution or correction. The rights of the theologian as an academician become real only when situated in this ecclesial framework.

There is the other whole complex question of how the pastoral judgments of the hierarchy should be implemented within the university. The question has to be answered in different ways for universities of different types. In each case, the charter "and statutes of the university must be considered, as well as the terms of the contract entered into between the university and the faculty member in question." Unless the statutes so provide, I do not see how the Holy See or the bishops could intervene directly in the working of a civilly chartered university by dismissing a professor or preventing a course from being taught. Whether the officers or trustees could dismiss a professor whom the hierarchy judged to be lacking in orthodoxy would depend upon the variables just mentioned. On the other hand, a given university might by its statutes engage itself publicly to hire in its department of theology only professors who have received some kind of license or mission from ecclesiastical authorities. In the United States, this type of arrangement will presumably be rare and will normally be accompanied by provisions to ensure due process. Here, as in other countries, ecclesiastical control can be, has been, and is fully compatible with a high level of theological research. Theologians of the stature of Karl Rahner and Bernard

Lonergan regularly taught, I believe, with a canonical mission or its equivalent.

I conclude, therefore, that the prevailing secular model, as described by standard authorities, requires some modification before being applied to Catholic or other Church-related institutions. The model shows signs of having been constructed with a laudable but one-sided purpose of protecting university professors from incompetent outside authorities, who might unjustly seek to impose their own ideas. This model overlooks the responsibility of theology to the community of faith and the mandate of the ecclesiastical magisterium to ensure the doctrinal soundness of theology.

The secular model, moreover, is somewhat narrowly based on a theory of knowledge more suited to the empirical sciences than to theology, which rests primarily on divine revelation. The dogmas of faith do not have the same status in theology as the currently accepted theories have for secular science. Those who practice theology with the conviction that revealed truth exists and is reliably transmitted by authoritative sources will see the need to work out a properly theological concept of academic freedom. A properly adapted version will protect authentic theology but will not separate theologians from the Body of the Church; it will not set them in opposition to the community of faith or its pastoral leadership. Theologians and bishops, in spite of their different roles in the Church, are fundamentally allies because they are alike committed to maintain and explore the unfathomable riches of Christ, in whom alone is given the truth that makes us free.

14. THE THEOLOGIAN

April 18, 2005

A s bishop and later pope, John Paul II did not have the freedom to propose purely personal theological positions in his official documents. When acting as a pastoral teacher, he sought rather to defend and proclaim the doctrine of the faith. But since doctrine always has to be expressed, justified, and interpreted in a theologically colored language, official teaching and theology always interpenetrate. Even in their proclamation of the Christian message, popes and bishops have regularly relied upon theological advisers or upon their personal competence in theology. Karol Wojtyla was outstanding among the popes of modern times for his reliance on his own competence and insights. Even in his official documents one can usually hear the voice of Wojtyla, their author.

Among the personal gifts that Wojtyla brought to his office one must reckon his exceptional qualifications in philosophy and theology. He completed a doctoral degree in theology at the Angelicum in Rome in 1946, followed by a doctorate in ethics at the Jagiellonian University in Krakow in 1954. He began to teach social ethics in the faculty of philosophy at the Catholic University of Lublin in 1953, and continued to do so, as time permitted, even after his appointment as bishop in 1958. In 1978, as cardinal, he received the title of "honorary professor," a position he retained for life.

Trained as he was in both theology and philosophy, Wojtyla was sensitive to the dual claims of faith and reason. The light of faith, he maintained, could bring reason to its highest fulfillment and sustain it in its quest for wisdom. Conversely, faith was dependent on reason to give intelligibility to the Word of God, received through revelation.

The distinctive traits of Wojtyla's theology may be ascribed to three sets of influences. As a child and young man he was nurtured by the strongly Catholic piety of southern Poland; he steeped himself in prayer and savored the high spirituality of St. John of the Cross. As a graduate student of theology in Rome, he espoused the metaphysical realism of St. Thomas Aquinas. Later, as a doctoral student in philosophy, he came to appreciate personalist phenomenology. This threefold derivation has made John Paul II's theology mystical, ontological, and dialogical or, to put the same ideas in different terms, devotional, metaphysical, and phenomenological. Linking all these dimensions together is a pervasive personalism.

In February 1968 the recently appointed Cardinal Karol Wojtyla wrote to Henri de Lubac, S.J.:

> I devote my very rare free moments to a work that is close to my heart and devoted to the metaphysical sense and mystery of the PERSON. It seems to me that the debate today is being played on that level. The evil of our times consists in the first place in a kind of degradation, indeed in a pulverization, of the fundamental uniqueness of each human person. This evil is even much more of the metaphysical order than of the moral order. To this disintegration, planned at times by atheistic ideologies, we must oppose, rather than sterile polemics, a kind of "recapitulation" of the inviolable mystery of the person. (See Henri de Lubac, At the Service of the Church [San Francisco: Ignatius, 1993], 171–72.)

Wojtyla's personalism, matured by his familiarity with the Thomism of the Lublin school and the writings of Max Scheler (1874–1928), the German phenomenologist, was confirmed by his encounters with Marxism. In post–World War II Poland, the Church, he found, was the chief defender of the dignity and rights of persons in opposition to totalitarian oppression. As a philosopher, Wojtyla taught that human persons stand above the rest of the visible world by virtue of their capacity to make responsible decisions—a task that required them to envisage the true and the good. As a theologian he knew that our human dignity comes from our creation in the image and likeness of God. We are called to yet closer union with the divine, thanks to the Incarnation, whereby the Son of God became our brother, paid the price for our redemption, and sent his Spirit into our hearts.

In his days as a student priest, Wojtyla developed close pastoral relations with young married couples. In informal conversations with them he developed a very positive assessment of the body and of human sexuality. The human person, he asserted, was not created to be solitary but to live in communion with others. By God's design, male and female are complementary. This complementarity comes to its fullest expression in the marital act, which is intrinsically ordered toward procreation—an activity whereby human beings are privileged to participate in the creative action of God. The total self-giving of the partners demands openness to the generation of new life. In his first book, *Love and Responsibility* (1960; English translation 1981), Bishop Wojtyla strongly supported the traditional Catholic teaching on the objective immorality of contraception—a position he would reaffirm as a cardinal and a member of Pope Paul VI's "birth control" commission.

As a young bishop, Wojtyla attended all four sessions of the Second Vatican Council (1962–65). The event deeply marked the rest of his career. He formed friendships with prominent theologians, including the Dominican Yves Congar (1904–95) and the Jesuit Henri de Lubac (1896–1991), both of whom he would later raise to the cardinalate. The two documents that most engaged his attention were the 1965 *Declaration on Religious Freedom* and the 1965 *Pastoral Constitution on the Church in the Modern World*. While esteeming these documents for their assertion of human freedom and self-determination, he defended them against false interpretations. Freedom, he insisted, is not an end in itself; it is given to us in order that we may personally embrace the truth and live by it. The truth is objective and transcendent; it demands our reverent submission. When freedom becomes arbitrary and self-willed, it destroys itself.

Shortly after Vatican II, Cardinal Wojtyla held a synod for his archdiocese of Krakow for the sake of implementing the council. His *Sources of Renewal*, composed as a guide for this synod, displays his mastery of the conciliar texts, his perfect fidelity to their teaching, and his personalist interpretation of the council as an event. Vatican II, he held, marked a dramatic advance in the self-consciousness of the Church, corresponding to a fresh moment in human history. The Church, seen as a believing subject rather than simply as an object of faith, has accepted fuller responsibility for the faith it professes. At the council, the Church recognized itself as "the social subject of responsibility for divine truth" (see John Paul II's first encyclical, issued in 1979, *Redemptor Hominis*, 19).

In *Sources of Renewal* and subsequent writings, John Paul II showed a marked predilection for the idea of the Church as a spiritual communion of persons, modeled on the divine Trinity as a *communio personarum*. The Church exists in order to make its members holy—that is to say, sharers in the divine Trinitarian life. While the whole Church is a great family of persons bound together by the love of God, each Christian household is called to be a Church in miniature, an *ecclesia domestica*. Like the Church itself, the family is a communion of persons. It should be an efficacious and fruitful sign mirroring the loving union between Christ and the Church.

In his theology of office in the Church, John Paul II maintained his personalist perspective. The sacramental and institutional elements in the Church, he insisted, exist for the sake of fostering personal holiness in the whole people of God. Popes and bishops, as hierarchical leaders, stand at the meeting point between Christ and other members of the Church. Through their faith and prayer they must be personally responsive to the mysterious presence of Christ through the Holy Spirit. The entire body of bishops, moreover, is bound together in a communion of grace and love, technically expressed in the doctrine of collegiality. The "hierarchical communion" of the pastors gives expression to the communion of their Churches. Collegiality, most perfectly expressed in ecumenical councils, receives true though limited expression in synods of bishops and episcopal conferences.

Episcopal collegiality and papal primacy, in Wojtyla's vision, were two sides of the same coin. Collegiality itself requires a primatial office charged with special responsibility for maintaining unity among the bishops. The bishops should not be isolated from their head, nor the head from the bishops. Convinced of this reciprocity, John Paul II made extraordinary efforts to keep in close contact with the bishops of every nation. In teaching he refrained from invoking his personal infallibility in *ex cathedra* pronouncements. He preferred to use his office as supreme pastor to declare what was already taught by the bishops. On several occasions John Paul II proclaimed doctrines that should be firmly believed by all the faithful by reason of the constant and universal consensus of the bishops, grounded in scripture and tradition.

While recognizing that perfect communion requires the fullness of the means of grace available only in the Catholic Church, John Paul II insisted that the communion of grace extends beyond the visible borders of Roman Catholicism. Orthodox and Protestant Christians, thanks to their faith, sacraments, and ministry, are in various degrees of communion with Catholics. According to the will of Christ, all believers should be conjoined in a single visible Church. The aim of the ecumenical movement, according to John Paul II, was to pass from incomplete to full communion among separated Christians. Respectful dialogue is a privileged means of bringing this about.

As a personalist, John Paul II had great confidence in dialogue and sought to promote it not only among Christians but with non-Christians as well. Conscious of the dignity of every human person and of the workings of grace among all peoples, he called attention to what Vatican II, following the early Fathers, called "seeds of the Word" and "rays of divine truth" in the various religions and philosophies of humankind. Dialogue seeks to identify these seeds and bring them to maturity so that they may bear fruit.

Seeking a productive dialogue with scientists, John Paul II sponsored interdisciplinary colloquia with cosmologists about the origin of the universe. He was convinced that the ancient quarrels between science and religion rested on unfortunate confusions. Just as scientists had sometimes intruded into the sphere of theology, so churchmen had occasionally trespassed on the territory of science. Each discipline, he contended, should remain within its own sphere of competence and respect the relative autonomy of other disciplines. From the beginning of his pontificate, Wojtyla defended the Polish astronomer Copernicus (1473–1543) and took steps to retract Pope Paul V's condemnation of Galileo in 1616. In dialogue with anthropologists, he expressed his readiness to accept the evolution of the human body, provided that the process was not understood in atheistic or materialistic terms.

As a theologian of dialogue, John Paul II drew on the personalism of Jewish philosophers such as Martin Buber and Emmanuel Lévinas. Like them he taught that sincere dialogue demands candor in manifesting one's own positions. Dialogue therefore appeared to Wojtyla as fully compatible with the Church's mission to evangelize all peoples. In dialogue, he noted, we give witness to our own convictions while listening respectfully to the testimony of others. To bear witness to Jesus Christ is an essential task and privilege of the Church and of all its members. The Gospel, according to John Paul II, should be proclaimed to all peoples, because all have a right to hear the message of divine love and redemption that has been entrusted to the Church. Our times call for a "new evangelization" that expresses the

Gospel in new language and makes full use of the new media of communication.

Evangelization, in the perspectives of John Paul II, was always closely linked with social teaching. In his social doctrine, he built on human dignity and freedom as basic presuppositions. He was not content to propound a negative ethics based on divine prohibitions. Our obligations toward others, he believed, are positively grounded in the inherent dignity of every human person. From earlier popes, and especially John XXIII, Wojtyla took over the concept of the Church as a champion of human rights.

The right to life, in Wojtyla's view, was fundamental because life is the primary good, presupposed by all others. Above and beyond biological life, people have the right to a truly human existence. On various occasions John Paul II set forth rather comprehensive lists of human rights, such as those to food, shelter, clothing, education, religious freedom, employment, and political participation. He also championed the rights of nations, families, women, workers, and oppressed minorities. These rights, while deeply inscribed in the nature of reality, are enhanced by the biblical message of creation and redemption. The inviolability of human rights, for Wojtyla, demanded that they be grounded in the transcendent, that is to say, in God.

In espousing the sacredness of human life, John Paul II emphatically repudiated evils such as abortion and euthanasia. Without going to the extreme of pacifism, he showed a consistent aversion to war and a reluctance to approve of capital punishment.

Perhaps because of his own experience doing forced labor during the Nazi occupation of Poland, Wojtyla spoke with special feeling about the rights of labor. As a personalist he protested against the instrumentalization of work, whether by the state or by a capitalist class. According to his theology, work should be perfective of laborers themselves, even when it is burdensome. The difficulty of toil can itself be redemptive, especially when united to the sufferings of Jesus on the Cross.

Although he criticized the extremes of laissez-faire capitalism, John Paul II never espoused socialism. From his experience under a Marxist regime in Poland, he saw firsthand the inefficiency and corruption of the planned economy. As a personalist, he believed that entrepreneurs should be free and creative. In his encyclicals he spoke of the advantages of the free market economy while at the same time pointing out the necessity for government intervention to prevent economic injustices.

The theme of culture was dear to John Paul II as a poet, dramatist, and actor. Poland, he believed, preserved the faith by means of its culture, which remained authentically Christian and Catholic even when the political order was militantly atheistic. Faith, in his view, had a natural tendency to become incarnate in cultures and in so doing to purify and elevate cultures themselves. Conversely, faith tended to be weakened when culture was debased. John Paul II wrote a stirring "Letter to Artists," exhorting artists to seek out new epiphanies of beauty, "opening the human soul to the sense of the eternal." Contemporary culture in the West, in his estimation, showed alarming signs of becoming materialistic and hedonistic. Cultures, he believed, were always in need of being evangelized.

Wojtyla's thought unfolded in light of his vision of God's personal self-disclosure through his action in human history. Prior to the coming of Christ, God manifested his mercy and fidelity by his dealings with Israel. In the life and ministry of Jesus, God presented himself as the Son, obedient to the Father in carrying out his redemptive mission. And after the resurrection of Jesus, God revealed himself even more fully as the tri-personal mystery of love. The Spirit bestowed at Pentecost, in Wojtyla's view, discloses the inner depth of the divinity. Human beings are thus enabled to understand themselves and their destiny in reference to the triune God.

Wojtyla's Christology was framed in universalist perspectives. Christ for him was the center and goal of all history and indeed of the whole cosmos. No individual could attain fulfillment without communion with Jesus Christ, the universal redeemer. With this conviction, John Paul II opened his pontificate with the bold summons "Be not afraid. Open wide the doors for Christ. To his saving power open the boundaries of states, economic and political systems, the vast fields of culture, civilization, and development." It is fear, he believed, that drives individuals, parties, and nations to set up barriers to the truth, goodness, and beauty of God, shining forth on the face of Jesus Christ.

Wojtyla had a deep Marian piety based in part on his early study of St. Louis Grignion de Montfort. In his 1987 encyclical on Mary, he extolled her as the fairest daughter of the Father, the Mother of the Son, and the Spouse of the Holy Spirit. By reason of her intimate relationship with the three divine persons, she is the exemplar and the supreme realization of the Church, which reflects in itself her virginal motherhood. Just as on earth Mary exercised a maternal role toward Jesus, so in heaven she intercedes in a maternal way for the mystical Body. At Vatican II Wojtyla's voice was one of the many that successfully urged Pope Paul VI to confer on Mary the title "Mother of the Church."

A notable feature of Wojtyla's thought is the importance he attached to particular times and places. He made much of shrines and pilgrimages. The crucial turning points of salvation history, in his assessment, had abiding efficacy. Devoutly recalled in the prayer of the community, these saving mysteries can continue to impart their specific graces to the Church. The mysteries of the new covenant, according to John Paul II, are reactualized in the Church's liturgy.

According to Wojtyla's theology of time, the history of the Church is punctuated with weekly, yearly, and jubilee celebrations of the foundational events. Sunday, as the Lord's Day, should be specially observed by the assembly of the community at the Holy Eucharist as a living memorial of the paschal mystery. The authenticity of the Eucharist requires that it be celebrated by priests ordained in succession to the Twelve who were present at the Last Supper. The priest at the altar acts in the very person of Christ, the covenant partner and spouse of the Church. Following Vatican II, the pope treasures the eucharistic sacrifice as "the source and summit of the Christian life."

John Paul II saw his own pontificate as spanning the interval between Vatican II and the jubilee of the year 2000. Suitably prepared for, that jubilee could be a moment of special grace and renewal for the Church. In his 1994 apostolic letter The Coming of the Third Millennium, the pope indicated ways whereby the Church could dispose itself for the graces of the occasion. He called for gratitude for past favors, for an examination of conscience on the part of the whole Church, for acts of repentance, for hope of forgiveness, and for a renewal of trust in God. Over the heads of some nervous cardinals, he insisted that the Church should corporately express sorrow for unjust and violent acts that had been performed with its blessing in the past. The celebration of the millennial jubilee, the pope believed, could usher in an age of greater unity among Christians and a new springtime of evangelization.

At the end of the great jubilee, John Paul II issued a new apostolic letter, The Beginning of the New Millennium, in which he sought to harvest the graces of the previous year. Calling for prayerful contemplation, he taught that effective proclamation of Christ requires deep insertion into the Christian mystery. Personal holiness is the primary vocation of the Church, which proclaims Christ more by what it is than by anything it does. In his last years the pope sought to show forth the meaning of old age and suffering in his own patient perseverance.

So vast and multiform is the doctrinal legacy of John Paul II that it defies easy assessment. Perhaps the world will have to wait another century before it can pronounce on the positive achievements and limitations of this brilliant and energetic pope. Even today, however, it can be said that he brought the teaching of the Church to bear on almost every area of modern life. While firmly adhering to the Catholic doctrinal tradition and the positions of

Vatican II, he advanced Catholic teaching in several areas, such as the theology of the body, the sacredness of human life, the theological meaning of culture, work, and leisure. He urged Catholics to be open to respectful dialogue, confident of their own heritage, and critical of the spirit of the age. While seeking to reach out to the whole world, he never compromised on matters of doctrine for the sake of winning acclaim. On unpopular issues he was content to be, like his Master, a "sign of contradiction."

LECTURES AND ADDRESSES

15. EPISCOPAL CONFERENCES: THEIR TEACHING AUTHORITY

January 6, 1990

(Address delivered at the Seminary of the Immaculate Conception, in Huntington, New York, on October 15, 1989.)

Much of the difficulty surrounding the question of the teaching authority of episcopal conferences stems from the ambiguities in the documents of Vatican Council II's *Constitution on the Church* (*Lumen Gentium*) which makes it clear in article 25 that only the universal college of bishops or the pope speaking *ex cathedra* can demand the absolute assent of faith. But the same article declares that popes and councils, when they do not call for divine faith, may require a religious submission of mind (*obsequium animi religiosum*). The same is true, said the council, of the individual bishop speaking as the teacher of his diocese.

Lumen Gentium, though it alluded to episcopal conferences in article 23, nowhere mentioned them as having authority to teach. Nor can one find reference to their teaching authority in the *Constitution on the Liturgy* or in the *Decree on the Church's Missionary Activity*, both of which speak of episcopal conferences. The most extensive treatment of the conferences is in the *Decree on the Pastoral Ministry of Bishops* (*Christus Dominus*). In article 38, this decree describes an episcopal conference as a gathering in which the bishops of a given nation or territory jointly exercise their pastoral ministry. This language can be interpreted so as to include joint teaching, but the power of conferences to teach is not specifically mentioned. To all appearances Vatican II wished to leave open the question whether or not episcopal conferences possess the power to teach with authority in the Church.

The 1983 Code of Canon Law, in its chapter on the nature and authority of episcopal conferences (canons 447–59), makes no mention of conferences as doctrinal instances. In speaking of the legally binding decrees (*decreta*) of episcopal conferences (canon 455), the code seems to have in view only legislative acts and practical norms.

In book III, however, on the Teaching Office of the Church, the code in one canon (753) speaks of the bishops in conference as having the power to teach with authority and states that such teaching, like that of an individual bishop of a particular council, calls for religious submission of mind. The term here used (*religiosum animi obsequium*) is the same as that used in *Lumen Gentium* 25. This canon is not supported by anything else in the code, and some authors have tried to interpret it in ways that deny teaching authority to the conferences as such. Like most other commentators, I am personally convinced that the canon must be interpreted as conferring on the conferences as such a certain power to teach with authority. I conclude, therefore, that according to current canon law episcopal conferences are true doctrinal instances in the Church.

Some questions, however, remain. Book II of the code, in canon 455, lays down very stringent conditions for legislative acts on the part of episcopal conferences. Such acts require, ordinarily, a special mandate from the Holy See to legislate on the particular matter, passage by a two-thirds majority of those entitled to a deliberative vote and a subsequent review of the decree by the Holy See. Canon 753, by contrast, does not specify the conditions under which episcopal conferences can teach with obligatory force. Must the bishops all agree, or must there be at least a moral unanimity in favor of the doctrine? Does a two-thirds majority suffice? Or a simple majority? Is any kind of prior approval or subsequent review by the Holy See required? Are the individual bishops who belong to the conference entitled to dissent from their colleagues and to teach their own dioceses according to their own convictions? Until these and similar questions are answered, it is difficult to apply canon 753 in practice.

In the past few years some very distinguished theologians, including Cardinal Henri de Lubac, Cardinal Jerome Hamer, and Cardinal Joseph Ratzinger, have cast doubts on the theological basis for episcopal conferences, on the collegial nature of their activity, and especially on their doctrinal authority. Fears have been raised that the conferences tend to undermine the teaching authority of the pope, that they introduce an unhealthy nationalism into the Church, that they breed an ambitious and power-hungry bureaucracy, and that they frustrate the ministry of individual diocesan bishops as teachers of their people. Conscious of these criticisms, the Extraordinary Synod of Bishops, meeting at Rome in 1985, requested a theological study to clarify the status of the conferences and especially their teaching authority. The Congregation for Bishops was placed in charge of that project, and in 1987 it circulated the first draft of the results of its study. That draft, however, was so unsatisfactory that bishops and theologians all over the world reacted with anger and dismay. In the United States, a committee consisting of all the previous presidents of the National Conference of Catholic Bishops (NCCB) was unsparing in its criticism. As a result of all this negative feedback, the draft has, to all appearances, been withdrawn. But the whole future of the study now seems to be in limbo.

While the theoretical problems cannot be solved without further clarifications from Church authorities, the actual practice of the conferences is less problematical. I can think of no instance in which an episcopal conference has tried to impose its own teaching as obligatory on the faithful of its territory, as canon 753 suggests that it might do. Frequently, of course, the conferences restate for the people of their territory what is already the doctrine of the Church and seek to bring out special emphases or implications to meet the current pastoral problems. But in so doing the conferences make no effort to establish doctrine that is binding only upon the faithful of their own territory. Catholics in the United States, for example, are not held to any beliefs over and above the common faith of the Church all over the world.

For the most part, the teaching of the conferences has been pastoral rather than strictly doctrinal. That is to say, the aim has been to state common Catholic doctrine in a manner persuasive and meaningful to the people of their territory. The NCCB in this country has sought to mediate between the universal teaching of the Church, as found in papal and conciliar documents, and the prevalent culture, or cultures, of the United States.

Beginning with its first collective pastoral of 1967, "The Church in Our Day," the NCCB has consciously engaged in pastoral teaching of this kind. A number of other instances come to mind: the collective pastoral "Human Life in Our Day" (1968), the pastoral letter on the Blessed Virgin Mary (1973), the pastoral on Moral Values (1976), and the National Catechetical Directory (1977). In the present decade, the conference has involved itself to some degree in social and economic questions, notably in its letter on Marxist Communism (1980) and in its two recent pastorals, "The Challenge of Peace" (1983) and "Economic Justice for All" (1986). In these last two letters, the bishops attempted to distinguish between their social doctrine and the applications they made to the concrete circumstances of the time and place. The applications, they stated, were prudential judgments not binding in conscience on the faithful. They asked only that Catholics seriously consider the views of the conference when forming their own conscientious opinions in the light of the Gospel.

In my judgment the NCCB has not exceeded its teaching authority. It has not tended to establish a doctrinally independent Church in this country. On the contrary, it has consistently supported the Holy See and has made the universal teaching of the Church more acceptable to American Catholics. The bishops of my acquaintance seem to agree that the conference has strengthened rather than weakened their teaching authority in their dioceses. Thus the criticisms of certain European theologians mentioned above do not seem fully applicable to the episcopal conference in the United States. Yet these criticisms should be taken seriously insofar as they point to abuses that can easily occur.

If I could express one reservation about the operations of the NCCB, I would suggest that it has not drawn as clear a line as might be desired between its teaching statements and its statements on public policy issues. In the public policy area the bishops have less authority than in matters of doctrine, and they are more dependent, generally speaking, on specialized staff. The conference statements on public policy issues have attracted wide notoriety and have given the NCCB a reputation of being politically biased. It would be well if the conference could somehow make it clear that its policy statements do not enjoy the kind of authority that belongs to teaching statements.

Let me end with one final comment. The de facto influence of conference statements does not depend primarily on their formal or juridical authority but rather on the persuasiveness and relevance of their contents. The faithful of the territory, and perhaps those of other territories, will assess the statements in the context of their sense of the faith and their total life experience. Statements enjoying little or no juridical authority may gain great influence and be cited with approval for generations to come. Other statements issued with the same juridical formalities may be simply forgotten.

16. CATHOLICISM AND AMERICAN CULTURE: THE UNEASY DIALOGUE

January 27, 1990

(Lecture delivered at Fordham University on December 5 and 6, 1989.)

After several centuries of increasing centralization, Vatican Council II set the Catholic Church on a course of inner diversification. It depicted Catholicism in terms that were pluralistic rather than monolithic, multiform rather than uniform. The Church of Christ, said the council, should be incarnate in many cultures, all of which were in a position to enrich one another and to bring the wealth of the nations to the feet of Christ the King.

In the decade after Vatican II, "inculturation" became a buzzword. Although popes have used the word only with caution, they have said on journeys to Asia and Africa that the Catholic Church in those continents ought not to be a slavish copy of the European Church. As a consequence American Catholics began to conclude that Catholicism in this country should develop its own distinctive traits. In the past it had been a mosaic of importations from various "Old World" nations—Ireland, Germany, France, Poland, Italy, and others. Even if the efforts of Isaac Hecker and Archbishop John Ireland to Americanize the Church in the nineteenth century proved abortive, perhaps the time had now come for a new and more sober effort. Would not such Americanization, far from undermining authentic Catholicism, serve to solidify and strengthen it? This question is being asked in many places at the present time.

The importance of an encounter between faith and culture has been a major theme of the present pontificate. The meeting among the United States archbishops, the pope and the heads of Roman congregations last March took as its theme "Evangelization in the Context of the Culture and Society of the United States." Thus our topic is one that the Holy See places very high on its agenda.

Our analysis must begin with a brief discussion of the nature of the American culture into which the Catholic faith might be inserted. This culture is extremely diverse. Catholics in the United States come not only from the various Western European countries already named, but some are American Indians, some are African Americans, some are Vietnamese or Filipinos, and very many are Spanish-speaking people from the Caribbean or Latin America. Thus we cannot easily find a common denominator.

Even the white, Anglo-Saxon, Protestant (WASP) culture that has played a preponderant part in shaping the habits of the nation is not all of a piece. It has gone through a number of major shifts in the centuries since the first settlers came to New England and Virginia. Four major stages may here be pointed out:

1. The Puritanism of Congregationalist New England, which underlies much of our history, was anything but liberal. The Pilgrims looked upon the New World as a promised land where the covenant people could build the City of God. The culture of seventeenth-century Massachusetts was bound by a rigorous code of belief and morality founded upon the Bible as read in the Calvinist tradition. The Church dominated civil society in Boston as firmly as it had done in Calvin's Geneva.

This Calvinist heritage has been, for the most part, cast off. And yet it remains a living memory. It fueled many nineteenth-century exhortations about the "Manifest Destiny" of the United States, and it continues to reappear in Thanksgiving Day proclamations, in campaign oratory, and in anniversary

celebrations of the Declaration of Independence or the Constitution. Because of this vibrant tradition, it is still possible to speak
of the United States, with Chesterton, as "a nation with the soul
of a church."

2. By the time that the United States received its foundational
documents (the Declaration of Independence, the Constitution,
and the Bill of Rights), the Enlightenment was in full swing. The
common faith of the founding fathers was no longer that of the
Pilgrims but that of Christians profoundly influenced by the deis-
tic religion of "nature and of nature's God." The religion of reason was, however, understood with clearly Christian overtones,
as can be seen from the Declaration of Independence. There and
in other documents God was depicted as creator and ruler of all.
Human beings were considered to be endowed by their creator
with certain inalienable rights that demanded universal respect.
Among these rights was listed the free exercise of religion, which
in turn required that no one church be established as the religion of the state. The law favored certain generically Christian
institutions, such as monogamous, indissoluble marriage. Commitment to these traditional religious and moral values gave a
transcendent basis to the claim that the country should be free
and independent.

3. Certain elements in the Lockean philosophy of the founding fathers disposed the nation for a major incursion of individualistic utilitarian philosophy in the nineteenth century. The
common good was reconceived as the net result of a balancing of
contrary interests. The pursuit of private gain by individuals and
groups was seen as contributing, in the long run, to the prosper-
ity of all. The Puritan moralism of the seventeenth century, and
the cult of civic virtue in the eighteenth century, now yielded to
a system in which material wealth became the dominant value.
The role of the government was seen as that of an arbiter, laying
down the conditions under which competition could be fairly
conducted. At its worst, this new mentality spawned a kind of
social Darwinism. The great capitalists amassed fortunes for

themselves, but, having done so, they were driven by their residual Puritan conscience to a pursuit of philanthropy, no less arduous than their previous self-enrichment.

4. In the twentieth century, still another major shift has occurred. A new mass culture, largely determined by technological advances, is superimposing itself on the three layers already examined. The whole syndrome of contemporary culture is well described by the term "consumerism." Each individual is seen primarily as a consumer, and heavy consumption is viewed as the key to social well-being. Wealth becomes a function of sales, which are increased to the extent that people can be induced to buy new goods. To provide such inducement, business sponsors a gigantic advertising industry, which in turn supports and dominates journalism and mass communications. Advertising is funneled into programs that have the widest popular appeal. Nearly everything, from sports to education and religion, succeeds to the extent that it can arouse interest and provide entertainment. The desire for pleasure, comfort, humor, and excitement is continually escalated. The traditional work ethic becomes tributary to, and is to some extent undermined by, the quest for affluence and sensory gratification. While the entertainment industries and business grow ever more fiercely competitive, alcoholism, drug abuse, and obsessive sex proliferate in large sectors of the consumerist society.

This fourth layer of culture has not totally displaced the previous three, but it threatens to modify them profoundly. The culture that the Church faces today cannot be understood as that of the previous three centuries, though some elements of the earlier American heritage still survive.

In the Catholic literature on American culture published in the past twenty years or so, it is possible to detect four major strategies. For short they may be called traditionalism, neoconservatism, liberalism, and prophetic radicalism.

1. Traditionalism is the posture of those Catholics who are highly critical of what they find in the dominant American

culture, and who wish to restore the more centralized and author-itarian Catholicism of the years before World War II. James F. Hitchcock and Ralph Martin are representative of this tendency at its best. Confusion in the Church, they lament, has resulted from attempts to make peace with contemporary culture. Amer-ica today, in their judgment, is less hospitable to Catholic values than in the recent past, when John Courtney Murray wrote about the American proposition. Today it is necessary to be more divi-sive and to make the Church a "sign of contradiction." True to its vocation to judge the culture of the day, the Church must run the risk of being considered a ghetto. Within their own families, par-ishes, and communities of prayer, Catholics must pass on their religion by providing an experience of living faith. Liturgy must be celebrated with dignity and convey "the beauty of holiness." The young should be familiarized with the Latin Mass and with time-honored devotions. Doctrine must be clearly taught, with authority and not simply as a matter of opinion. Moral norms, especially in the area of sexuality, must be strictly maintained. Ecumenical contacts should be sought especially with conserva-tive evangelicals, with a view to reinvigorating Christian influ-ence on American culture.

In contrast to the moderate traditionalism just described, cer-tain more extreme traditionalists such as Archbishop Marcel Lefebvre frankly dismiss Vatican Council II as a capitulation to the ideals of the French Revolution. These traditionalists repudi-ate all forms of ecumenism and interreligious cooperation. Some American disciples of Archbishop Lefebvre have followed him into schism.

In either of these forms Catholic traditionalism is self-con-sciously countercultural. It seeks to maintain a Christian and Catholic culture alongside a secular culture that it deplores.

2. The neoconservative strategy rejects as unrealistic the res-torationism of the paleo-conservatives. Thinkers such as George Weigel, Archbishop J. Francis Stafford, and, to some degree, Michael Novak belong to this category. They exalt the powers

of natural reason and the value of civility in argument. They
espouse an optimistic, world-affirming humanism. While recognizing that the Church's first task is to proclaim and embody
the Gospel, these authors focus their attention especially on
the second task, the renewal of American democracy. The cul-
ture-forming task facing the Church today, they assert, is that of
"constructing a religiously informed public philosophy for the
American experiment in ordered liberty."

The American experiment, according to these writers, has
its roots in the Catholic natural law tradition. Several presidents
of the United States, as John Courtney Murray pointed out, officially proclaimed God's sovereignty over the nation and urged
the nation to make a public acknowledgment of its dependence
on God. Human rights are inalienable because they have their
source in God's eternal law. For democracy to succeed, human
passions must be curbed by moral values. Rights cannot be safeguarded without public virtue and care for the common good.

The neoconservatives are confident that the Catholic Church,
with its liturgical, personalist, and communal heritage, and
with its long tradition of moral reflection on the proper ordering
of human society, has unique resources for the renewal of the
American experiment. By using these resources courageously,
this policy hopes to bring about what the Lutheran theologian
Richard John Neuhaus, in his 1987 book, hailed as the "Catholic
moment."

The American experience, in the neoconservative view, is harmonious with some current trends in the universal Church. John
Paul II has accepted the human rights tradition and has praised
the American experiment of freedom. The Congregation for the
Doctrine of the Faith, in its 1986 "Instruction on Christian Freedom and Liberation," calls for political freedom, human rights,
pluralism in institutions, private initiative, and the separation
of governmental powers. Thus there seems to be some convergence between the present Roman agenda and authentic Americanism. Neoconservatives express optimism that the system

of democratic capitalism is beginning to enrich official Catholic teaching on political economy.

3. The third option, Catholic liberalism, can be verified in the work of many leading scholars, such as the Rev. Richard P. McBrien, the Rev. Charles E. Curran, Daniel Maguire, and Jay Dolan. The Detroit Call to Action conference sponsored by the American bishops in 1976 was a triumph for liberal Catholicism. Not satisfied to concentrate on what the Catholic tradition can contribute to the American experiment, Catholic liberals are primarily intent on showing how Americanism can help to modernize the Church. They propose to reform Catholicism along the lines of participatory democracy.

Dennis P. McCann provides a showcase exhibit of the liberal Catholic position in his book *New Experiment in Democracy*. He overtly aligns himself with the optimism of Archbishop Ireland. Americanism, he holds, was not a phantom heresy but a reality against which Leo XIII delivered a preemptive strike. Yet the strike was not fatal, because Americanism can never be extirpated from the soul of the nation. "What they condemned in Rome as the Americanist heresy," he says, "is the key to our historic development within the family of Christian churches." Vatican II, while it promoted religious liberty against state control, failed to address the question of religious freedom within the Church. Such freedom can eventuate if the Church democratizes itself on the basis of the "republican blueprint" drawn up by Archbishop John Carroll and the lay trustees of the early nineteenth century. The United States bishops in their recent pastoral letters on peace and the economy have introduced a dialogic method that promises to transform the Catholic Church into an open "community of moral discourse." The same method of consulting the faithful, if transferred to other sensitive areas such as birth control, abortion, and divorce, could result in a broader moral consensus. In the name of the principle of subsidiarity, the hierarchy should be made subordinate to the people and accountable to them. Whenever Rome or the bishops fail to speak credibly, the faithful are

justified in adhering to Catholic doctrine on a selective basis. The
Church, after all, is a voluntary association.

4. In the past, Catholics, generally speaking, have shunned
the sectarian stances of American Protestantism. But as the Catholic Church has become more solidly rooted in American culture,
it has begun to take on the characteristics of its new environment. It has made room for radical expressions bordering on the
sectarian. Dorothy Day, a convert to the Church from Marxist
Communism, founded the Catholic Worker Movement, which
has inspired numerous Catholic pacifists and Catholic socialists. Daniel Berrigan, S.J., a leader of radical protest movements
since the 1960s, has been relentlessly countercultural. The Cross
and the world, he maintains, can never meet otherwise than in
conflict. Christ, he adds, cannot enter our sinful world except
under a cloud that blinds the eminences and authorities. These
power holders typically don the mantle of Dostoyevsky's Grand
Inquisitor, hounding and crushing the authentic witnesses of the
Gospel.

Fr. Berrigan's apocalypticism is only one variety of radical Catholicism. Some radicals espouse a theology of violence
and revolution modeled on heroes such as Che Guevara. More
recently we have seen the budding of New Age theology and
of a creation-centered spirituality. Repudiating spiritualities
based on the fall and redemption, Matthew Fox, O.P., advocates
a creationist paradigm. Although he seems far more optimistic about nature and creation than Fr. Berrigan, and far less oriented toward suffering and sacrifice, Fr. Fox speaks out with a
similar prophetic vehemence against capitalism, consumerism,
militarism, racism, and the genocide of native peoples. Like Fr.
Berrigan, he champions the rights of homosexuals and other
oppressed minorities. Fr. Berrigan and Fr. Fox alike, as radicals,
set themselves against every establishment, whether secular or
ecclesiastical.

While calling for the total conversion of Church and society,
radical Catholics seek to legitimate their positions by invoking

historical precedents, both religious and civil. Catholic pacifists point to the early Christians who refused to bear arms for the Roman Empire; they make common cause with Quakers and Mennonites, and they praise the nonviolence of Gandhi. Catholic radicals draw inspiration from the Franciscan spirituals, from Utopian socialists, and from the Abolitionists of the Civil War period. Fr. Berrigan, besides looking to the crucified Jesus, sees himself as a disciple of the Jesuit martyrs of Elizabethan England. The creationist and green movements find their historical roots in Genesis, in the nature psalms, in Francis of Assisi, and in Hildegard of Bingen. They find allies among the native Americans and the nature worshipers of many peoples, ancient and modern. Creationists also include in their roster of the saints American writers such as Henry David Thoreau and Walt Whitman. Thus they are not totally countercultural. They identify with selected streams of the cultures they wish to reform.

The strategies I have examined are easily identifiable in contemporary American Catholicism. The four positions could easily be arranged in a logical square of opposition. For the neoconservatives, both Catholicism and American secular culture are basically good; for the radicals, both are fundamentally corrupt. For the Catholic traditionalists, the ecclesiastical culture is holy, but American secular culture is demonic. For the liberals, the American experiment is fundamentally healthy, but traditional Catholicism is diseased.

In the square of opposition, therefore, the neoconservatives are diametrically opposed to the radicals; the traditionalists are diametrically opposed to the liberals. The other pairs, though opposed on some points, can agree in part. For example, the neoconservatives can agree with the liberals on the value of the American experiment in democracy! Neoconservatives and traditionalists can agree on the importance of stability and on the need for authority in any society. Liberals and radicals can agree about the Church's need for continual self-criticism and reform. Traditionalists and radicals vie with each other in denouncing the evils of our pleasure-loving consumerist society. Militants of the peace movement and of the pro-life movement have more than a little in common.

None of the four strategies, I submit, is simply wrong. The realities of American Catholicism and of American culture are complex and many-faceted. American life has aspects that we can praise with the neoconservatives and the liberals, and other aspects that we must deplore with the traditionalists and the radicals.

Regarding the Church, I would hold with the traditionalists and neoconservatives that it is basically healthy and that we should let it shape our convictions and values. The first loyalty of the Catholic should be to the Church as the Body of Christ. But the liberals are correct in holding that the Church stands in reciprocal relations with secular culture. Roman Catholicism, as it has come down to us, has been significantly shaped by the social institutions of medieval and early modern Europe, and this very fact suggests that the Church might have something to learn from the American experiment of ordered liberty. Liberal Catholics and neoconservatives alike insist that the Vatican II's *Declaration on Religious Freedom* is due in part to the influence of the American system. Further influences of this kind might be beneficial to world Catholicism.

The radicals also have some valid points to make. The Church, like secular society, is continually tempted to settle for mediocrity. To the extent that it has adopted the values and attitudes of middle-class America, the Church deserves to be admonished by prophetic reformers. Repentance needs to be preached to those within the household of God.

Just as all four of the strategies have their strengths, so too, taken in isolation, they have weaknesses. Catholic traditionalism is on the whole too regressive. It looks nostalgically back to a past that can hardly be recovered. In its typically American expressions, moreover, traditionalism offers little guidance to Catholics who live amid the secular realities of our day. While adhering to the strictest canons of orthodoxy in their beliefs and personal morality, many affluent Catholic traditionalists want the Church to say nothing about politics, economics, business, or professional life. They effectively divorce their religious convictions from their day-to-day activities.

The neoconservatives, with their patriotic attachment to the American heritage, are inclined to minimize the extent to which the tradition of public virtue has been eroded by the quest for private pleasure and material gain. Intent upon maintaining civility in the orders of law and politics, they neglect the urgency of renewing the faith commitment and devotional life of contemporary Americans. They could be understood as holding that some kind of generalized civil religion suffices and that personal commitment to a specific religious tradition is a purely private matter, even a matter of personal taste. To point out this danger is not to accuse all representatives of the model of falling into the error, but simply to indicate that the neoconservative model needs to be supplemented and balanced by other models.

Liberal Catholicism, with its enthusiasm for participatory democratic models, runs the risk of introducing into the Church the ideologies and interest groups that compete for power in civil society. Americanist Catholics easily forget the New Testament warnings against personal ambition and partisanship. In their zeal for updating, the liberals too easily assume that Catholicism can and should do away with its traditional structures, its reverence for the sacred, its docility to authority, and its esteem for sacrifice, prayer, and contemplation. Finally the Catholic radicals, with their strident apocalyptic denunciations, cannot hope to play more than a marginal role in Catholicism, which is and must remain an essentially incarnational faith. According to the famous phrase attributed to James Joyce, Catholicism means "here comes everybody." Sectarian militancy lacks the broad popular appeal needed for it to be effective in such a large and traditional institution.

The most fundamental question raised by the preceding discussion is whether the Church in this country should become more countercultural, as the traditionalists and radicals would wish, or more accommodationist, as the liberals and some neoconservatives propose. The tide since Vatican Council II has been running heavily toward accommodationism. Middle-aged adults constitute the last generation of Catholics raised with a strong sense of Catholic identity. Most younger Catholics look upon themselves first of all as Americans and only secondarily as Catholics. Their culture has been predominantly formed by the secular press, films, television, and rock music. Catholicism is filtered to them through these screens. Catholic schools are becoming less numerous and less distinctively Catholic. Catholic colleges and universities, while in some cases expanding, have lost much of their religious character. A certain vague religiosity perdures among the young, but it is that of "communal Catholics" not strongly committed to the doctrines and structures of their Church.

Under these circumstances parents and teachers, fearful of being rejected as old-fashioned, are understandably reluctant to confront the young with the challenge of official Church teaching, especially in the area of sexuality. Religious educators often feel powerless in the face of the sexual revolution and the passion for affluence that possesses their students. Bishops and pastors find it increasingly difficult to shape the convictions and attitudes of the faithful. Apart from the issue of abortion, on which they are willing to risk a measure of unpopularity, the bishops increasingly shift their attention to social issues, adopting agendas that in many ways resemble those of the liberal intelligentsia, notably in their teaching on peace and on the economy. They seek to appeal to a broad public that includes non-Catholics, non-Christians, and nonbelievers.

Many sociologists of religion speak of a crisis of identity among American Catholics of our day. In the opinion of Joseph P. Fitzpatrick, S.J., the strength and stability of the Catholic Church in this country has hitherto rested on the religious symbols and practices that the immigrants brought with them. "Now, as these supports weaken and disappear, there is nothing in the American culture which provides a similar support for Catholic belief and practice." Another sociologist of religion, John A. Coleman, S.J., traces the current identity crisis to the jettisoning of many elements of Catholic tradition and disregard for historic Catholic sensibilities. "Today," he writes, "Catholic America, like the larger nation, is a land without adequate symbols." Classical Catholic wisdom concerning asceticism, contemplation, and mysticism has been largely forgotten. "Finally and most importantly, the church seems to have suffered pastoral bankruptcy in dealing with a specifically religious agenda at a time when a kind of religious revival of interiority is occurring outside the church." Fr. Fitzpatrick and Fr. Coleman alike recognize that the middle-class American values that have been accepted by most contemporary Catholics are not an authentic fulfillment of genuine Catholic aspirations.

In this context the problem of accommodation takes on rather concrete implications. There can be no question of simply rejecting accommodation as a strategy. It has always been an honored principle of pastoral and missionary practice. The Christian message must be presented, insofar as possible, in forms that make it intelligible, credible, interesting, and relevant to the hearers. Vatican II, in its *Decree on Missionary Activity*, recommended that the younger churches should borrow "from the customs and traditions of their arts and sciences . . . all those things which can contribute to the glory of their Creator, the revelation of the Savior's grace or the proper arrangement of human life." Accommodation becomes a problem only when the hard sayings of the Gospel are watered down, and when immoral or dehumanizing practices are tolerated.

As I have said, there are healthy elements in American society. Liberals and neoconservatives have good grounds for maintaining that the Church in this nation will be stronger to the extent that it builds these elements into its own life and makes them available for the universal Church. Our American traditions of freedom, personal initiative, open communication, and active participation can undoubtedly be a resource for the renewal of Catholicism in an age when authoritarian structures, repression, and conformity are in general disrepute.

On the other hand, it can be at least equally important to guard against the dangers of accommodation. To the degree that it adjusts to the dominant culture, the Church has less to say. By simply echoing the prevailing opinions and values, the Church undermines the credibility of its claim to present a divine message and weakens people's motivation for seeking membership. A church that no longer issues a clear call for conversion is only dubiously Christian. Traditional Catholicism has convictions and priorities very different from those embedded in contemporary American culture. The more thoroughly Catholics become inculturated in the American scene, the more alienated they become from their religious roots and the hierarchical authorities. Accommodation, therefore, can increase the crisis of identity felt by American Catholics.

Because of all these factors, there is reason to believe that the greatest danger facing the Church in our country today is that of excessive and indiscreet accommodation. Catholics will be well advised to cultivate a measured, prudent counterculturalism. Traditionalists rightly insist on this. The first and most urgent priority, they would say, is for the Church to socialize its members into its own tradition by immersing them in the symbols and meaning systems of scripture and Catholic tradition. Only so can communities be formed in which the Gospel, the sacraments, and pure doctrine are taken seriously.

Pope John Paul II, like Paul VI before him, has repeatedly called upon Catholics everywhere to evangelize their cultures. He recognizes that faith cannot survive without cultural embodiment, and that faith can have no home in a culture untouched by the Gospel. To carry out their assignment from these popes,

Catholics must first of all become firmly rooted in their own religious tradition. They must, through their parishes, their families, prayer groups, or basic ecclesial communities, find an environment in which they can interiorize their religious heritage. In this way they can prepare themselves to become agents in the evangelization of the secular culture. Such cultural evangelization, in turn, may help to establish an atmosphere in which Catholic Christianity can be lived out more faithfully by greater numbers.

The neoconservative program, more outgoing than that of the traditionalists, has its proper place in the Catholic agenda. Neoconservatism, if it allows itself to be enriched by the sacramental piety and prayerful interiority of the traditionalists, has great potential for the evangelization of American culture. But these two strategies, even in combination, do not exhaust the possibilities. As I have already indicated, the Catholic Church stands to gain from a prudent introduction of certain American democratic values and practices as urged by the liberals. The neoconservatives do not deny this, and traditionalists would be well advised to concede the point. Catholic radicalism, finally, serves as a needed gadfly. Both Church and secular society need to be challenged by the radicals' call to higher standards of evangelical perfection.

In summary, the four strategies are not reciprocally exclusive. They can and should be pursued concurrently. Although American Catholics can disagree about the extent to which each strategy is appropriate at a given time and place, they should be on guard against mutual hostility and recrimination. Each group should respect the intentions of the others and humbly recognize its own limitations. The internecine struggles between opposed factions are a scandal and a waste of energies that could more profitably be devoted to the common mission of the Church as a whole to minister to the salvation of the world. By generously recognizing the diverse gifts of the Holy Spirit, all can help to build up the Body of Christ in unity and strength. Traditionalists and radicals, liberals and neoconservatives, by their joint efforts,

can enable the Catholic Church to enter into dynamic and fruitful relations with American culture in its full complexity.

17. JOHN PAUL II AND THE NEW EVANGELIZATION

February 1, 1992

(Lecture delivered at Fordham University on December 4 and 5, 1991.)

The majority of Catholics are not strongly inclined toward evangelization. The very term has for them a Protestant ring. The Catholic Church is highly institutional, sacramental, and hierarchical in its structures. Its activities are primarily directed toward the instruction and pastoral care of its own members, whose needs and demands tax the institution to its limits. Absorbed in the inner problems of the Church, and occasionally in issues of peace and justice, contemporary Catholics feel relatively little responsibility for spreading the faith.

The Catholic Church has, of course, a long history of missionary involvement. In the early Middle Ages, the Benedictine monks evangelized much of Europe. Since the sixteenth century, the extension of Christianity beyond Europe was considered to be the special vocation of missionary orders and societies rather than the responsibility of all members of the Church. Even in these restricted circles, Catholics before Vatican II spoke rarely of evangelization. They used terms such as "missionary activity," "the propagation of the faith," and "the planting or extension of the Church."

In predominantly Christian territories, Catholics showed no lack of interest in convert-making, but again the thrust was not evangelical; the Gospel was hardly at the center. This apostolate was mainly directed to showing, against Protestants, that Christ had founded a hierarchical Church that was to be accepted as the organ of divine revelation. The focus was more on authority than on content. Catholics were instructed to believe whatever the Church taught precisely because it was Church teaching.

The terminology of evangelization came into Catholic literature toward the middle of the present century, partly through the influence of Protestant theologians such as Karl Barth. In the face of de-Christianization, many pastoral theologians and religious educators in Western Europe became convinced that the best remedy was a confident proclamation of the basic message of salvation through Jesus Christ. The kerygmatic sermons of Peter and Paul, as reported in the first chapters of the Acts of the Apostles, were studied as models.

Some religious educators and missiologists of this period distinguished three stages of initiation into the faith. The first, called pre-evangelization, was concerned with arousing interest in religious questions and disposing people to hear the Christian message. Then came the stage of evangelization, the proclamation of the basic Christian message. After faith in this message had been elicited came the stage of catechesis, or elementary doctrinal instruction, which in principle should precede the reception of the sacraments.

Building on the kerygmatic theology of the preceding decade, Vatican II made use of evangelical terminology. A comparison with Vatican I, which reflected the nineteenth-century mentality, is instructive. Vatican I used the term "Gospel" (*evangelium*) only once and never used the terms "evangelize" or "evangelization." Vatican II, by contrast, mentioned the "Gospel" 157 times, "evangelize" 18 times, and "evangelization" 31 times. When it spoke of evangelizing, Vatican II seems generally to have meant what the kerygmatic theologians meant by the term: the proclamation of the basic Christian message to those who did not yet believe in Christ.

In the very first sentence of its constitution on the Church (*Lumen Gentium* [LG]), Vatican II affirmed that Christ had sent the Church to preach the Gospel to every creature (LG 1; cf. Mk

16:15). Since the Church is missionary by its very nature, evangelization, according to the council, is a duty of every Christian (LG 16–17; cf. *Ad Gentes* [AG] 23, 35). The bishops, in union with the pope, are charged with leading in the process (LG 23; *Christus Dominus* [CD] 6; AG 29, 30); priests are to stir up zeal for the evangelization of the world (*Presbyterorum Ordinis* [PO] 4; AG 39); and all the laity are expected to cooperate in the work of evangelization, especially in the environment of their work and family life (LG 35; *Apostolicam Actuositatem* [AA] 2–3, 6; AG 41). Without slighting the ministries of sacramental worship and pastoral leadership, Vatican II gave clear primacy to the preaching of the word among the responsibilities of bishops (LG 25) and priests (PO 4).

Following the lead of the council, Pope Paul VI (1963–78) gave even greater emphasis to evangelization. In choosing the name of Paul, he signified his intention to take the Apostle of the Gentiles as the model for his papal ministry. In 1967, when he reorganized the Roman curia, he renamed the Congregation for the Propagation of the Faith the Congregation for the Evangelization of Peoples. He was the first pope in history to make apostolic journeys to other continents—first to the Holy Land (1964), then to India (1964), New York (1965), Portugal, Istanbul, and Ephesus (1967), Colombia (1968), Geneva and Uganda (1969), and finally (1970) a long journey including Tehran, East Pakistan, the Philippines, West Samoa, Australia, Indonesia, Hong Kong, and Sri Lanka. For good reason he was often called the "Pilgrim Pope." At his burial an open book of the gospels was fittingly laid on his coffin, a sign of the evangelical quality of his ministry.

Wishing to orient the Church more toward the dissemination of the Gospel, Paul VI chose as the theme for the Synod of Bishops in 1974 the evangelization of the modern world. From materials provided by that synod, he composed in 1975 his great apostolic exhortation on evangelization, *Evangelii Nuntiandi* (EN). That document proposed a very comprehensive concept: "Evangelization is in fact the grace and vocation proper to the Church, her deepest identity. She exists in order to evangelize, that is to say in order to preach and teach, to be the channel of the gift of grace, to reconcile sinners with God and to perpetuate Christ's sacrifice in the Mass, which is the memorial of his Death and glorious Resurrection" (14).

Paul VI's notion of evangelization is more inclusive than that of the kerygmatic theologians. In his view, proclamation and catechesis, while occupying an important place in evangelization, are only one aspect of it (22). Evangelization, moreover, should be directed not simply at individuals but also at cultures, which need to be regenerated by contact with the Gospel (20). The tasks of human development and liberation, according to the apostolic exhortation, are profoundly linked with evangelization, but they are not the same thing. Against all secularizing tendencies, Paul VI warned that evangelization can never be reduced to a merely temporal project (30–34). It must always include a clear and unequivocal proclamation of Jesus as Lord (22). It must be directed to eternal life in God (26, 35).

Pope John Paul II, at the opening of his pontificate, attended the general conference of the Latin American bishops at Puebla, near Mexico City, in January 1979. The theme of that conference was "Evangelization at Present and in the Future of Latin America" (see "Third General Conference of Latin American Bishops, Puebla: Conclusions," National Conference of Catholic Bishops, Washington, DC, 1979). While accepting Paul VI's identification of evangelization with the very mission of the Church, Puebla emphasized that through evangelization the Church intends to "contribute to the construction of a new society that is more fraternal and just."

In his opening address at Puebla, John Paul II quoted extensively from *Evangelii Nuntiandi*. Like Paul VI, he warned against acceptance of secular ideologies and sociological reductionism, but at the same time he declared that the Church "does not need to have recourse to ideological systems in order to love, defend and collaborate in the liberation of the human being." An indispensable part of the Church's evangelizing mission, he said, "is made up of works on behalf of justice and human promotion." "We cry out once more: Respect the human being, who is the image of God! Evangelize so that this may become a reality, so that the Lord may transform hearts and humanize political and economic systems, with the responsible commitment of human beings as the starting point." In March 1979 the pope sent the Latin American bishops a letter with a ringing endorsement of the conclusions of the Puebla conference.

Beginning with the Puebla conference, John Paul II has made himself the principal evangelizer in the Catholic Church. In his arduous apostolic journeys, in his annual messages for World Mission Sundays and on many other occasions, he has continued to build on the themes articulated by Paul VI. He speaks of the evangelization of cultures and a "synthesis between faith and culture" (see Letter to Cardinal Casaroli establishing the Pontifical Council for Culture, May 20, 1982). While insisting on the priority of eternal salvation, he maintains that human promotion is inseparably bound up with evangelization.

On March 9, 1983, John Paul II first mentioned the "new evangelization." Speaking at Port-au-Prince, Haiti, to the bishops of the Latin American churches, he observed that the year 1992, when the Latin American bishops were to hold their next general conference, would mark the half millennium of the first evangelization of the Americas. This anniversary, he added, would gain its full meaning with the commitment of the Church in this hemisphere to a new evangelization—"new in ardor, methods and expression."

A year and a half later, in a speech at the Olympic Stadium in Santo Domingo, the pope expanded on this theme. The very day, October 12, 1984, he recalled, was the anniversary of the landing of Columbus at San Salvador Island, which initiated "the encounter between two worlds." The jubilee of 1992, he said, would be an occasion to recall the first evangelization of the Americas without triumphalism and without false modesty. That evangelization, he observed, had essentially marked the historical and cultural identity of Latin America. But today, in the face of secularization, corruption, and grinding poverty, the Church was called to redouble its efforts to lead the faithful to "the word of Christ and the founts of grace which are the sacraments." The new evangelization should generate hope in the future "civilization of love" which Paul VI had proclaimed.

Since 1984, John Paul II, in addressing audiences in North and South America, Asia, Africa, and Europe, has frequently referred to the need of a new evangelization. In several of his addresses since 1987, the pope has linked the new evangelization with the preparation for the jubilee celebration of the Incarnation in the year 2000. In his apostolic exhortation on the laity, *Christifideles Laici* (December 30, 1988), he summarized many of his ideas regarding the new evangelization. At a time when whole countries were falling into religious indifference, he declared, the laity had a special responsibility to demonstrate how Christian faith constitutes the only fully valid response to the problems and hopes that life poses to every person and society (34). Participating as they did in the prophetic mission of Christ, lay men and women should make their daily conduct a shining and convincing testimony to the Gospel (34, 51). He exhorted the laity to narrow the gap between faith and culture and to make use of new media of communication to proclaim the Gospel that brings salvation (44).

The theme of the new evangelization is spelled out in greater detail in two major papal documents of 1990. In the first of these, a letter of June 29 to the religious of Latin America, the pope connects this effort with the novena of years that he had announced in 1983 to prepare for the anniversary of 1992 ("Toward the Fifth Centenary of New World Evangelization," *Origins* 20 [September 6, 1990], 208–16). Cordially inviting the religious of our day to emulate the generosity and commitment of the pioneers of evangelization, he called attention to the special needs of the present time. The new evangelization, he said, must deepen the faith of

Christians, forge a new culture open to the Gospel message, and promote the social transformation of the continent.

Then, at the end of 1990, John Paul II issued his encyclical on the Church's missionary activity, *Redemptoris Missio* (RM). He distinguished more clearly than before between situations requiring pastoral care and others requiring evangelization (33). In some places, he said, the Church is adequately equipped with ecclesial structures and is able to devote itself to the pastoral care of the faithful, but in other regions the people are still in need of being evangelized. The situations of evangelization, he observed, are two. Primary evangelization is called for in regions where Christ and the Gospel are not yet known. A second evangelization, or re-evangelization, is required in areas where large groups of Christians have lost a living sense of the faith and no longer consider themselves members of the Church.

In this encyclical, the "new evangelization" seems to be identified especially with the re-evangelization of formerly Christian areas. But the compartmentalization is not rigid. When the pope speaks of the new audiences requiring first evangelization, he mentions not only new geographical areas but also new cultural sectors such as the inner cities, migrants, refugees, young people, and the "new humanity" whose formation depends greatly on the mass media of communication (37).

Drawing on scattered statements in different documents, one may attempt a synoptic overview of what the pope seems to have in mind by the "new evangelization." (In the remainder of this article, numbers in parentheses will refer to volume and page number in *Origins*, the documentary service published by the Catholic News Service, except that apostolic exhortations [*Catechesi Tradendae, Christifideles Laici*] and encyclicals [*Sollicitudo Rei Socialis, Centesimus Annus, Redemptoris Missio*] will be cited by the initials of the Latin title followed by paragraph number.) It is new, in part, because it is occasioned by the forthcoming commemoration of Christopher Columbus and, eight years later, the jubilee of the Incarnation. Grateful for the achievements of the past, the new evangelization must avoid denigrating the work of the early missionaries or judging them by the behavioral standards of our own day (20:209–10). No matter how well others did for their own age, the new evangelization cannot be a mere return to the missionary tactics of a former era. The persuasive heralding of the Gospel message today requires a new quality of evangelization (15:546) and methods attuned to the sensibility of our times (15:544). This adaptation is clearly implied in the idea of "new evangelization."

John Paul II sees the new evangelization as having a deeply theological motivation. It rests on a recognition that the living Christ is, through the Holy Spirit, the chief agent. To be effective bearers of the Gospel, ministers of the Church must have a close personal relationship to the Lord. "Missionary dynamism," according to John Paul II, "is not born of the will of those who decide to become propagators of their faith. It is born of the Spirit, who moves the church to expand, and it progresses through faith in God's love." The new evangelization, he says, "is not a matter of merely passing on doctrine but rather of a personal and profound meeting with the Savior." Although the name of Jesus Christ must be explicitly proclaimed (RM 44), evangelization can never be a matter of words alone. "The witness of a Christian life is the first and irreplaceable form of mission" (RM 42). Before we can pass on the Gospel to others, it must first have permeated our own lives. "It is important to recall that evangelization involves conversion, that is, interior change." It must emanate from a deep experience of God (20:214).

Animated by Christ and the Holy Spirit, the new evangelization is for that very reason a work of the Church. It "is the witness which the Son of Man bears to himself, perpetuated in the mission of the Church," which is sent by Christ to evangelize. Looking upon the Church as such, as the corporate evangelizing subject, John Paul II insists that the effort must be borne by the entire membership—clerical, religious, and lay. Members of the Church act not as isolated individuals but in communion with the whole Church (at Puebla; also RM 45) and in subordination to the bishops (20:213) and the Holy See (14:579).

As a task of the universal Church, it is also the primary responsibility of each local church, under its own diocesan bishop (18:250). Parish priests must see themselves as charged with the evangelization of fellow citizens who do not yet belong to the flock of Christ (RM 67). Basic ecclesial communities can be important centers of evangelization, provided that they live in harmony with the Church (RM 51). The family, as a kind of "domestic church," can be a powerful instrument of evangelization (10:637; cf. *Christifideles Laici* [CL 62]). Since the family is the primary cell of the Christian community, it follows that families should evangelize families.

Our times offer special challenges and special opportunities. Because of current demographic trends, the non-Christian population of the world is becoming proportionally greater every year. Yet, as the Catholic Church has explicitly recognized, seeds of the Word and rays of divine truth are present in the nonbiblical religious traditions (RM 55). In the Day of Prayer at Assisi (October 27, 1986), and on other occasions, John Paul II has sought to bring the religions into a more cordial and cooperative relationship (16:370). He repeatedly insists that in proclamation and dialogue Christians should respect the freedom of their hearers (RM 8, 39). Dialogue, however, should not limit or impede evangelization; rather, it should be seen as a component in the Church's evangelizing mission (RM 55). The Christian in dialogue will have no reason for minimizing the conviction that all grace and salvation come from God through Jesus Christ (ibid.).

John Paul II frequently refers to disunity among Christians as an obstacle to evangelization. Christ prayed that his disciples might be one in order that the world might believe (Jn 17:21; RM 1). The effort to bring the Gospel to all nations can serve as "a motivation and stimulus for a renewed commitment to ecumenism" (RM 50). The real but imperfect communion already existing among Christians permits a significant degree of common witness and collaboration in social and religious matters.

Among the other challenges of our time the pope mentions the spread of secularism, religious indifference, and atheism (CL 34). In some countries there is a scarcity of qualified ministers; in others, efforts at evangelization are hampered by legislation that forbids the free profession of faith (14:309). Additional difficulties arise from the prevalence of political ideologies and from a culture of violence, drugs, and pornography (ibid.). In many cities the teeming masses experience degrading poverty and paralyzing anonymity (RM 37). The faithful are influenced by systems of communication that glorify the affluent life, instilling hedonism and consumerism (17:308). This new cultural world constitutes the kind of challenge that Paul encountered when he addressed the Athenians at the Areopagus (RM 37). The challenges themselves, according to the pope, may be seen as opportunities. While on the one hand, people seem to be sinking more deeply into materialism and despair, we are witnessing, on the other hand, an anxious search for meaning, the craving for an inner life, and a desire to experience the presence of God in prayer (RM 38). Evangelization must cultivate the seeds of the Word wherever they are present, and interpret them as manifestations of an imperative need for salvation in Jesus Christ (18:28). In answer to people's anxious questioning and unsatisfied hopes, "the Church has an immense spiritual patrimony to offer mankind, a heritage in Christ, who called himself 'the way, the truth and the life' (Jn 14:6)" (RM 38). Evangelization, says the pope, "is the primary service which the church can render to every individual and to all humanity in the modern world" (RM 2).

Within the immense field of evangelization, the evangelization of culture occupies a position of special preeminence (18:33). Faith cannot take root, express itself, and grow unless it incarnates itself in cultural forms (Letter to Cardinal Casaroli; *Catechesi Tradendae* [CT] S3). In every culture, the pope remarks, there are seeds of the Word that tend to bear fruit in harmony with the Gospel (18:28). Whoever seeks to evangelize must be able to understand the mentality and attitude of the modern world, to illuminate them from the perspective of the Gospel, and purify and elevate the sound elements in the light of Christian revelation (14:541; 15:121–22, 171; CL 44). The missionaries of the past, the pope reminds us, did much to raise the level of the arts, including dance, music, and the theater (14:308). They rightly saw this as falling within their evangelizing mission.

John Paul II consistently teaches that Catholic social doctrine, since it is rooted in the revealed concept of the human, is a valid means of evangelization (*Centesimus Annus* [CA] 54). "Teaching and spreading her social doctrine are part of the church's evangelizing mission" (*Sollicitudo Rei Socialis* [SRS] J41). Authentic human development must be grounded in an ever deeper evangelization (RM 58). By exposing the roots of unjust political and economic systems (14:579), evangelization goes to the very heart of social imbalances (9:175). It includes a dynamic commitment to the common good of society (19:32) and to the ways of peace and justice (14:583; 15:588; 17:305–9). Just as some missionaries of former centuries raised their voices prophetically against the violation of the rights of indigenous peoples (20:209–10), so those who evangelize in our own day, by insisting on human dignity and integral development (CA 55), help to build a new civilization of love (14:310; 15:124; RM 51).

John Paul II is quite aware of the problems inherent in the modern means of communication and of the incapacity of mass media to take the place of direct contact between persons. But notwithstanding their limitations, the new media may be responsibly used in the service of truth, solidarity, and peace, and may thereby contribute to evangelization. "The communications media," he says, "have a wonderful power to bring the people of the world together. The power of the communications media is undoubtedly very great, and it depends on us to guarantee that they will always be instruments at the service of truth, justice and moral decency." Because of its rapid development and deep formative influence, the world of the media requires the attention of the Church (CL 44). The Gospel and its values must be made more present in the world of public communication (20:29), which may be seen as a new frontier for the evangelizing mission of the Church (CL 44). To integrate the Christian message into the new culture created by the mass media is a highly complex task involving new languages, new techniques, and a new psychology (RM 37).

In my judgment, the evangelical turn in the ecclesial vision of Popes Paul VI and John Paul II is one of the most surprising and important developments in the Catholic Church since Vatican II. This development, as I have indicated, did not take place without a degree of preparation in Vatican II and preconciliar kerygmatic theology. But Paul VI went beyond the council in identifying evangelization with the total mission of the Church. John Paul II, with his unique familiarity with world of Catholicism, assigns the highest priority to evangelization in the mission of the Church.

While both popes have notably broadened the concept of evangelization, they have retained the main emphasis of the earlier kerygmatic concept. For them, as for the kerygmatic theologians, the heart and center of evangelization is the proclamation of God's saving love as shown forth in Jesus Christ. Where the name of Jesus is not spoken, there can be no evangelization in the true sense (EN 22, 27; RM 44). But it is not enough to speak the name. Christian initiation is incomplete without catechesis, which is a moment in the whole process of evangelization (CT 18). Evangelization must take account of the full implications of the Gospel for individual and social existence.

All of this constitutes a remarkable shift in the Catholic tradition. For centuries evangelization had been a poor stepchild. Even when the term was used, evangelization was treated as a secondary matter, the special vocation of a few priests and religious. Even these specialists were more concerned with gaining new adherents for the Church than with proclaiming the good news of Jesus Christ. Today we seem to be witnessing the birth of a new Catholicism which, without loss of its institutional, sacramental, and social dimensions, is authentically evangelical.

Will the shift toward the evangelical model meet with general acceptance and successful implementation? In many parts of the Church the response has been clearly positive: In April 1974, the Federation of Asian Bishops' Conferences, preparing for the Synod of Bishops of 1974, issued a ringing declaration on "Evangelization in Modern Day Asia." The Latin American bishops at Medellín (1968) and Puebla (1979) gave a clear priority to evangelization. Their Fourth General Conference at Santo Domingo in 1992 will have as its theme "New Evangelization, Human Advancement and Christian Culture."

In 1986, an international organization known as "Evangelization 2000" was founded with a headquarters in Rome, having as its principal purpose to promote a Decade of Evangelization that will end on December 25, 2000. This organization has already sponsored worldwide retreats for thousands of priests in Rome in 1984 and 1990. It is establishing networks of schools of evangelization and prayer groups to promote the success of the evangelization program.

In our own country, the National Conference of Catholic Bishops, which has long possessed a Committee on the Missions, has set up a Committee on Evangelization. Originally formed as an ad hoc committee in response to Paul VI's *Evangelii Nuntiandi*, it has since been made a standing committee. Another ad hoc committee has been formed to make preparations for the observance of the Fifth Centenary of the Evangelization of the Americas. In 1986, the United States bishops published a pastoral statement on world mission, "To the Ends of the Earth," and on November 15, 1990, they approved a pastoral letter, "Heritage and Hope," looking forward to the anniversary of 1992. A national plan for evangelization is being formed. The bishops of the United States have responded to statements on evangelization issued by Hispanic-American Catholics and by Black Catholics. In 1989, the episcopal conference of Texas issued an important pastoral letter urging parishes to establish evangelization committees and to become welcoming communities celebrating vital and inspiring Sunday liturgies.

Quite evidently the new evangelization will encounter inertia and resistance. As I mentioned already, the Catholic Church, especially in modern times, has been principally oriented toward the pastoral care of its own members. U.S. Catholics are wary of evangelization for a variety of reasons. They see it as the chosen trademark of revivalist and fundamentalist sects, some of them virulently anti-Catholic. They distrust the biblicism, the individualism, the emotionalism, and the aggressive proselytism of certain Protestant evangelistic preachers. Many are repelled by recent revelations about the financial dealings and private lives of several prominent televangelists. In addition, Vatican II put many Catholics on guard against anything smacking of triumphalism. Attempting to be modest and self-critical, they often fail to proclaim their faith with confidence. Some have been going through a process of doubt and reappraisal and are groping for ways of making better sense of their own heritage. Influenced by the conviction that the assent of faith must be a free and personal response to grace and by American tradition that religion is a purely private matter, they do not wish to bring pressure on anyone to undergo a deep conversion of mind and heart.

Notwithstanding all these difficulties, I submit that the popes of our time have correctly identified God's call to the Church in our day and have hit upon an effective remedy for the Church's present ills. The Church has become too introverted. If Catholics today are sometimes weak in their faith, this is partly because of their reluctance to share it. Unless the Gospel message was a truth to be communicated to others, it would not be of great value for believers themselves. Once we grasp the universal validity of the message and its significance for the whole of human life, we gain a new appreciation of the privilege of being its bearers and a new eagerness to share it. As John Paul II asserts, "Faith is strengthened when it is given to others" (RM 2).

Evangelization, by concentrating on the basic Christian message, helps us to see what is supremely worthwhile in our religion. If we believe simply on the authority of the Church, without caring what the contents are, we can hardly be enthusiastic about our faith. But if we focus on the God of Jesus Christ, as disclosed in the Gospel, our faith becomes a loving assent to an extraordinary piece of good news intended by God for all the world. It is a message that we have no right to monopolize, to keep to ourselves (RM 11; cf. 44).

Catholic spirituality at its best has always promoted a deep personal relationship with Christ. In evangelizing we are required to raise our eyes to him and to transcend all ecclesio-centrism. The Church is of crucial importance but is not self-enclosed. It is a means of drawing the whole world into union with God through Jesus Christ.

Too many Catholics of our day seem never to have encountered Christ. They know a certain amount about him from the teaching of the Church, but they lack direct personal familiarity. The hearing of the Gospel, personal prayer, and the reception of the sacraments should establish and deepen that saving relationship. When Catholics regard religious worship as a mere matter of duty or routine, they become an easy prey for sectarian preachers who, notwithstanding their faulty understanding of the Christian message, give witness to a joyful encounter with the Lord.

The evangelical turn in Catholicism can make Catholics less vulnerable to the sects. It also has considerable ecumenical possibilities. The most vigorous branch of Protestantism in the United States today is evangelicalism, the faith of many conservative Christians, especially in the southern states. Until recently, conservative evangelicals have not been greatly interested in dialogue or collaboration with Catholics. Some, indeed, are anti-Catholic, partly because they have had so little contact with Catholicism.

Yet there is increasing recognition that Catholics and conservative evangelicals share many things in common, including a reverence for the canonical scriptures and adherence to the central doctrines of the Trinity, the Incarnation, and the atoning death and bodily resurrection of Jesus. In the realm of moral teaching, conservative evangelicals, like Catholics, tend to be opposed to abortion and to defend traditional family values.

A number of authors have begun to call for a new ecumenism between Roman Catholics and evangelical Protestants. Kenneth Craycroft, in a recent article, writes:

> The new ecumenism can be successful because of the peculiar qualities that each tradition brings with it. Catholics have an ancient and rich moral vocabulary; it formed the great philosophical and theological traditions of the (pre-modern) West. The institutional memory and current organization of Catholicism make it effective at organizing and implementing its agenda. Evangelicals bring a sense of urgency and fervor to the project. They are converts and children of converts, with all the energetic zeal that that entails. Their emphasis on active personal discipleship and commitment to Sacred Scripture make evangelicals the yeast in the dough. Even committed Catholics have become complacent in recent years. Evangelicals will call us to a more energetic expression of our faith. ("Our Kind of Ecumenism: Why Catholics Need to Be More Evangelical and Vice Versa," *Crisis* 9 [October 1991], 32)

In the dialogue here envisaged, Protestant evangelicals can help Catholics overcome their excessive preoccupation with inner Church issues, while Catholics can help Protestants overcome their own imbalances. Many of them have focused too narrowly on God's Word in scripture, and some have fallen into fundamentalistic literalism. Catholics can help evangelicals to achieve a deeper grounding in tradition, a richer sacramental life, a more lively sense of worldwide community, and a keener appreciation of sociopolitical responsibility. These values, which are praised in the recent writings of certain evangelicals, are prominent in the evangelization programs of Paul VI and John Paul II.

Several authors have written about "the Catholic moment" in the life of our nation. This moment is often described in terms of the Church's potential contribution to a religiously informed public philosophy. Without denying the importance of this project, I would recall that the Catholic moment was originally, and rightly, described by the Rev. Richard John Neuhaus as "in which the Roman Catholic Church in the world can and should be the lead Church in proclaiming and exemplifying the Gospel." The first and highest priority is for the Church to proclaim the good news concerning Jesus Christ as a joyful message to all the world. Only if the Church is faithful to its evangelical mission can it hope to make its distinctive contribution in the social, political, and cultural spheres.

18. THE PROPHETIC HUMANISM OF JOHN PAUL II

October 23, 1993

(Lecture delivered at Fordham University on September 28, 1993.)

For some time I have been asking myself whether there is a single rubric under which it might be possible to summarize the message of the present pontificate. I have thought about the pope's concern for the inner unity of the Catholic Church, the new evangelization, the dialogue between faith and culture, and reconstruction of the economic order. All these themes are clearly important to John Paul II, but no one of them permeates his teaching as a whole. In seeking a more comprehensive theme, I have hit upon the idea of prophetic humanism.

In the case of this pope, as in the case of any other, it is difficult to ascertain which of his statements are actually composed by himself and which are simply accepted by him after having been drafted by others. I have no inside information to help me in this discernment. My method will be to rely principally on books and articles that he published under the name of Karol Wojtyla before he became pope, and then inspect documents from his papacy that closely resemble these in style and in substance. Several of his encyclicals are so personal in tone that it seems safe to attribute them to him, even though he presumably had assistants in the final process of editing. Most of his major documents are amply furnished with footnotes that he would scarcely have had time to compose.

1. THE CONCEPT OF PROPHETIC HUMANISM

The concept of prophetic humanism requires some explanation. Any humanism must be a system of thought centered on the human person. The pope himself generally uses the term "man," which, at least in Latin, has no reference to gender. In quoting or paraphrasing his statements I shall sometimes use the English word "man" to mean an individual member of the human race. Near synonyms such as "person" are not always satisfactory, given the pope's understanding of personalization.

Humanism, moreover, implies a high esteem for the human as having intrinsic value. As we shall see, the defense of the dignity of the human person and the promotion of human rights stand at the very center of the pope's program.

This program may be called prophetic for several reasons. A prophet is someone who speaks out of a strong conviction and with a sense of vocation. John Paul II evidently sees himself and the Church as divinely commissioned to be advocates of authentic humanity. The prophet speaks with a certain sense of urgency. Karol Wojtyla, even when he writes as a philosopher, is never the detached academic. He is conscious of speaking to a world that is in the throes of a crisis—a crisis of dehumanization. Like most prophets, he senses that he is faced with enormous opposition and that his is perhaps a lonely voice. He is not afraid to confront others in his struggle to salvage human dignity.

Yet the pope is no pessimist. He is convinced that in the face of human needs God has provided an answer in Christ, who came that we might have life to the full. He sees the Gospel as a message of hope, love, and truth, not for Christians or Catholics alone, but for every human being. The Church, he believes, has an essential contribution to make to the task of making the world more human. He repeatedly quotes from Vatican II the statement that the Church is called to be a sign and safeguard of the transcendence of the human person (*Pastoral Constitution on the Church in the Modern World*, 76).

The central and unifying task of the Church, for John Paul II, is to rediscover and promote the inviolable dignity of every human person. "Man," as he puts it in his first encyclical, is the way of the Church—"man in the full truth of his existence, of his personal being and also of his community and social being" (*Redemptor Hominis* [1979] 14). The Church's mission must therefore be carried out with a view to humanity, and for that very reason with a view to God. Following Christ, who is both God and man, the Church must link anthropocentrism and theocentrism in a deep and organic way (*Dives in Misericordia* [1980] 1).

2. HUMAN DIGNITY

The first point to consider is the pope's understanding of what it means to be human. Especially in his major philosophical work *The Acting Person* (1969, revised 1977, English version 1979), he develops an original anthropology that owes something to classical Thomism and something to modern personalist phenomenology, especially as represented by Max Scheler (1874–1928). He is also conscious of points of contact with the philosophy of action of Maurice Blondel (d. 1949). In place of the Cartesian *cogito* ("I think"), which begins with the thinking subject, John Paul prefers to begin with action. "I act, therefore I am" might fairly characterize his starting point. Through action, he maintains, one can come to know the real character of the human being as a free, creative, responsible subject. By my free actions, he asserts, I make myself what I am.

Although John Paul's focus is initially on man as subject, his analysis brings out the necessary role of the object. As free and intelligent beings we are called to make decisions, and for these decisions to be meaningful they must conform to the truth. The root of human dignity consists in the capacity to transcend mere self-interest and embrace what is objectively true and good. One element in this objective order is the existence of other human beings with the same essential dignity as my own. With an explicit reference to Kant, Wojtyla declares that human beings must always be treated as ends, never as mere means. He frequently quotes from Vatican II the statement that, alone among all creatures on earth, man exists for his own sake.

For Wojtyla the ethical dimension is determinative for the value of all human action. When I act according to truth, I fulfill the deepest dynamism of my being and become good. When I do not act according to the truth, I do not fulfill myself and I become bad. In his philosophical works, Wojtyla does not explain very clearly how a person intuits the truth. As George Huntston Williams remarks, he "fails to provide the reader with what the conditions are for coming to the truth" (*The Mind of John Paul II*, 1981). Williams hints that the operative ethics behind Wojtyla's proposal come from Christian revelation and Catholic tradition, and I suspect he is correct.

Speaking prophetically, the pope formulates his doctrine of freedom in opposition to a merely negative concept, according to which freedom would consist in not being coerced or not being obligated by law. Already at Vatican II Bishop Wojtyla had pleaded successfully for amendments to the *Declaration on Religious Freedom* to specify that freedom is not a mere entitlement to do whatever one pleases. During his first visit as pope to the United States in 1979, he warned that the concept of freedom should not be used as a pretext for moral anarchy, as though it could justify conduct that violates the moral order. Freedom, he insisted, is not an end in itself. It is a capacity to fulfill one's deepest aspirations by choosing the true and the good. In this connection the pope likes to quote the saying of Jesus, "The truth shall make you free" (Jn 8:32). When freedom is rightly understood, moral norms do not appear as a limitation. Truth is the guide to meaningful action, action in accordance with conscience.

We can, of course, disobey the voice of conscience and act against the truth as we perceive it. Violations of conscience do not bring about self-fulfillment; they result in anti-values and frustration. The very ability to commit sin testifies in favor of the dignity of the person. Because we have the capacity freely to embrace the good, we also have the power to reject it. "To erase the notion of sin," says the pope, "would be to impoverish man in a fundamental part of his experience of his humanity" (*"Be Not Afraid!": Andre Frossard in Conversation with Pope John Paul II*, 1984). The loss of the sense of sin, which seems to be an affliction of our time, is evidence of the failure to see man as a responsible moral subject oriented toward truth and goodness.

Thus far, we have been looking at human dignity from a philosophical point of view, without reference to revelation, which confirms and enhances human dignity. As a theologian, John Paul II draws initially on the creation narratives of Genesis. Man, he holds, was created to the image and likeness of God and destined to have dominion over the rest of creation (Gn 1:26–28). But the full meaning of human life cannot be grasped except in the light of Christ, who, in revealing God, reveals humanity to itself (*Redemptor Hominis* 8–9). There is no more impressive evidence for the value that God sets upon the human than God's gift of his own Son as the price of our redemption (20). Every human being is intended by God to be redeemed and to come through Christ to final self-realization.

Some philosophers, influenced by Feuerbach and his school, have contended that God must die in order for man to attain his full stature. The present pope, like Henri de Lubac (*The Drama of Atheist Humanism*), argues just the contrary. The world must be reminded, he says, that while men and women can organize the world without God, without God it will always in the last analysis be organized against humanity. In denying the transcendent source and goal of our being, we would deprive man of the source of his true dignity (*Centesimus Annus* [1991] 13). Without God as creator there would be no inviolable human rights. Without Christ as savior, human hope would no longer extend to everlasting union with the divine. In this connection John Paul II quotes from Augustine the famous sentence "You have made us for yourself, O Lord, and our hearts cannot find rest until they rest in you" (*Confessions* 1.1).

3. HUMAN EXISTENCE AS COMMUNAL

Against excessive individualism John Paul II insists that human existence is essentially communal. He writes: "Man's resemblance to God finds its basis, as it were, in the mystery of the most holy Trinity. Man resembles God not only because of the spiritual nature of his immortal soul but also by reason of his social nature, if by this we understand that he 'cannot fully realize himself except in an act of pure self-giving'" (*Sources of Renewal*, 1981). The pope then goes on to explain that human beings are intended to exist not only side by side, but in mutuality, for the sake of one another. The Latin term *communio* indicates the reciprocal giving and receiving that goes on within this relationship.

Human community is realized on many different levels, from the family to the state and the international community. Vatican II, in its *Pastoral Constitution on the Church in the Modern World* had four separate chapters dealing with family, culture, economy, and political community. On each of these levels conscience obliges us to transcend the narrow limits of our own self-enhancement and to contribute to the good of others. In a small unit such as the family, the members act primarily for the individual good of their partners, but in larger groups the primary objective is the well-being of the group as such. As distinct from the "I-thou" community, the "we"-society comprises a group that exists and acts together for the sake, primarily, of the common good.

4. THE FAMILY

The family, according to John Paul II, is the basic cell of society and for that reason the primary locus of humanization (*Christifideles Laici* [1988] 40). The pope's doctrine of the family, adumbrated in his early work *Love and Responsibility* (1960), is amplified in several documents from his papacy. He sees the family in a state of crisis, especially because of the reigning consumerist mentality that leads to false concepts concerning freedom and sexual fulfillment (*Familiaris Consortio* [1981] 6, 32). He draws on the traditional Catholic teaching regarding conjugal morality, divorce, and remarriage in order to protect the family as a stable community of generous love. Sexuality, he asserts, is realized in a truly human way only if it is an integral part of the loving communion by which a man and a woman commit themselves to one another until death. The sexual relationship between married persons should always promote human dignity. The unitive meaning of marriage cannot be separated from the procreative. The deliberate exclusion of procreation, according to the pope, is detrimental to the unitive relationship between the couple.

Although Christian preachers have often proclaimed that wives should be subject to their husbands, John Paul II goes to some pains to point out that the domination of the husband is a sign and effect of original sin. In the Christian order there should be an equality of mutual service between wives and husbands (*Mulieris Dignitatem* [1988] 10). In this connection the pope sets forth a doctrine of women's rights based on the complementarity and communion between male and female.

5. THE ORDER OF CULTURE

Culture has been a major concern of John Paul II from his early days, when he developed his talents for music, poetry, and drama. Between 1977 and 1980 he published several important papers on the philosophy of culture. In 1982, when establishing the Pontifical Council for Culture, he wrote in a letter to Cardinal Agostino Casaroli: "Since the beginning of my pontificate I have considered the church's dialogue with the cultures of our time to be a vital area, one in which the destiny of the world at the end of the 20th century is at stake."

The pope's theory of culture is thoroughly humanistic. "Man lives a really human life thanks to a culture" (address to

UNESCO, Paris, 1980). Man is the subject of culture, its object and its term. Culture is of man, since no other being has culture; it is from man, since man creates it; and it is for man, since its prime purpose is human advancement. Everyone lives according to some culture, which determines the mode of one's existence.

Culture, as a human achievement, involves our capacity for self-creation, which in turn radiates into the world of products. Culture is a materialization of the human spirit and at the same time a spiritualization of matter. It thus serves to render our world more human.

We should not imagine that every culture, just because it is a culture, is above criticism. John Paul speaks of a dialogue between faith and culture. Like everything human, culture needs to be healed, ennobled, and perfected through Christ and the Gospel (*Redemptoris Missio* [1991] 54). Because culture is a human creation, it is also marked by sin. The Church must prophetically oppose what the pope, at his visit to Denver last August, called "the culture of death." On another occasion (1984) he said: "More than ever, in fact, man is seriously threatened by anti-culture which reveals itself, among other ways, in growing violence, murderous confrontations, exploitation of instincts and selfish interests." In technologically advanced societies, people tend to value everything in terms of production and consumption, so that man is reduced to an epiphenomenon. Authentic culture, on the contrary, resists the reduction of man to the state of an object. "It signifies the march towards a world where man can achieve his humanity in the transcendence proper to him, which calls him to truth, goodness and beauty."

One aspect of the contemporary crisis of culture is the crisis in education. To an alarming degree, education has become focused on having rather than being. All too often it turns people into instruments of the economic or political system. In the alienated society, education is in danger of becoming a form of manipulation (UNESCO Address, 1980).

The term "alienation," which the pope borrows from Marxist literature, is central to his social philosophy. For him it is the opposite of participation. In the good society all the members contribute to the common good and share in its benefits. Alienation arises when the society does not serve the dynamism of its own members, but unfolds at their expense, so that they, or some of them, feel cut off. The neighbor becomes the stranger, even the enemy.

6. THE ECONOMIC ORDER

The dynamics of participation and alienation, which are the key to John Paul II's theory of culture and education, are also central to his economic analysis. While he does not purport to give lessons in economics, he insists that any sound economy must accept the primacy of the human person and the common good as guiding principles. His teaching on this subject is set forth in three important encyclicals.

In the first of these, *Laborem Exercens* (1981), he concentrates on the theological meaning of work, as a fulfillment of the biblical mandate to subdue the earth (Gn 1:28). He protests against systems in which man is treated as an instrument of production rather than as the effective subject of work. By transforming nature, says the pope, man can achieve greater fulfillment as a human being. All too often labor is regarded as a mere means to the production of capital and property, to the detriment of workers themselves. As a champion of human dignity, the Church has a duty to speak out in defense of the rights of labor.

In his second encyclical on economics, *Sollicitudo Rei Socialis* (1987), John Paul II recognizes personal economic initiative as a fundamental human right, stemming from the image of the Creator in every human being. Does not the denial of the right to take initiatives in economic matters, he asks, "impoverish the human person as much as, or more than, the deprivation of material goods?" (15). Drawing, no doubt, on his experience behind the Iron Curtain, he castigates systems in which citizens are reduced to passivity, dependence, and submission to the bureaucratic apparatus. He likewise criticizes consumerist societies in which things take priority over persons. "To 'have' objects and goods," he writes, "does not in itself perfect the human subject unless it contributes to the maturing and enrichment of that subject's 'being,' that is to say, unless it contributes to the realization of the human vocation as such" (28).

In *Centesimus Annus* (1991), his third social encyclical, John Paul II returns to many of the same themes. He points out that while the natural fruitfulness of the earth was once the primary source of wealth, today the principal resource is rather the initiative and skill of human persons. He defends private property, profit, and the free market as against the socialist alternatives. At the same time he cautions against consumerism, "in which people are ensnared in a web of false and superficial gratifications rather than being helped to experience their personhood in an authentic and concrete way" (41). He speaks at some length of the alienation that can arise in capitalist as well as in socialist societies.

From the beginning of his pontificate, the present pope has shown a constant concern for the environment. Unlike some creationists, he bases this concern less on the inherent goodness of nature than on what is genuinely good for humanity. In *Redemptor Hominis* (1979) he noted that the power of humanity to subdue the earth seems to be turning against humanity itself. Many seem to see no other meaning in the natural environment than its immediate use and consumption. Such exploitation, however, instead of making our life on earth more human, carries with it the threat of an "environmental holocaust" (15). At the root of our senseless destruction of the natural environment, he observes, lies a prevalent anthropological error, further described in *Centesimus Annus*. We are often driven by a desire to possess things rather than respect their God-given purpose. We lack the disinterested attitude, born of wonder, which would enable us to find in nature the message of the invisible God. We also violate our obligations toward future generations.

7. THE POLITICAL ORDER

The thinking of John Paul II about politics and the state is closely intertwined with his reflections about culture and economics. Emphasizing the human dimension, he consistently speaks of the personalist values of participation, dialogue, and solidarity. The common good, he maintains, is threatened on the one hand by selfish individualism and on the other hand by totalitarian systems that trample on the rights of the individual person. No single group may be allowed to impose itself by power upon the whole of society. The enormous increase of social awareness in our day requires that the citizens be allowed to participate in the political life of the community (*Redemptor Hominis* 17). The pope accordingly praises the democratic system "inasmuch as it ensures the participation of citizens' in making political choices, guarantees to the governed the possibility both of electing and of holding accountable those who govern them and of replacing them through peaceful means when appropriate" (*Centesimus Annus* 46). Yet even his endorsement of democracy contains a warning against certain popular misunderstandings. Too often our contemporaries assume that agnosticism and skeptical relativism are the philosophy and basic attitude that best correspond to democratic forms of political life. John Paul II replies that, on the contrary, a democracy without objective values and ethical responsibility can easily turn into open or thinly disguised totalitarianism. The rights of the human person must be acknowledged as inviolable.

The pope has repeatedly praised the Universal Declaration of Human Rights that was adopted by the United Nations in 1948. In his address to the United Nations in 1979, he enumerated, among the human rights that are universally recognized, "the right to life, liberty and security of person; the right to food, clothing, housing, sufficient health care, rest and leisure; the right to freedom of expression, education and culture; the right to freedom of thought, conscience and religion." This list (too long to be repeated here) ended with the "right to political participation and the right to participate in the free choice of the political system of the people to which one belongs." In speaking of human rights, the pope frequently alludes to the evils of abortion and euthanasia, which he regards as scandalous violations of human dignity (address to the United Nations, 1979). All these declarations of human rights are abstract. The pope clearly recognizes that philosophical and theological principles cannot be automatically translated into positive law or judicial practice. The talents of statesmen and jurists are needed to determine the extent to which a given right—for example, the right to education or free expression—can be implemented in a given situation.

8. THE CHURCH

Thus far, we have been speaking of essentially natural societies, whose existence does not rest on the Gospel and on faith. In dealing with them, John Paul II speaks primarily as a philosopher. As a theologian and teacher of the people of God, he extends his theory of personal action, participation, and community into the order of revealed truth, where it becomes the basis of an ecclesiology. John Paul II's ecclesiology is not a simple corollary from his general doctrine of society. The Church has a unique status and mission. In a memorable phrase he calls it "the social subject of responsibility for divine truth" (*Redemptor Hominis* 19). The Gospel, he reminds us, does not spring spontaneously from any cultural soil. It always has to be transmitted by apostolic dialogue, because it comes to the Church through the apostles. The message is that of Christ, who declared, "The word that you hear is not mine but is from the Father who sent me" (Jn 14:24).

The idea of the Gospel as a word coming down from above might appear to conflict with the view that the human vocation is to active self-realization. John Paul II is aware of this difficulty, and he replies that God's redeeming action in Christ comes to meet the deepest longings of the human heart for truth, freedom, life, and community. The gift of divine adoption enables us to fulfill our deepest identity in a surpassing manner. The Church as communion is the locus of this personal and communal participation in the divine. It reflects and shares in the Trinitarian communion of the divine persons among themselves.

Thanks to the presence of the Holy Spirit in the hearts and minds of the faithful, the people of God experience a unique awareness of their divine adoption. "The Christian bears witness to Christ not 'from outside' but on the basis of participation" (*Sources of Renewal*, 1981). The entire people of God shares in the threefold office of Christ as prophet, priest, and king (*Christifideles Laici* 14). Each individual member is called to share in the life-giving mystery of redemption, to make a perfect gift of self and thereby to achieve definitive self-realization. For it is always in giving that one finds one's true self.

The members of the Church share in the threefold office of Christ in differentiated ways. All the ministries, whether hierarchical or charismatic, serve to build up the one community in unity. The Holy Spirit gives the Church a corporate "sense of the faithful" to discern the meaning of God's Word. This "supernatural sense of the faith," however, is not a matter of majority opinion. It is a consensus achieved through the collaboration of the various orders in the Church. In this process "pastors must promote the sense of the faith in all the faithful, examine and authoritatively judge the genuineness of its expressions, and educate the faithful in an ever more mature evangelical discernment" (*Familiaris Consortio* 5).

The special role of the hierarchy within the Church is reiterated by John Paul II. Instituted by Christ, the episcopal order, together with the pope as successor of Peter, has an irreplaceable responsibility for ensuring the unity of the Church in the truth of the Gospel (*Sources of Renewal*, 1981). Like charismatic gifts, hierarchical office is essentially a service toward the community. Its whole task is to build up the community of the people of God. The pope warns against a laicism that denies the proper role of the hierarchy. The contrary error is clericalism, which arises either when the clergy usurp the competence of the laity or when the laity shirk their responsibilities and throw them on the clergy.

In his Christology and ecclesiology, John Paul II frequently appeals to the category of prophetic testimony. Jesus Christ, he says, is the great prophet, the one who proclaims divine truth. The Church and all its members are called to share in his prophetic mission. The transmission of the sacred heritage of saving truth can be an extremely demanding task. When asked to preach a retreat to the papal curia, Cardinal Wojtyla chose as his title "Sign of Contradiction" (*Crossroad*, 1979). After describing the burdensome vocation of ancient prophets such as Jeremiah, he went on to say that the Church and the pope himself are often called to be signs of contradiction in our day. Secular society exerts heavy pressures on the Church and its hierarchy to relax moral norms and permit unbridled self-indulgence.

The then cardinal's answer was typically firm:

> In recent years there has been a striking increase in contradiction, whether one thinks of the organized opposition mounted by the anti-Gospel lobby or of the opposition that springs up in apparently Christian and "humanistic" circles linked with certain Christian traditions. One has only to recall the contestation of the encyclical *Humanae Vitae*, or that provoked by the latest declaration by the Sacred Congregation for the Doctrine of the Faith, *Personae Humanae*. These examples are enough to bring home the fact that we are in the front line in a lively battle for the dignity of man—it is the task of the church, of the Holy See, of all pastors to fight on the side of man, often against men themselves!

In an important speech on Catholic universities, John Paul II made a special appeal to them to be a "critical and prophetic voice" in confronting the increasingly secularized society of our day. It would be a mistake, he says, for such universities to attenuate or disguise their Catholic character. They must take full cognizance of their responsibility to affirm a truth that does not flatter but is absolutely necessary to safeguard the dignity of the human person (see John Paul II's apostolic constitution on Catholic higher education *Ex Corde Ecclesiae* [1990] 32).

In the end, therefore, authentic humanism is compelled, for the sake of its own integrity, to become prophetic. Conscious that the dignity of the person rests both upon freedom of conscience and upon a transcendent order of truth most perfectly revealed in Christ, the faithful Christian must protest against dehumanizing forces, whether collectivistic or individualistic, whether absolutistic or relativistic. The testimony of the Church, like that of Christ, must be against the world for the world. By courageously taking up this task, John Paul II has made himself, in my estimation, the leading prophet of authentic humanism in the world today.

19. THE IGNATIAN CHARISM AND CONTEMPORARY THEOLOGY REFLECTIONS

April 26, 1997

(Lecture delivered at Fordham University on April 10, 1997.)

W here would theology be except for the works of the Jesuits Pierre Teilhard de Chardin (1881–1955) and Henri de Lubac (1896–1991) of France, Karl Rahner (1904–84) of Germany, Bernard Lonergan (1904–84) of Canada, and John Courtney Murray (1904–67) of the United States?

The Swiss-born Hans Urs von Balthasar (1905–88) may be appropriately added to this group because for several decades he too was a Jesuit. After taking a doctorate at the University of Zurich in 1929, he entered the Society of Jesus and was ordained in 1936 in Munich. The approach of World War II forced him to return to Switzerland, where he became a chaplain to students of the University of Basel. Here he met Adrienne von Speyr, a physician and convert to Catholicism who had remarkable mystical gifts. Some ten years later, Balthasar left the Society of Jesus in order to join Speyr in the founding of a secular institute.

These great giants of the mind unquestionably belong to the advance guard of the Second Vatican Council and, except for Teilhard, who had died in 1955, were among the leading interpreters of the council's work. And if one asks what these men had in common, the obvious reply is that all of them were deeply formed by the Spiritual Exercises and the teaching of St. Ignatius of Loyola, whom they took as their spiritual guide. Teilhard de

Chardin, Rahner, de Lubac, and Balthasar, upon whose achievements I shall focus my remarks, give clear manifestations of this intellectual genealogy.

De Lubac, in a short book on Teilhard de Chardin, notes that his *The Divine Milieu* is permeated by Ignatian motifs such as passionate love of Jesus Christ, ardent longing for Christ's kingdom, and boldness in conceiving grand designs to serve him (*Teilhard de Chardin: The Man and His Meaning*). Balthasar, in a volume on de Lubac, remarks on the centrality of the Church in that author's theological vision and comments: "One could show that this center—a pure passageway for pure transmission of the gift—is also the center of the Ignatian spirit. Henri de Lubac lives so intimately in and from this spirit that he diffidently refrains from quoting the holy founder of the Society of Jesus among the thousands who throng his footnotes" (*The Theology of Henri de Lubac: An Overview*). Even this statement is not strong enough. As we shall see, de Lubac in his *The Splendor of the Church* refers to various passages in the Spiritual Exercises and to the Ignatian "Letter on Obedience."

Speaking of himself, Balthasar likewise gladly confesses his indebtedness as a theologian to St. Ignatius, whose Spiritual Exercises he translated into German. Referring to his experiences as a student at Lyons, he says: "Almost all of us were formed by the Spiritual Exercises, the great school of Christocentric contemplation, of attention to the pure and personal word contained in the Gospel, of lifelong commitment to the attempt at following" (*My Work in Retrospect*). The Spiritual Exercises, he writes, provide "the charismatic kernel of a theology of revelation that could offer the unsurpassed answer to all the problems of our age that terrify Christians."

As for Rahner, he declared in an interview at the age of seventy-five: "In comparison with other philosophy and theology that influenced me, Ignatian spirituality was indeed more significant and important. . . . I think that the spirituality of Ignatius himself, which one learned through the practice of prayer and religious formation, was more significant for me than all the learned philosophy and theology inside and outside the order" (interview in *America*, March 10, 1979; reprinted in *Karl Rahner in Dialogue*).

These expressions of appreciation on the part of twentieth-century theologians are in some ways surprising, since Ignatius, though he was a great spiritual leader, scarcely comes up for mention in histories of Catholic theology. He aspired to no theological originality. For the training of Jesuit students he recommended the doctrine of Thomas Aquinas. Instead of calling for innovation, he directed that Jesuit professors should adhere to the safest and most approved opinions, avoiding books and authors that were suspect.

What inspire the creativity of modern systematic theologians are not primarily the theological views of Ignatius but rather his mysticism. Modern authors speak frequently of this as a Christ-centered mysticism, a sacramental mysticism and an ecclesial mysticism. They mention Ignatius's mysticism of service, of reverential love, of the Cross, and of discernment. Whereas other mystics may find communion with God by withdrawing from activity in the world, the contrary is true of Ignatius. He seeks union with God primarily by dwelling within the mysteries through which God makes himself present in our world—especially the mysteries of the incarnate life of the eternal Son. It is a mysticism of action, whereby we unite ourselves with the mission of Christ in the Church. I should like to comment on four themes from the Spiritual Exercises that have particularly inspired twentieth-century theologians: finding God in all things, the immediacy of the soul to God, obedience to the hierarchical Church, and lastly, the call to glorify Christ by free and loving self-surrender into his hands. I shall illustrate each of these themes—the cosmic, the theistic, the ecclesial, and the Christological—from the writings of one of the theologians already mentioned.

FINDING GOD IN ALL THINGS

To the best of my knowledge the expression "finding God in all things" does not appear verbatim in the writings of St. Ignatius. But there are many similar expressions in the Spiritual Exercises, Ignatius's letters, and the constitutions Ignatius wrote for the Society of Jesus (e.g., *Constitutions* 288).

In the "First Principle and Foundation" at the opening of the Exercises, St. Ignatius teaches that sickness and health, poverty and riches, dishonor and honor, a short life and a long life, can all serve as means to that union with God that makes for our eternal salvation (23). In the "Examination of Conscience," he writes that those advanced in the spiritual life constantly contemplate God our Lord "in every creature by His essence, power, and presence" (39). In the "Contemplation to Obtain Divine Love" at the end of the Exercises, Ignatius reflects on how God dwells in all creatures and especially in human beings, who are "created in the likeness and image of the Divine Majesty" (235). Indeed, says Ignatius, God works and labors not only in human persons, but also in the elements, the plants, and the animals (236; cf. 39). From this and similar passages it seems evident that God can be found in all things.

St. Ignatius's close disciple, the Majorcan Jerome Nadal (1507–80), contended that Ignatius was endowed with a special grace "to see and contemplate in all things, actions, and conversations the presence of God and the love of spiritual things, to remain a contemplative even in the midst of action." Nadal believed that to be a contemplative in action and to find God in all things were graces or charisms especially proper to the Society of Jesus.

Among modern Jesuit authors, none has extolled the sense of the divine omnipresence more eloquently than Pierre Teilhard de Chardin in his classic work *The Divine Milieu*, first published in English translation in 1960. This work was written, according to the author, with the intention of instructing the reader "how to see God everywhere, to see Him in all that is most hidden, most solid and most ultimate in the world." The divine milieu, Teilhard declares, "discloses itself to us as a modification of the deep being of things"—a modification that does not alter the perceptible phenomena, but renders them translucent and diaphanous, so that they become epiphanies of the divine.

In successive chapters Teilhard explains how to find God in the positive experiences of successful activity and in the negative experiences of failure and diminishment. The Cross, he maintains, enables sickness and death to be paths to victory. His is a mystical spirituality that involves detachment from all creatures for the site of union with the divine. As he wrote in a private letter of October 22, 1925, "After all, only one thing matters, surely, 'to see' God wherever one looks." The Protestant pastor Georges Crespy observes quite correctly: "It is not difficult to recognize the Ignatian inspiration of the *Milieu Divin*."

For Teilhard, the realization of God's universal presence was not simply an ascetical principle for his own interior life. It was the inspiration of his lifelong quest to build a bridge between Christian faith and contemporary science. Having meditated deeply on the kingdom of Christ, as set forth in the Spiritual Exercises, Teilhard was filled with ardent longing to set all things on fire with the love of Christ (see Henri de Lubac, *The Religion of Teilhard de Chardin*). Aflame with this missionary zeal, he saw the worlds of science beckoning to him as the new territory to be evangelized. In 1926, referring to a recent lecture by a Harvard professor on the dawn of thought in the evolution of species, he wrote in a letter: "However farfetched the notion might appear at first, I realized in the end that, *hic et nunc*, Christ was not irrelevant to the problems that interest Professor Parker: it only needed a few intermediate steps to allow a transition from his positivist psychology to a certain spiritual outlook. This realization cheered me up. Ah, there lie the Indies that draw me more strongly than those of St. Francis Xavier."

Just as the early Jesuit missionaries sought to adopt all that was sound in the cultures of India and China, so Teilhard sought to utilize the new findings of science as points of access to faith in Christian revelation. In his enthusiasm he identified Christ as the Omega Point toward which all the energies of religion and science were converging. This hypothesis certainly went far beyond anything that St. Ignatius would have imagined, but it may be in part an outgrowth of the Ignatian vision of Christ in glory as the "eternal Lord of all things" (Spiritual Exercises 98); it recalls the universalistic horizons of the meditations on the kingdom of Christ, the Incarnation and the Two Standards.

Whatever the weaknesses of the Teilhardian synthesis, it should not be dismissed as a kind of secularism. He explicitly warned against this error: "The sensual mysticisms and certain neo-Pelagianisms (such as Americanism)," he wrote, "have fallen into the error of seeking divine love and the divine Kingdom on the same level as human affections and human progress" (*The Divine Milieu*). The Christ into whom all things must be gathered was for him none other than the historical Jesus, who had been crucified under Pontius Pilate. When he spoke of the convergence of all religions, he added that they must converge on the Christian axis, "the other creeds finding in faith in Christ the proper expression of what they have been seeking as they grope their way towards the divine." In an essay entitled "How I See," he presented the Catholic Church as "the central axis of the universal convergence and exact point at which blazes out the meeting of the Universe and the Omega Point." Repudiating every kind of vague syncretism, he insisted that Christianity is the phylum through which the evolution of the religions must pass in order to achieve its goal. From Rome in 1948 he wrote: "It is here in Rome that we find the Christie pole of the earth; through Rome, I mean, runs the ascending axis of hominization." As we shall see, this ecclesial and Roman spirituality is also thoroughly Ignatian. What inspires the creativity of modern systematic theologians is not primarily the theological views of Ignatius but rather his mysticism.

IMMEDIACY TO GOD

A second theme from the Spiritual Exercises is that of the immediacy of the soul to God. In the "Annotations for the Director" in the introduction to the Exercises, St. Ignatius admonishes the director to refrain from urging the retreatant to choose the more perfect way of life. "It is more suitable and much better," he says, "that the Creator and Lord in person communicate himself to the devout soul in quest of the divine will, and that He inflame it with love of Himself." The director should therefore "permit the Creator to deal directly with the creature, and the creature directly with its Creator and Lord" (15).

In choosing a way of life, Ignatius later declares, the individual should turn with great diligence to prayer in the presence of God our Lord (183) and assess whether the inclination one feels toward a given choice descends purely from above, that is, from the love of God (184). It is possible for God to act directly on the soul, giving spiritual joy and consolation that are not humanly prepared for by any preceding perception or knowledge on the part of the creature (329–30). Since God alone can act in this manner, such consolation can be a sure sign of God's will (336).

Among modern theologians who have built on this Ignatian theme, none is more explicit than Karl Rahner. On the ground that God can draw the soul suddenly and entirely to himself, Rahner argues that it is possible for the human mind to have an experience of God, as he immediately bestows himself in grace. Rahner rereads St. Ignatius, just as he rereads Thomas Aquinas, in light of a transcendental philosophy that has its roots in the work of the Belgian Jesuit Joseph Maréchal (1878–1944).

The basic idea of this philosophy is that the human spirit, while it knows objects in the world through sense experience, is oriented beyond all objects to a non-objectifiable divine mystery. The entire enterprise of theology, Rahner maintains, must be sustained and energized "by a previous unthematic, transcendental relatedness of our whole intellectuality to the incomprehensible infinite." "The meaning of all explicit knowledge of God in religion and in metaphysics is intelligible," he says, "only when all the words we use there point to the unthematic experience of our orientation toward the ineffable mystery" (*Foundations of Christian Faith*). All conceptual statements about God, for Rahner, live off the nonobjective experience of transcendence as such.

This nonobjective transcendental knowledge of God may be seen as the keystone of Rahner's whole theology. As Francis Fiorenza has noted, it forms the background of many of Rahner's characteristic theses: God's presence to man in grace and revelation, the "supernatural existential," the anonymous Christian, the ontological and psychological unity of Christ, the limitations of Christ's human knowledge, the historicity of dogma, the nonobjective factor in the development of dogma, and many other points.

Rahner recasts the theology of the sacraments on the ground that they do not mediate grace in a reified way but bring about and express an experience of grace that consists in a direct contact between the soul and God. He cautions against the trap of imagining that God should be identified with any one "categorially" mediated religious presence, such as the Bible or the sacraments. After all, Rahner might say, there is no such thing as bottled grace!

On the ground that every individual is in immediate contact with God through grace, Rahner develops an original theory of the relationship between the charismatic and the institutional elements in the Church. The charisms, or gifts of the Holy Spirit, he holds, are in principle prior to the institution. The charismatic element, in fact, is "the true pith and essence of the Church," the point where the lordship of Christ is most directly and potently exercised. The external structures of the Church, in his system, are seen as subordinate to the self-actualization of the transcendental subject, achieved by grace. Officeholders in the Church are obliged not to stifle the Holy Spirit but to recognize and foster the free movements of the Spirit in the Church.

Holding that the articulation of dogma always falls short of the reality to which it refers, Rahner pleads for a high level of tolerance for doctrinal diversity in the Church. He favors a pluriform Church with structures that are adaptable to local and transitory needs. The institutional forms, for him, are radically subordinate to the nonthematic experience of grace. The student of the Spiritual Exercises is reminded in this connection of the way in which Ignatius instructs the director to adapt the meditations to the age, education, and talents of those making the Exercises. Retreatants are encouraged to adopt whatever posture best enables them to pray. For Ignatius, external forms and practices were always secondary to spiritual fruits.

On the ground that the human spirit is always and everywhere open to God's gracious self-communication, Rahner draws a further consequence. All persons, he contends, have some experience of the immediate presence of the divine, and have the possibility of living by God's grace, even if they have failed to arrive at explicit belief in God or in Christ. Even those who have never heard the proclamation of the Gospel may be, in Rahner's famous phrase, "anonymous Christians." We have a right to hope for the salvation of all.

Rahner combines his conviction that God is found in transcendental experience with the characteristically Ignatian tenet of God's presence in all things. While insisting on the primacy of the inner experience of God in the depths of consciousness, Rahner holds that this experience is actualized through encounters with inner-worldly realities. The transcendental is not the remote: it continually mediates itself through particular historical experiences.

In an early essay on "Ignatian Mysticism of Joy in the World," Rahner celebrates the distinctively Jesuit affirmation of the world and its values, the disposition to accept the achievements of culture, to esteem humanism, and to adapt to the demands of varying situations. Once we have found the God of the life beyond, he concludes, we are able to immerse ourselves in the work required of us in our world today. Since God is active at all times and places, he argues, there is no need to flee to the desert or return to the past to find him. Like Teilhard, therefore, Rahner interprets Ignatius as having laid the foundations of a lay theology that discovers God's presence in worldly realities.

Rahner, again like Teilhard, accepts the Ignatian theology of the Cross. He insists that God is to be found not only in the positive but also in the negative experiences of life, including failure, renunciation, sickness, poverty, and death. Just as the passion and death were central to Christ's redeeming work, so privation and self-denial can be paths to the ultimate renunciation that each of us will have to undergo in death. God is greater than either our successes or our failures. He, the *Deus semper maior*, is our only lasting hope. The drama of the following of Christ through his sufferings to ultimate victory is central to the entire theological project of Hans Urs von Balthasar.

ECCLESIAL OBEDIENCE

St. Ignatius of Loyola, while recognizing the immediacy of the individual soul to God, strongly emphasizes the mediation of the Church. He repeatedly speaks of the Church as the Mother of Believers and the Bride of Christ (Spiritual Exercises 353). "In Christ our Lord, the Bridegroom, and in his Spouse the Church," he asserts, "only one Spirit holds sway" (365). Ignatius in the Exercises speaks of serving Christ in the Church militant and on two occasions refers to it as the hierarchical Church" (170, 353), a term apparently original with Ignatius. On one occasion he adds that the hierarchical Church is "Roman" (353, some manuscripts). He takes it for granted that no one could be called by the Holy Spirit to do anything forbidden by the hierarchical Church (170). This ecclesial mysticism is recaptured in the theology of the French Jesuit Henri de Lubac, as well as in that of his friend and disciple Hans Urs von Balthasar.

De Lubac, like Rahner, was strongly influenced by Maréchal's view that the human spirit is constituted by a dynamic drive to transcend all finite objects in quest of that which is greater than everything conceivable (see *The Discovery of God*). The dynamism of the human spirit toward the vision of God, he believed, surpasses all the affirmations and denials of both positive and negative theology. A ceaseless inquietude of the soul toward God drives the whole process forward. Primordial knowledge comes to itself in reflexive concepts, but these concepts are never final; they are always subject to criticism and correction (see Balthasar, *The Theology of Henri de Lubac*).

Conscious though he is of this inner drive, de Lubac does not fall into religious individualism. Picking up the Ignatian designations of the Church as Bride of Christ and as Mother of all Christ's faithful, he affirms that a "mystical identity" exists between Christ and the Church. He repudiates every tendency to introduce an opposition between the mystical and the visible, between spirit and authority, or between charism and hierarchy. Although the Church has an invisible dimension, it is essentially visible and hierarchical. "Without the hierarchy which is her point of organization, her organizer and her guide," he declares, there could be no talk of the Church at all (*The Splendor of the Church*).

In a celebrated passage of *The Splendor of the Church*, de Lubac paints a glowing portrait of the loyal Christian, one who seeks to be what Origen termed a "true ecclesiastic." Like St. Ignatius, such a person will always be concerned to think with and in the Church, cultivating the sense of Catholic solidarity, and accepting the teaching of the magisterium as a binding norm. The ecclesiastical person, according to de Lubac, will not only be obedient but will love obedience as a way of dying to self in order to be filled with the truth that God pours into our minds. De Lubac discountenances negative criticism and complaint. "Today," he writes, "when the Church is in the dock, misunderstood, jeered at for her very existence and even her sanctity itself, Catholics should be wary lest what they want to say simply to serve her better be turned into account against her." A certain delicacy will prompt them to refrain from public criticism. In these assertions de Lubac echoes the teaching of St. Ignatius in his "Rules for Thinking with the Church."

THE CALL OF THE KING

A final theme in the Spiritual Exercises that has inspired modern disciples of St. Ignatius is the call of Christ in the meditation on the kingdom. All persons with good judgment, Ignatius maintains, will offer themselves entirely to labor with Christ in order to share in his victory (96). But those who wish to distinguish themselves in service will wish to imitate Christ in bearing all wrongs, and suffering abuse and poverty, in order to give greater proof of their love (97–98). The drama of the following of Christ through his sufferings to ultimate victory is central to the entire theological project of Hans Urs von Balthasar. Balthasar's theology of revelation is centered about the self-manifestation of the divine majesty, a theme he himself connects with the Ignatian motto *ad maiorem Dei gloriam*. The glory of God, he holds, overwhelms and captivates all who perceive it. The culminating manifestation of God's glory is Jesus, the crucified and risen one. Jesus glorifies God by the faithful execution of his mission, which is the prolongation in time of his own origin from the Father.

The perfection of human beings cannot be measured by abstract ethical rules but only by their response to the call that Christ addresses to them. That call is always to share in the lot and mission of the Lord. The Church incorporates its members into Christ, first of all through baptism into his death. Christians achieve the freedom of children of God by renouncing their self-will, putting on the mind of Christ. In Balthasar's ecclesiology, therefore, obedience is central and constitutive. To be Church is to be, like Mary, the "handmaid of the Lord." The Church's task, like hers, is to hear the word and do it. In developing his theology of obedience, Balthasar draws extensively on the Spiritual Exercises of St. Ignatius, especially on the "Rules for the Election" and the "Rules for Thinking with the Church." Christian perfection, he has learned from Ignatius, consists in a faithful and loving response to God's call. The love of Christ, in his view, requires not only the observance of the commandments but the following of the evangelical counsels, which are nothing but the form of Christ's redeeming love.

Balthasar's large volume *The Christian State of Life* is an extended commentary on the call of Christ described in the Ignatian meditation on the kingdom. The vocation to the consecrated life, in the view of Balthasar, is a fundamental feature of the Church. Since Jesus called the Twelve to poverty, chastity, and obedience during his public ministry, the state of the evangelical counsels existed even before the priestly state. By renouncing every desire of their own, Christians are best able to share in the absolute freedom that is in God. The prayer of St. Ignatius, "Take, Lord, and Receive," magnificently expresses the sacrifice of personal freedom for the sake of living by the divine will alone.

The following of the crucified Lord takes on concrete form in the hierarchical Church, which retains its Christological form thanks to the authority of officeholders over other members of the Church. If this opposition between hierarchy and faithful were dissolved, he writes, "all that would remain would only be a formless mush of ethical instructions." Like de Lubac, therefore, Balthasar holds that office and charism belong together. From one point of view, office may be seen as a special charism for coordinating other charisms and bringing them into the unity of the Church as a whole.

Recognizing the centrality of the office of Peter, Balthasar wrote a thick volume against what he describes as the "venomous" and "irrational" anti-Roman feeling that has been spreading among Catholics since Vatican II. Within the Christological mystery, he asserts, the Jesuit ideal of combining personal maturity with loving submission to ecclesial authority does not involve the absurdity that some have found in it (The Office of Peter and the Structure of the Church). In its vow of special obedience to the pope, the Society of Jesus, he notes, as a body practices the "disponibility," or universal availability, that lies at the heart of the Ignatian ideal of "indifference."

These reflections on four Ignatian themes as found in four twentieth-century Catholic theologians suggest authentic and apostolically fruitful ways of thinking about God, Christ, Church, and world. In a longer presentation, many other themes and authors could be studied. One might wish to survey the missionary theology of Pierre Charles and Jean Daniélou, the ecumenism of Augustin Bea, the theology of conversion of Bernard Lonergan, and the views of John Courtney Murray on religious freedom. In all these authors it would be possible to trace Ignatian motifs based on the Spiritual Exercises. Reference should also be made to theological disciples of Ignatius who are teaching and writing today. Considerations of space and the limitations of my own knowledge prevent me from exploring these interesting questions in this essay. Ignatian principles, as I have tried to indicate, can lead to a variety of theological systems. In the Spiritual Exercises themselves, there seems to be an inbuilt tension between immediacy and mediation, between personal freedom and obedience, between universalism and ecclesio-centrism, between horizontal openness to the world and reverence for the sacred and the divine. Some theologians, such as Teilhard de Chardin and Rahner, put greater emphasis on immediacy to God, personal freedom, and universalism; others, like de Lubac and Balthasar, especially in their later work, insist more on ecclesial mediation, sacramentality, and obedience. The "Rules for the Discernment of Spirits" seem to point in one direction, the "Rules for Thinking with the Church" in the other. But because both emphases are valid and are held together in the Exercises, they must be harmoniously reconciled in theology.

The Ignatian charism, as I understand it, consists in the ability to combine the two tendencies without detriment to either. A purely mechanical obedience without regard for the movements of the Spirit and a purely individualistic reliance on the Spirit without regard for ecclesiastical authority would be equally foreign to the heritage we have been exploring. For Ignatius it was axiomatic that Christians are called to achieve authentic freedom by surrendering their limited freedom into the hands of God. The theologian who is most prayerfully open to the impulses of the Spirit is best able to enter into the mind of the Church and by this means to interpret the Christian faith in fullest conformity with the intentions of the Lord himself.

20. MARY AT THE DAWN OF THE NEW MILLENNIUM

November 19, 1997

(Lecture delivered at Fordham University on November 19, 1997.)

For Pope John Paul, Mary is the primary patroness of the advent of the new millennium. As the mother of Christ she is preeminently an advent figure—the morning star announcing the rising of the Sun of Righteousness. Like the moon at the dawn of a new day, she is wholly bathed in the glory of the sun that is to come after her. Her beauty is a reflection of his.

The glories of Mary have only gradually been discovered by the Church in the course of nearly two thousand years of study and contemplation. The basic lines of Catholic Mariology are by now beyond dispute, enshrined as they are in the scriptures; in the liturgy, in prayer, poetry, song, and art; in the writings of saints and theologians; and in the teaching of popes and councils. Mary holds a secure place as the greatest of the saints, conceived and born without original sin and free from actual sin at any point in her life. Full of grace, she is exemplary in her faith, hope, love of God, and generous concern for others. Having virginally conceived the Son of God in her womb, she remained a virgin throughout life. At the end of her earthly sojourn she was taken up body and soul into heaven, where she continues to exercise her spiritual motherhood and to intercede for the needs of her children on earth. This body of teaching, constructed laboriously over long centuries, belongs inalienably to the patrimony of the Church and can scarcely be contested from within the Catholic tradition. It goes without saying that John Paul II accepts this heritage without question.

WOJTYLA'S MARIOLOGY

These convictions have not come to the present pope only as a result of being installed in his office. He has been a devoted son of Mary ever since early youth, when he worshiped at her shrines in the neighborhood of his native Wadowice. During the Nazi occupation of Poland, as a chaplet leader in a "living rosary," he joined in prayers to Mary for peace and liberation. He also studied the works of St. Louis Grignion de Montfort (1673–1716), from whom he takes his motto as pope, *totus tuus* ("I am wholly yours"). It would be a mistake to think of Karol Wojtyla's attachment to Mary as the fruit of sentimentality. He emphatically denies that Marian teaching is a devotional supplement to a system of doctrine that would be complete without her. On the contrary, he holds, she occupies an indispensable place in the whole plan of salvation. "The mystery of Mary," writes the pope, "is a revealed truth which imposes itself on the intellect of believers and requires of those in the Church who have the task of studying and teaching a method of doctrinal reflection no less rigorous than that used in all theology" (*L'Osservatore Romano,* January 10, 1996).

A bishop at Vatican II, Wojtyla made several important interventions regarding Mary. He favored the inclusion of Mariology within the *Dogmatic Constitution on the Church* but he pleaded for a different location of the text, so that, instead of being a final chapter, it would immediately follow chapter 1 on the Mystery of the Church. Mary, he declared in a written intervention in September 1964, having built up Christ's physical body as mother, continues this role in the mystical body. Since she is mother of Christ and of Christians, she ought to be considered early in the document, he said in a joint submission with the other Polish bishops in the fall of 1964, rather than be relegated to a kind of appendix at the end.

"For practical reasons," however, the theological commission judged it necessary at that stage to keep the section on Mary at the end of the constitution—a decision that unfortunately made it possible for some commentators to say that Vatican II had demoted the status of Mary. The commission also rejected several proposals to designate Mary formally as Mother of the Church, and even to make that term the title of the chapter. But in the *Dogmatic Constitution on the Church* (1964), the council did declare that "the Catholic Church, taught by the Holy Spirit, honors her with the affection of filial piety as a most loving mother" (53). To the great satisfaction of Archbishop Wojtyla, Paul VI at the end of the third session, on November 21, 1964, explicitly proclaimed Mary to be Mother of the Church.

The Mariology of John Paul II appears in concentrated form in his encyclical *Redemptoris Mater* (1987) and more diffusely in a series of seventy Wednesday audience catecheses on Mary delivered between September 6, 1995, and November 12, 1997. In general, his teaching may be called pastoral rather than speculatively theological. The pope is more concerned with communicating the faith of the Church and fostering authentic piety than with proposing new theories. But rather frequently one comes across phrases and statements that reflect personal insights of his own.

The key term that unifies the pope's Mariology, as I see it, is that of "motherhood." Mary is the mother of the Redeemer, mother of divine grace, mother of the Church. The Council of Ephesus in the fifth century established the foundational dogma of Mariology that Mary is Mother of God, *theotokos* (literally, "God-bearer"). In *Redemptoris Mater*, the pope calls attention to the ecumenical value of this dogma (30–32): it is accepted by practically all Christians, and has given rise to beautiful hymns, especially in the Byzantine liturgy, which in turn inspired the salutation in the great Anglican hymn "Ye Watchers and Ye Holy Ones":

O higher than the cherubim. More glorious than the seraphim.
Lead their praises. Alleluia! Thou bearer of the eternal Word,
Most gracious, magnify the Lord, Alleluia!

With his great interest in the theme of redemption, John Paul
II frequently calls attention to Mary's involvement in the saving
mission of her Son, beginning with the annunciation, when she
consented to the plan of the Incarnation and received the signal
grace of divine motherhood. As the virgin mother, she conceived
through faith and obedience to the divine Word that came to her
from on high (*Redemptoris Mater* 13).

Like Christ's own redemptive mission, Mary's role in salvation history was not exempt from sorrow. In many texts John
Paul II recalls how, at the presentation of the infant Christ in the
Temple, Simeon prophesied that Mary's soul would be pierced
by a sword. This prophecy was to be fulfilled on Calvary, where
Mary's compassion perfectly mirrored the passion of her Son,
whose sufferings reverberated in her heart.

After the death of Jesus, according to the pope, Mary's motherly office assumes a new form. In saying to the Beloved Disciple "Behold your mother," Jesus places the apostles under her
maternal care (Jn 19:25–27). In the days following the Ascension,
we find Mary in the company of the apostles prayerfully and
confidently waiting for the Holy Spirit, who had already over-
shadowed her at the annunciation, to descend upon the Church.
There is a mysterious correspondence, therefore, in Mary's maternal relationships to Jesus and to the Church. By her unceasing
intercession she cooperates with maternal love in the spiritual
birth and development of the sons and daughters of the Church
(*Redemptoris Mater* 44). "Choosing her as Mother of all humanity," writes the pope, "the heavenly Father wanted to reveal the
maternal dimension of his divine tenderness and care for men
and women of every age" (*L'Osservatore Romano*, weekly English
edition, October 22, 1997).

MARIAN DOGMAS?

As the present millennium draws to a close, certain groups of Catholics are pressing for new dogmatic definitions officially conferring upon Mary the titles "coredemptrix," "mediatrix of all graces," and "advocate of the people of God." A Dutch mystic, Ida Peerdeman, who died in 1995, predicted that John Paul II would proclaim this threefold title of Mary as the "final dogma." A group calling itself Vox Populi Mariae Mediatrici, based in the United States and headed by Mark Miravalle, a lay professor of theology at Steubenville, Ohio, has been gathering signers, including many cardinals and bishops, calling for this triple definition. According to *Newsweek* for August 25, 1997, the pope has received 4,340,429 signatures from 157 countries requesting him to make this dogmatic proclamation. Miravalle is quoted as claiming that the date of the proclamation has actually been set: May 31, 1998, a day when the feast of Pentecost coincides with the former feast of Mary Mediatrix of All Graces.

There is nothing unusual about campaigns to confer more exalted titles on Mary. The dogmas of the Immaculate Conception and the assumption were preceded by floods of petitions. After World War I, the Belgian Cardinal Désiré-Joseph Mercier took the leadership in a drive for a dogmatic definition that Mary was universal mediatrix of grace. Pius XI appointed three commissions to study this question, but no further action was taken. Many bishops, however, obtained permission for the Mass and Office of Our Lady Mediatrix of All Graces to be celebrated in their dioceses. In 1950 the first International Mariological Congress, meeting in Rome, asked for a dogmatic proclamation of Mary's universal mediation. But Pius XII did not implement this request. In fact he replaced the feast of Mary Mediatrix with that of the Queenship of Mary in 1954.

In order to assess the acceptability of the three proposed titles, it will be helpful to glance at their past usage in Catholic theology and magisterial teaching.

THE PROPOSED TITLES

Of the three proposed titles, "advocate" is the least burdened
with difficulties. It was used in the patristic age by Irenaeus and
John Damascene, and in the Middle Ages by Bernard and many
others. In the Salve Regina we implore Mary as "most gracious
Advocate" to turn her eyes of mercy toward us. The fact that the
title "advocate" is applied to the Holy Spirit in the fourth gospel
(Jn 14:16, 26; 15:26; 16:7) and to Christ in the First Letter of John (1
Jn 2:1) can hardly constitute an objection, since Mary's advocacy,
as that of a created person, takes place on a different level. If she
is not our advocate, what could her intercession mean? To deny
her this title would be in effect to reject the whole doctrine of the
intercession of the saints. The title "mediatrix" is likewise very
ancient. It goes back to the fifth century (Basil of Seleucia) and
was in common usage by the eighth century (Andrew of Crete,
Germanus of Constantinople, and John Damascene). Medieval
saints such as Bernard of Clairvaux, Bonaventure, and Bernar-
dine of Siena frequently used the title. In modern times it was
further popularized by St. Louis Grignion de Montfert and St.
Alfonsus Liguori.

The designation of Mary as "mediatrix" is a commonplace in
papal documents. Leo XIII in 1896 said of her, "No single individual can even be imagined who has ever contributed or ever will
contribute so much toward reconciling man with God. . . . She is
therefore truly his [Christ's] mother and for this reason, a worthy and acceptable 'Mediatrix to the Mediator.'" Pius X in 1904
said that by reason of the union she had with Jesus she is "the
most powerful mediatrix and advocate of the whole world with
her divine Son." Benedict XV in 1915 in an address to the Consistory of Cardinals declared: "The faith of her believers and her
children's love consider her not only God's mother, but also the
mediatrix with God." Pius XI in 1928 declared that Christ willed
"to make his mother the advocate for sinners and the dispenser
and mediatrix of his grace." Pius XII in 1940, without actually

using the term "mediatrix," urged faithful Christians to have recourse to Mary since, as Bernard had taught, "it is the will of God that we obtain all favors through Mary."

In preparation for Vatican II, and in response to many petitions, the Theological Commission in 1962 proposed a schema formally declaring that Mary was mediatrix, but several eminent cardinals, including Augustin Bea, Paul Emile Léger, and Bernard Alfrink, argued that the title was not yet sufficiently clarified in theology to warrant a conciliar pronouncement and that a formal declaration would be ecumenically counterproductive. In the final text, therefore, the council contented itself with the very moderate statement that because of her motherly care, Mary is invoked in the Church by titles such as "advocate" and "mediatrix" (*Dogmatic Constitution on the Church*, 62).

In his sixty-fourth catechesis on Mary (September 24, 1997), John Paul II affirms that Mary is indeed mediatrix inasmuch as she "presents our desires and petitions to Christ, and transmits the divine gifts to us, interceding continually on our behalf." In his encyclical on Mary, the pope characterizes Mary's mediation as maternal; it is motherhood in the order of grace (21, 38). It is intercessory in nature, since it reaches out toward the Son and has a universal embrace corresponding to his saving will for all humanity (40). From these statements we may conclude that Mary's mediation, according to John Paul II, extends in some way to all the gifts of grace.

The difficulty is often raised that to speak of Mary in these terms derogates from the unique mediatorship of Jesus Christ, which is formally affirmed in scripture (1 Tm 2:5). Mary's mediation might even seem to interfere with an immediate union between the Christian and the Lord. In replying to this difficulty, the pope repeats the teaching of Vatican II that "all the saving influences of the Blessed Virgin . . . originate from the divine pleasure; they flow forth from the superabundance of the merits of Christ, rest on his mediation, depend entirely upon it, and draw all their power from it. In no way do they impede the immediate union of the faithful with Christ. Rather, they foster this union" (*Dogmatic Constitution on the Church*, 60). Mary's mediation, according to the council, "takes nothing away from the dignity and power of Christ the one mediator, and adds nothing to it" (62). If these principles are kept in mind, the doctrinal objections to the title "mediatrix" lose much of their force.

As for the title "coredemptrix," this has a more checkered history. Having first appeared in theology toward the end of the fourteenth century, it becomes prominent in papal teaching in the first half of this century. Benedict XV in 1918 went so far as to assert that Mary "with Christ redeemed mankind," and Pius XI, addressing a group of pilgrims in 1933, declared: "From the nature of his work the Redeemer ought to have associated his mother with his work. For this reason we invoke her under the title of Coredemptrix. She gave us the Savior, she accompanied him in the work of Redemption as far as the Cross itself, sharing with him the sorrows of the agony and of the death in which Jesus consummated the redemption of mankind." Again in 1935, he addressed Mary in prayer, "Mother most faithful and most merciful, who as coredemptrix and partaker of thy dear Son's sorrows didst assist him as he offered the sacrifice of our redemption on the altar of the cross."

But Pius XII studiously avoided the term. Instead he spoke of Mary as the loving Mother, "inseparably joined with Christ in accomplishing the work of man's redemption." Paul VI and Vatican II made no mention of Mary as coredemptrix. The very term seemed to contradict the common teaching that although there are many mediators of intercession, there is but one mediator of redemption, Jesus Christ. All Catholics agree that Christ was the sufficient cause of our redemption. The question concerns the manner in which he associated his mother with himself in this action.

In line with previous popes, John Paul II holds that Mary cooperated with Christ at every stage from his coming into the world to his death upon the Cross, where her soul was pierced with grief as his heart was pierced with a lance. Although the pope does not speak of Mary as "coredemptrix" in any of his encyclicals or other major documents, he did use the term in occasional speeches, at least until 1985. (The only case since 1985 known to me is in a meditation on the Angelus, October 6, 1991, commemorating the sixth centenary of the canonization of St. Bridget of Sweden. Here the pope mentions that Bridget invoked Mary under various titles, including that of "Coredemptrix.") For example, in an address at the Marian shrine of Guayaquil, Ecuador, on January 31, 1985, he declared: "As she was in a special way close to the cross of her Son, she also had to have a privileged experience of his Resurrection. In fact, Mary's role as coredemptrix did not cease with the glorification of her Son."

In the few cases where the present pope has used the term "coredemptrix," it seems to be a concise way of referring to Mary's intimate association with her Son in his redemptive action. This interpretation is borne out by his Wednesday audience catechesis of April 9, 1996:

> Moreover, when the Apostle Paul says, "For we are God's fellow workers" (1 Cor. 3:9), he maintains the real possibility for man to co-operate with God. The collaboration of believers, which obviously excludes any equality with him, is expressed in the proclamation of the Gospel and in their personal contribution to its taking root in human hearts.
>
> However, applied to Mary, the term "co-operator" acquires a specific meaning. The collaboration of Christians in salvation takes place after the Calvary event, whose fruits they endeavor to spread by prayer and sacrifice. Mary, instead, co-operated during the event itself and in the role of mother; thus her co-operation embraces the whole of Christ's saving work. She alone was associated in this way with the redemptive sacrifice that merited the salvation of all mankind. In union with Christ and in submission to him, she collaborated in obtaining the grace of salvation for all humanity.

Whether he is speaking of Mary's mediation or of her role in redemption, the pope always makes it clear that he is referring to her participation in Christ's own action, which is by itself incomparable and sufficient. The doctrine of Mary as coredemptrix cannot mean that she stands on the same level with Christ or makes up for any deficiency in his redemptive action. But since Christ's mediation does not exclude the cooperation of subordinate mediators, so it would seem, he could freely associate others with his redemptive action without ceasing to be the full and sufficient cause. If this point is clearly understood, it is acceptable to speak of Mary as having been in some way conjoined with Christ in his redemptive work, and in that qualified sense as "coredemptrix."

WILL THE TITLES BE DEFINED?

As things presently stand, however, I think it unlikely that the pope will dogmatically proclaim any or all of the three proposed titles, especially the title of coredemptrix. My first reason for thinking so is the pope's complete loyalty to the intentions of Vatican II, which was cautious in its use of Marian titles and made no reference to "coredemptrix." Following the council, John Paul II has thus far been careful to avoid both maximalism and minimalism and to refrain from personally deciding issues that are still subject to theological debate. Like John XXIII and Paul VI before him, he has until now abstained from making any *ex cathedra* pronouncements and attaching anathemas to his teaching. Although he recognizes his power as pope to speak authoritatively to the universal episcopate, he evidently prefers to teach collegially and without canonical censures, expressing what he perceives as being the consensus of the episcopal college.

Second, it must be noted that these dogmas would provoke considerable confusion among Catholics and great ecumenical dismay, especially in Protestant and Anglican circles. Some might think that Mary was being exalted to become a fourth person in the godhead or at least that the unique mediatorship of Christ or the sufficiency of his redemptive act was being obscured. Even the Orthodox, who might agree with the substance of the proclamation, would be opposed to the manner of its issuance if it came from the pope speaking *ex cathedra*. The pope, who places ecumenism high on his agenda, would surely take account of these sentiments. (See John Paul's 1995 encyclical *Ut Unum Sint* on the importance of ecumenical dialogue about the Virgin Mary.)

Third, the exact content of the proposed dogmas is still unclear. Mary's mediation or advocacy could be understood, or misunderstood, as implying that she can make God change his plans or that she is more merciful than her Son. It raises the question whether all prayers must be channeled through Mary in order to be heard by God. If she is coredemptrix, does that mean that she cooperates directly and immediately in the redemptive action of Christ, offering him up on the Cross, or only indirectly and remotely—for example, by becoming mother of the Redeemer and consenting to his sacrificial death? What, if anything, does her cooperation add that would not be present without it? Mariologists have debated points like this with great subtlety, without, however, reaching any full agreement. These unsettled points suggest that any dogmatic definition might be premature.

Fourth, the community of Mariology scholars seems to be opposed. At Czestochowa in Poland in August 1996 a commission of fifteen Catholic theologians from the Pontifical International Marian Academy, chosen for their specific competence in this area, together with three officers of the society and five non-Catholic theologians, unanimously recommended against any dogmatic definition of the Marian titles of mediatrix, coredemptrix, and advocate. Their reason was partly ecumenical, but more substantively that the titles are ambiguous and lend themselves to misunderstanding. Using similar arguments, an International Mariological Symposium, meeting at Rome on October 7–9, 1997, registered overwhelming opposition to the proposed papal definitions and especially to that of coredemptrix. Finally, we have a statement of the papal press secretary, Joaquín Navarro-Vails, on August 18, 1997, declaring that no proclamation of any new Marian dogmas is at present planned or under study by the pope or any Vatican commission. It is "crystal clear"—he is quoted as saying—that the pope will not solemnly define any of these three titles as dogmas.

If the pope wishes to honor Mary in some special way at the approach of the new millennium, he would have other possibilities than to proclaim new dogmas. He could, for example, declare that these beliefs are worthy of credence, or he could establish some new liturgical feast honoring Mary by one or another of these titles. Due recognition of Mary in the celebration of the great jubilee does not, however, necessitate any doctrinal or liturgical innovations.

THEMES FOR 1997-99

In his apostolic letter The Coming of the Third Millennium, John Paul II makes a number of concrete suggestions with implications for Marian practice and devotion. He relates the last three years of the current millennium to the three divine persons and the three theological virtues. The year 1997, he declares, is a time to concentrate on faith with special reference to Jesus Christ as the divine Son. The year 1998 would then be a time for emphasizing the Holy Spirit and the virtue of hope. And 1999 is to be an occasion for turning to God the Father and for special emphasis on the virtue of charity.

Each of these three years, according to the pope, has a Marian dimension. She is the virginal mother of the Son, the immaculate spouse of the Holy Spirit, and the fairest daughter of the Father. She is also exemplary in her faith, hope, and charity.

In the year 1997, therefore, we were urged to contemplate Mary's journey of faith in relation to the incarnate Son. At the annunciation, she responded in faith to the angel's message that she was chosen to become the mother of the redeemer. In uttering her *fiat* she entered the history of the world's salvation through the obedience of faith (see the 1986 encyclical *Dominum et Vivificantem*). At the visitation she was praised by Elizabeth with the words: "Blessed is she who believed that there would be a fulfillment of what was spoken to her from the Lord" (Lk 1:45).

Mary's faith was to be severely tested by the flight into Egypt, the loss of the child Jesus in the Temple, his rejection at Nazareth, and especially his crucifixion at Golgotha, which the pope describes as "perhaps the deepest kenosis of faith in human history" (*Redemptoris Mater* 18). But her faith continually grew as she pondered the meaning of the words addressed to her. Her obedient submission in faith was, in the expression of Irenaeus, the act that untied the knot of Eve's disobedience, thus enabling humanity to rise again to communion with God. Mary's faith is perpetuated in the Church as it makes its own pilgrimage of faith.

By pondering Mary's faith in Christ in 1997, Christians disposed themselves for meditation on the Holy Spirit and on hope, the themes proposed for 1998. Mary's faith, itself a gift of the Holy Spirit, enabled her to conceive her Son by the power of that same Spirit. Her faith flowered in an ardent and unfailing hope. Just as Abraham hoped against hope that he would become the father of many nations (Rom 4:18), so Mary trusted against all appearances that the Lord would place her Son upon the throne of David, where he would reign in unending glory (Lk 1:32–33). The hope of the whole people of ancient Israel came to its culmination in Mary, who in her Magnificat praised God's fidelity to the promises he had made to Abraham and to his posterity forever (Lk 1:55). She is thus a radiant model for all who entrust themselves to God's promises. The image of the Virgin praying with the apostles in the Cenacle, says John Paul II, can become a sign of hope for all who call upon the Holy Spirit to deepen their union with God.

Finally, as the most highly favored daughter of the Father, Mary may be viewed as the supreme model of love toward God and neighbor—the theme proposed for 1999. Out of affection for her cousin Elizabeth, she hastens into the hill country to assist her and share with her the good news of the annunciation. In the Magnificat she expresses her joy of spirit in God her savior, who has looked upon her lowliness and done great things for her. In the same hymn she expresses solidarity with Yahweh's beloved poor, thus anticipating the Church's preferential option for the poor. At Cana she manifests her active charity by helping to relieve the embarrassment of her hosts, thus occasioning the miracle by which Christ first displayed his messianic power over nature. Mary's love for God is brought to its deepest fulfillment in heaven, where she continues to intercede lovingly for her children on earth. This she will continue to do until all things are subjected to the Father, so that God will become all in all.

The Church follows in the paths marked out for it by Mary. Like her the Church believes, accepting with fidelity, the Word of God. It preserves the faith by keeping and pondering in its heart all that God speaks to it. Sustained by the Holy Spirit amid the afflictions and hardships of the world, the Church unceasingly looks forward in hope to the promise of future glory. In imitation of Mary, the fair daughter of Zion, the Church continually praises the Father's mercies and imitates his love for men and women of every nation, the righteous and the unrighteous. The Church's prayers for the needs of the whole world blend with Mary's petitions before the throne of God.

Besides being an icon of the whole Church, Mary is in a particular way a model for women. The contrasting vocations of virginity and motherhood meet and coexist in her (see John Paul II's 1988 apostolic letter *Mulieris Dignitatem*). The single, the married, and the widowed can all look to her for inspiration. In Mary women can find an exemplar of "the loftiest sentiments of which the human heart is capable: the self-offering totality of love; the strength that is capable of bearing the greatest sorrows; limitless fidelity and tireless devotion to work; the ability to combine penetrating intuition with words of support and encouragement" (*Redemptoris Mater* 46).

MEANING OF THE JUBILEE

The Mariology of John Paul II is closely interwoven with his theology of time. Mary could receive the fullness of grace because the fullness of time had arrived (Gal 4:4). This fullness, says the pope, "marks the moment when, with the entrance of the eternal into time, time itself is redeemed." Jubilee years are more than sentimental recollections of the past. They are woven into the texture of salvation history. Christ began his public ministry by proclaiming the arrival of the great jubilee, the year of the Lord's favor predicted by the prophet Isaiah (Lk 4:16–30). We continue to live in this era of redemption, this jubilee season of grace and liberation. Just as the scripture was fulfilled in the hearing of those gathered in the synagogue of Nazareth, so it is fulfilled anew in our hearing, if we will only listen. Every jubilee celebration of the Church recalls and reactivates the arrival of the fullness of time.

Like the Incarnation itself, the coming jubilee has a Marian as well as a Christological dimension. The child does not enter the world apart from Mary his blessed mother, the *Theotokos*. In her pilgrimage of faith, hope, and love she blazes the trail on which the Church is to follow. She continues to go before the people of God (*Redemptoris Mater* 6, 25, 28), coming to the help of her clients who seek to rise above their sins and misery. Just as before the coming of Christ she was the "morning star" (*stella matutina*), so she remains, for us who are still on the journey of faith, the "star of the sea" (*stella maris*), guiding us through the dark journey toward the moment when faith will be transformed into the everlasting vision in which we look upon God our Savior "face to face" (*Redemptoris Mater* 6).

21. ORTHODOXY AND SOCIAL CHANGE

June 20, 1998

(Lecture given on March 19, 1998, at Loras College in Dubuque, Iowa.)

T he magisterium was never intended to seek popularity. It would forfeit all credibility if it taught only what people wanted to hear.

The question whether the secularization of society normally brings about a decline of religion has been much debated. The renowned sociologist Peter Berger during the 1960s answered this question in the affirmative, but soon he changed his mind. Since the 1970s he has maintained that the sociological process of secularization is not necessarily detrimental to religious faith and practice. His prime example is the United States, which remains a highly religious country even though secularization has gone as far here as anywhere else in the world.

POLITICAL SECULARIZATION

It may be helpful to make a distinction between two types of secularization—political and cultural. In the political sense the term means recognition of the state as a purely secular entity. The disestablishment of religion in the American system involves obvious problems, but on the whole it has worked out well both for religion and for secular society. To have a lively religious community, it is important that the members belong to it for religious motives, not because of any kind of social constraint or legal penalties. The churches thrive better in the United States than in countries where some form of Christianity is the official religion of the state. Religious groups are free not only to hold services of worship (as they can in some totalitarian states) but also to publish their views and to conduct schools, hospitals, and charitable organizations. Many Americans devote a large portion of their time, energy, and income to religious causes. Church attendance remains relatively high. It is a blessing for civil society as well to have a situation in which people of different religious faiths can live together peaceably in mutual respect and friendship.

In Western Europe the process of secularization has not worked out so favorably for religion. This is partly because it is seen as a setback for the Church, which in the past relied on the backing of the state. The people have not been prepared for a situation in which religion is a matter of choice. The national memory in most European countries is burdened by the involvement of the churches in struggles for political power. The history of religious wars has severely damaged the cause of religion, especially in those countries in which the Church relied upon the state to enforce its standards of belief and conduct.

In the long run, I would conclude, political secularization, far from being harmful to religious faith, is beneficial to it. Provided that its free exercise is safeguarded, religion can survive and prosper in a secularized state. But the kind of religion that will prosper depends to a large degree on the impact of cultural secularization, to which our consideration must now tum.

CULTURAL SECULARIZATION

Cultural secularization goes hand in hand with what sociologists describe as modernization, a phenomenon that can be clarified by several points of contrast between traditional or premodern cultures and those that are characteristically modern.

In traditional societies the religion, occupation, and customs of individuals are determined not by personal choice but by the family and neighborhood in which they were born and raised.

Modern society, by contrast, is highly mobile. People change their residence and occupation very freely, according to their personal inclination and the opportunities of the job market. The son of a fisherman from New Orleans can become a lawyer in New York; the daughter of an oil tycoon from Tulsa can become a movie actress in Hollywood.

Individual choice enters likewise into the sphere of religion. In parts of southern Asia one almost has to be a Buddhist or a Hindu, depending on the region where one lives. In much of the Middle East, Islam is the law of the land. But nothing similar exists in the United States. The Church becomes for all practical purposes a voluntary association. People belong to a church if they want to, not because they feel they have to. There are few if any social pressures to belong to one religion rather than another or even to any organized religion. Religion is considered a private matter, about which people can make their own choices. Many opt out of the church and the religion in which they were raised. Sometimes they come back to it; sometimes they join another religious body. This situation is not wholly bad because, in the words of the Second Vatican Council's *Pastoral Constitution on the Church in the Modern World*, it demands from individual persons "a more personal and explicit adherence to faith" (7).

A further aspect of modernization has to do with the division of life into separate spheres. Religion is seen as having a certain limited competence. It governs people's relationship to God, their prayer life, and their Sunday worship. But most believers do not want religion to interfere with the autonomy of their other activities. The various spheres—business, politics, social life, entertainment, and so forth—are relatively independent of one another. It is unusual to choose one's business partners, one's political allegiances, or one's recreational activities primarily on religious grounds.

In the modern situation religion tends to become marginalized, some would say trivialized. It has a very hard time maintaining itself in the public square or the marketplace. Any effort

by a church to say what is morally permitted, required, or prohib-
ited by the law of God in the spheres of politics, medicine, business, or family life is resented as an intrusion into alien territory.
It is considered improper for any private association to impose
its morality on people who do not belong to it. Thus religion is
progressively excluded from areas in which it formerly played
a decisive role. It has difficulty keeping a significant presence
in education. Even in domestic life, religion plays a diminished
part. As all these spheres become progressively secularized, religion retreats into its own corner. It survives as something one
might decide to do with one's leisure time—almost as a hobby
for people who want to be religious. Anyone who sees religion
as determinative for secular activities is likely to be regarded as
a fanatic. Teachers, businessmen, politicians, or judges who let
religion impinge in a major way on their professional activities
are considered eccentric.

In the kind of modern society I have described, people tend
to be selective in their adherence to their heritage, in the religious sphere as in other areas. They will be reluctant to commit
themselves to a whole "package" of doctrines and moral standards handed to them by tradition or by the official teachers.
The role of authority is greatly diminished. Even Christians who
belong to a particular church want to scrutinize the directives
coming from its office-bearers. Top-down management arouses
anger and irritation. Church members feel that they have a right
to be consulted and that they may choose for themselves which
doctrines they will accept.

THE SITUATION OF ORTHODOXY

Orthodoxy, in Christian terms, means adherence to a definite
body of truth certified by the Church as being consonant with
revelation. Like Muslims and Jews, Christians of various denominations have their own brands of orthodoxy, based on the confessional documents approved in their respective traditions. For

Catholics the principal criterion and judge of orthodoxy is the magisterium, which consists of the pope and the bishops who are in communion with him. The magisterium functions most authoritatively in the teachings of ecumenical councils, in which the pope and the universal episcopate act in unison.

The presupposition of Christian orthodoxy is that God has made a definite revelation that can, at least in part, be expressed in conceptual language. Creedal and dogmatic propositions articulate particular aspects or implications of divine revelation. Religious language, of course, is historically and culturally conditioned and may have to be translated for different times and places, but the truths expressed by it, inasmuch as they are warranted by God, transcend that conditioning. Admittedly, words like "Incarnation" and "Trinity" have highly technical meanings that have developed through centuries of discussion and are subject to further modification, but the reality to which these words refer is held to be objectively given in revelation.

The revelation of God in Christ, according to Christian faith, is permanently and universally true. It is addressed to all men and women and to all future generations. The Church has an obligation to preserve and transmit the deposit of faith. The magisterium has the responsibility of overseeing the whole process and enjoys the divine assistance needed to perform this indispensable function.

If the social analysis in the opening section of this article is correct, it should be evident that to be orthodox in our society it is necessary to be countercultural, at least in the sphere of religion. In the cultural situation that has developed in the United States and in great parts of the Western world, any kind of orthodoxy, and perhaps especially Catholic orthodoxy, is under enormous pressure. To indicate this, it may suffice to allude to five aspects of the contemporary mentality: relativism, historicism, subjectivism, individualism, and egalitarianism.

1. *Relativism* in extreme form maintains that truth is relative to the person who holds it: what is true for me may not be true for

you. In a more moderate form it maintains that we cannot know truth except in a manner conditioned by the particular environment in which we have been raised and educated. The logical consequence is that one should not profess to be certain of any religious belief that is contested in another social setting. In the face of religious pluralism, we should be modest enough to admit that our own faith is valid only within our limited horizons. The doctrines may be true for us, insofar as they work in our lives, but we cannot say that they ought to be believed and professed by those raised in other cultural environments. Because it runs directly counter to the universalism of Christian truth claims, relativism is incompatible with orthodoxy.

2. *Historicism* is simply a further specification of relativism. It means relativism in time. In extreme form it holds that what is true in one age can become false in another. In more moderate form it holds that ideas regarded as true and certain in one period of time may be seen as false or doubtful by a later age in light of further discoveries. For this reason, say the historicists, we should always be tentative in affirming religious truths and prepared to surrender them if the evidence runs against them. We can never be sure that they will not be overthrown by future intellectual progress. Historicism undermines the view of orthodox Christianity that the revelation given in Christ and the articles of Christian faith are permanently valid.

3. *Subjectivism.* According to the prevalent mentality of our day, there is no objective rule for determining religious truth. Religious knowledge does not arise through mathematical deductions from self-evident principles, as does geometry (according to the popular conception), nor can it be publicly verified by experimentation, as can scientific discoveries. Religion, according to this view, is essentially a matter of feeling and the heart. We are advised to adhere to the religion in which we find emotional satisfaction and growth experiences. By failing to acknowledge the objective truth-value of creedal and dogmatic statements, subjectivism opposes itself to orthodoxy.

4. *Individualism.* The reigning mentality of our age denies that we can make any institution or collectivity responsible for what we believe. Although we may join a church and accept its belief system, we have a right to choose the religious body, if any, to which we wish to belong. We also have a right to opt out of the body if its teaching seems incompatible with our own convictions. Individualism subordinates the faith of the Church to that of each particular member; it minimizes the duty to adhere to some divinely established way of salvation and to conform one's beliefs, as orthodoxy requires, to the teaching of a "true Church."

5. *Egalitarianism.* In civil society it has become practically a matter of dogma that all men and women are created equal, and that popularly elected government is necessary to protect the rights of all. Democracy may indeed be the best form of government for human societies that are set up by the people to secure the blessings of life, liberty, and the pursuit of happiness, but it is quite another question whether democratic principles can prevail in the Church, as a divinely established society that has a definite faith to preserve and propagate.

Egalitarianism, as applied to Christianity, seeks to refashion the Church in the image of democratic society. It denies that there is any order or class that has privileged access to the truth. Those who govern in the Church, it maintains, should be accountable to the membership at large and operate according to the rule of consensus. The officers of the Church, it is held, should adjust their teaching and precepts in light of the findings of public opinion polls or the results of a democratic vote. Democratization thus tends to subvert the teaching authority of the hierarchy.

The net result of these five pressures is to place Catholic orthodoxy in a difficult and highly unpopular position. Terms associated with orthodoxy, such as "dogma," "hierarchy," "priesthood," and "infallibility," evoke negative reactions. To cherish any of the four is considered to be a sign that one is not a really modern person but a survivor from some past era in which little value was placed on freedom, equality, and progress.

TWO CHRISTIAN MENTALITIES

The whole trend of modernization may be seen as eroding the foundations of orthodoxy. The ebullient secularity of our culture would seem to favor the more liberal and progressive styles of religion. Many, in fact, accept religion only on the terms set by the secular culture. For cultural Christians the Church is a voluntary society, comparable to the Masons or the Elks. They adhere to religion for its therapeutic and social value. It provides a way of celebrating certain occasions in secular life, such as baptisms (seen as ritual celebrations of birth rather than rebirth), weddings, and funerals. Some like to mark Sundays and holidays such as Christmas with attendance at church services.

For these secular Christians the Church does not function as an unquestioned authority governing their ideas or conduct. The Church, in their view, should not intrude into matters of domestic life, business, politics, and the like. They may be aware that ecclesiastical leaders and Church bodies sometimes make pronouncements on these subjects, but they do not feel bound by these directives. In their religious life cultural Christians rely heavily on their personal experience and give very limited scope to authority.

Orthodoxy is not a high priority for cultural Christians. If they recite the creed, they do so without deep conviction. They are acutely conscious that Christianity is a minority religion in the world and that each particular denomination is a minority within that minority. They are not sure that the minority to which they belong has any infallible access to the truth. They expect the Church to modify its doctrines as necessary to accommodate other points of view and keep pace with historical progress.

Such cultural Catholics do not adhere to the Church as it defines itself through its highest teaching organs. They do not accept its teaching at face value. They treat creedal and dogmatic statements as metaphors or vague approximations of a transcendent truth that remains elusive. Faith gives them a set of symbols by which to imagine the world. But for them it does not have any clear and definite content that is permanently and universally binding. Dissent appears to them as an acceptable option. Some, holding that the magisterium inhibits the Church from updating itself, are inclined to esteem dissenters as exemplary Catholics.

The phenomenon of dissent has increased exponentially in the thirty-odd years since Vatican II. In the Church that I remember from my youth, Catholics could be counted upon to support the teaching of the pope; public criticism of the magisterium by Catholics was almost unheard of, but if one goes back a little in history, dissent seems to have been almost normal. In the English-speaking world at the time of the American Revolution, many educated Catholics had an Enlightenment mentality. In France and elsewhere on the continent, Jansenism and Gallicanism were rife well into the nineteenth century. If Gallup polls had existed in the thirteenth century, it might have been possible to show that many of the laity failed to adhere to the teaching of the councils even on basic points of faith. Through long experience the Church has learned to live with dissent even while opposing it.

THE APPEAL OF ORTHODOXY

The prognosis for orthodoxy would seem to be dim if we looked only at the modern secular situation. But sociologists of religion report that the most vigorous branches of Christianity tend to be orthodox. Dean M. Kelley in his well-known book *Why the Conservative Churches Are Growing* (1972) set forth three main characteristics of the model religious group. First, its members are wholeheartedly committed to its ideals, to the extent that they are ready to suffer persecution and make great sacrifices for the organization and its goals. Second, the members willingly submit to the discipline of the group, obeying the decisions of the leadership without cavil. Third, the members exhibit an irrepressible missionary zeal, bathing the new members and the young with a nurturing stream of communications about the goals and life of the group. Dean Kelley's general thesis has been confirmed by many subsequent studies.

The very difference of these dynamic groups from the dominant culture makes them interesting and captivating. By contrast the progressive and culture-friendly institutions are flabby and colorless. The world has no need of a religious body that simply mirrors the dominant values of the society. A religion that lays claim to a divine revelation ceases to be credible if it teaches only what people would be inclined to believe without it.

In their hearts people long for something more than is offered by the secular order, with its passing pleasures and fluctuating opinions. They reach out for something higher, something universally and eternally good and true, to which they can give themselves permanently and totally. This is precisely what revealed religion has to offer. It tells us that God, the uncreated source of all truth and goodness, has freely communicated himself and his divine life by bestowing himself in his divine Son and his Holy Spirit. God has established in Christ a sacred order, a way of salvation. The Church, founded upon Christ, and secondarily upon Peter and the apostles, has been established in the world to give permanent testimony to the saving truth and to nourish the faithful with holy rites that put them in contact with the saving realities. The Church has been equipped by God with hierarchical structures to preserve its apostolic heritage and to prevent it from succumbing to the shifting tides of popular opinion. Faith, as a way to salvation, involves submission to the authoritative teaching that comes from God through the Church. Faith therefore cherishes orthodoxy.

Because of the deep hungers of the human spirit and the high claims of Catholic Christianity, there will continue to be countercultural Catholics. For them religion is not simply one department of life. It has an impact on everything they think, say, and do. They are not against culture as such, but they refuse to let their religion be denied by the culture in which they find themselves. For them it is axiomatic that faith rests on a divine revelation with a definite content that does not change to suit the culture or the times. Faith provides a basis for criticizing and even reforming the culture.

Some members of this countercultural group are persons who had a strong religious upbringing and are alarmed at the gulf between the mores of our society and traditional Christian principles. Other countercultural Christians are individuals who have been converted or reconverted to the faith at great personal cost and as a result of long and honest searching. Converts do not take their faith for granted; still less do they chafe at it as something forced upon them. For them it is the treasure hidden in the field, the pearl of great price, for which they joyfully sacrifice all lesser goods. Converts tend to remain very self-motivated even within the Church. They are so used to swimming against the tide that they sometimes become almost sectarian in their practice of Catholicism. They can be severely critical of other Catholics for conforming too much to the dominant culture.

With respect to orthodoxy, therefore, we have, and will continue to have, two basic tendencies. Cultural Christians tend to take anti-dogmatic stances. Only the countercultural Catholic can really embrace orthodoxy.

PROSPECTS FOR THE FUTURE

In a secularized society such as our own, consistently orthodox Catholics will constitute a minority, not only in the society at large but even, I would say, within their religious community. The majority are carried along by the tide of public opinion, which they receive daily in large doses through the popular media of communication. Although they are relatively few, these countercultural believers, because of the strength of their commitment, have an importance disproportionate to their numbers.

Revealed religion, beleaguered though it may be, has an indispensable role to play in the modern world. The secular relativism of our day stands on very weak grounds and holds no attraction for people looking for light and clarity. Many hear in a confused way the call to a higher life and feel in their hearts a craving for abiding truth. They welcome the Word of God because it comes from beyond and transcends the vicissitudes of time and culture. A religion that firmly adheres to its sacred heritage can make itself a sign of hope and a beacon of truth to the multitudes who are repelled by the easy relativism and cheap hedonism of popular culture. For these reasons I am convinced that orthodoxy rather than accommodationism offers greater promise for the future.

With the progressive de-Christianization of society, it is inevitable, I think, that the Church will suffer some defections and a measure of disaffection on the part of many who remain. Some of those who leave will join churches whose teaching seems more consonant with modern secular thinking. Others will find Catholicism too complicated and will embrace severer styles of Christianity, such as those found in biblicist sects. These negative developments will have to be countered by measures designed to increase the numbers and the loyalty of the Catholic faithful. Four particular steps occur to me as promising.

1. *Hierarchical Governance.* The hierarchical structures of the Church must be maintained and even strengthened so as to protect the teaching body from being unduly pressured by public opinion. Only the hierarchical form of government gives the official leadership the apostolic freedom that it needs to make decisions prayerfully in light of the Gospel and tradition.

For the unity of the Church it is essential for the bishops of each nation to be kept in close contact with the Holy See. Very careful screening of future bishops is needed to make sure that they adhere staunchly to the deposit of faith as officially interpreted and have the courage to stand up against the secular mentality. Stronger efforts must be made to recruit talented and loyal aspirants to the priesthood who will be able to exercise strong leadership in communion with the hierarchy while at the same time preserving good relations with their congregations.

2. *Doctrinal Firmness*. Jesus confronted his hearers with a stark choice between serving God and mammon, between accepting his "hard sayings" and withdrawing from his company. Paul taught that there could be no communion between Christ and Belial. Without unnecessarily alienating people of goodwill, the Church must clearly condemn unorthodox teaching.

In the face of dissent it might seem that the magisterium should mute its voice. Does it not weaken its own authority when it teaches doctrines that many practicing Catholics will predictably reject? The magisterium was never intended to seek popularity. It would forfeit all credibility if it taught only what people wanted to hear. The first and indispensable task of the hierarchical leadership is to bear witness to the deposit of faith so that the Church may always be "the pillar and the ground of truth." This the magisterium has done in the past and will continue to do. Its charism is to adhere constantly to the Gospel of Christ, to discern its implications for the present day and to proclaim it confidently, insistently, in season and out of season, even at the cost of becoming a sign of contradiction. In view of the divine promises to be with the apostolic leadership to the end of the age, I am convinced that the magisterium will not waver in this task.

3. *Formation*. In the secularized society of our day, it is imperative for the Church to mount vigorous educational programs so that its members may be nourished in their faith. Such an educational effort will require an active and forceful clergy assisted by a large body of well-trained and committed lay associates. Instruments such as the recent *Catechism of the Catholic Church* (1992) may profitably be used as norms for the revision of catechetical materials.

Parents must accept their role as the first educators of their children, not least in matters of religion. Educational institutions with a clear religious orientation can effectively supplement the formation received at home. Catholic schools, colleges, and universities should be supported and strengthened in their service to the Church. In addition to these academic endeavors, groups of laity should be encouraged to make days of recollection and retreats so that they can capture the full vision of the Gospel. Just as Jesus trained his apostles by taking them apart for prayer and special instruction, so must the Church do in our time. Jesus sought to arm the disciples against what he called "the leaven of the Pharisees." The Church must try to inoculate its members against the prevailing errors of our day.

Devout members of the laity should be encouraged to join organizations that support and intensify their life of faith, for example, third orders of religious congregations and movements such as Christian Life Communities, Communion and Liberation, the Focolare Movement, and other comparable associations.

4. *Evangelization.* Although it must stand for definite principles, the Church is not intended to become a pious remnant of faithful souls. It is called to be catholic and inclusive. The Gospel is intended for all men and women, whatever their race, language, nationality, or social status.

To compensate for the inevitable losses, the Church must carry on a vigorous plan of evangelization. Every parish must become a vibrant center of communication, and every believer should feel the impulse to spread the amazing good news of God's redemptive plan. By sharing our faith with others, we can do them an immense favor and strengthen our own faith in the process. As Pope John Paul II has said, faith is strengthened by being given away.

Whether these four steps will in fact be taken and will be successful is a matter for prophets to decide. It is not really important to know what the future holds. It is enough to know what we are called to do and what the Church is called to become. All of us can contribute to that end by striving to hear and internalize the Word of God as it has been handed down to us, so that we can pass it on to others. There will of course be struggles and setbacks, as there have been in every generation. But the assistance of the Holy Spirit will be given until the day when the Lord returns in glory.

22. JOHN PAUL II AND THE ADVENT OF THE NEW MILLENNIUM

October 31, 1998

(Lecture delivered at Fordham University on November 16, 1998.)

The Church celebrates different aspects of its relationship to God by recalling different events in the history of salvation. Every Sunday, for example, is a little Easter, a remembrance of the Resurrection, and every Friday a recollection of the Passion. On a larger scale, the liturgical year is arranged so as to provide occasions to ponder various phases of God's redemptive work, such as the birth of Christ, his suffering and death, his resurrection and ascension. We have now entered the season of Advent, in which we seek to dispose ourselves to receive more abundantly the graces connected with the Nativity, which we await at Christmastide, and also to prepare ourselves to meet the Lord as judge and savior at the end of time. Advent is a season of self-examination, hope, expectation, and intense prayer. If our preparation is successful, each Christmas can be for us a new Bethlehem.

Beyond the rhythms of the liturgical year, the Church designates holy years to commemorate major anniversaries of great events concerning our redemption. The bimillennium of the birth of Christ, which is now less than five years away, will be a particularly solemn jubilee. Because the birth of Christ was itself an outward event, the celebration of the jubilee, according to the present pope, should be outwardly manifested (see the apostolic letter *Tertio Millennio Adveniente*, November 19, 1994).

When John Paul II was elected pope, his friend and mentor, Cardinal Stefan Wyszynski of Warsaw, told him: "If the Lord has called you, you must lead the Church into the third millennium." The pope has taken this mandate to heart. His first encyclical, published early in 1979, began with a statement that the Church is already in a season of Advent, preparing for the great jubilee of the year 2000 (*Redemptor Hominis*, March 4, 1979, 1). More recently, he has spoken of the preparations for this celebration as "a hermeneutical key for my pontificate."

In his writings on the subject, John Paul II situates the coming jubilee within the framework of an imposing theology of history. The Christian faith, he points out, is eminently historical. Time has a beginning, a middle, and an end, and is at all points related to the eternity of God. St. Paul speaks of the coming of Christ as the fullness of time (Gal 4:4), because at that moment eternity actually enters time, and God becomes an actor on the stage of human history (*Tertio Millennio Adveniente* 9). Christ, the Lord of time, to whom all ages belong, plunges into the midst of time and becomes, in the words of Vatican II, "the focal point and goal of all human history" (*Pastoral Constitution on the Church in the Modern World* 10, quoted in *Tertio Millennio Adveniente* 59). Because Christ remains present through his Spirit, especially in the Church, all of us since Pentecost live in what scripture calls the last days, the final hour (Acts 2:17; Heb 1:2; 1 Jn 2:18). It is theologically correct to make a sharp distinction between the periods before and since the coming of Christ: BC and AD.

This does not mean, however, that the end of history is imminent. The Holy Father is very careful to avoid the excesses of millenarianism. Before the year 1000 a few preachers appear to have predicted that the reign of the Antichrist was about to begin, though there is no evidence of the widespread terror depicted by certain anticlerical French historians. Aware that we live today in a highly charged atmosphere in which the flames of mass hysteria can easily be ignited by fanciful speculations, the pope provides no basis for either Utopian prognostications or dire apocalyptic premonitions. Instead he calls upon the faithful to prepare soberly for "that new springtime of Christian life which will be revealed if Christians are docile to the action of the Holy Spirit" (*Tertio Millennio Adveniente* 18). "As the second millennium after Christ's coming draws to an end," he declares, "an overall view of the human race shows that this mission entrusted by Christ to the Church is still only beginning and that we must commit ourselves wholeheartedly to its service" (*Redemptoris Missio*, December 7, 1990, 1).

The pope evidently looks upon the Blessed Virgin Mary as the primary patroness of this new Advent. During the Marian year of 1986–87, celebrating the two thousandth anniversary of Mary's birth, he issued the encyclical *Redemptoris Mater* (March 25, 1987), in which he described Mary as the "morning star" (*Stella matutina*), whose appearance, like the dawn, announces the proximity of Christ, the "Sun of Justice" (*Sol justitiae*), before he rises visibly over the horizon. Throughout the years from 1986 to the end of the century, Mary's presence upon earth is to be gratefully recalled. Just as the Blessed Virgin carried the Christ child in her womb before his birth, so the present millennium, in its final years, bears within itself the seeds of the millennium now waiting to be born.

Already in 1983 John Paul II called up to Mary to inspire in the Church the same sentiments with which she awaited the birth of the Lord in the lowliness of our human nature (*Aperite Portas Redemptori* 9, a papal bull issued February 10, 1983). Every Christian is invited to look forward to this great jubilee with the deep faith, humility, and confidence in God that characterized the Virgin Mother in her days of expectancy.

Occasionally, but less frequently, John Paul II speaks in this connection of John the Baptist, who can also be considered a patron saint for Advent. By giving his life in witness to truth and justice, John became "the forerunner of the Messiah by the manner of his death" (encyclical *Veritatis Splendor*, August 6, 1993, 91; and see the Roman missal for August 29 and Mk 6:17–29). While the Church does not imitate the sternness of this holy prophet, it seeks, as he did, to move all who practice injustice to repentance and conversion. Christians now bear a fresh summons to prepare the way of the Lord, pointing anew to Jesus as "the one who was to come" (cf. Lk 7:20), "the Lamb of God who takes away the sins of the world" (Jn 1:29).

I have already referred to the coming anniversary as a jubilee. We are all familiar with the custom of silver, golden, and diamond jubilee anniversaries of weddings and ordinations. These are times of gratitude for the favors of past years, occasions for rededication and renewal of trust.

John Paul II points out that the custom of jubilees is a very ancient one, going back to Old Testament times. According to the law of Moses, as we find it in the books of Exodus, Leviticus, and Deuteronomy, every seventh year was dedicated in a special way to God, and every fiftieth year was a major jubilee celebration. During sabbatical and jubilee years, the earth was to be left fallow, slaves were to be liberated, and debts forgiven.

The prescriptions for the jubilee year represented hopes and ideals rather than actual facts, but they were valid insofar as they foreshadowed the work accomplished in an eminent way by Christ the redeemer (*Tertio Millennio Adveniente* 13). According to Luke's gospel, Jesus began his public ministry at Nazareth by announcing the fulfillment in his person of the prescriptions of the jubilee as set forth in Isaiah: "The Spirit of the Lord is upon me, because he has anointed me to preach good news to the poor. He has sent me to proclaim release to the captives and recovering of sight to the blind, to set at liberty those who are oppressed, to proclaim the acceptable year of the Lord" (Lk 4:18–19).

This quotation from Isaiah, which Jesus applies to himself, suggests appropriate ways of celebrating the coming jubilee. The year 2000 should be seen as a season of the Lord's favor, in which the presence of the Holy Spirit will be more deeply experienced, impelling Christians to preach the Gospel with new power, giving hope of liberation to the marginalized and the oppressed. According to John Paul II, the great jubilee of the year 2000 "contains a message of liberation by the power of the Spirit, who alone can help individuals and communities to free themselves from the old and new determinisms, by guiding them with the 'law of the Spirit, which gives life in Christ Jesus,' thereby discovering and accomplishing the full measure of man's true freedom" (encyclical *Dominum et Vivificantem*, May 18, 1986, 60). The relief of poverty, the liberation of captives, and the forgiveness of debts are means whereby the basic equality of all human beings is asserted, and whereby the rich are reminded that the earth and its fullness belong, in the final analysis, to God (see Ps 24:1). In the Catholic tradition jubilee years are times when the Church shows particular indulgence in granting the remission of sins and of the punishments due to them.

In the vision of Pope John Paul, "the Second Vatican Council was a providential event whereby the church began the more immediate preparation for the jubilee of the second millennium." From the point of view of the history of salvation, he writes, that council may be viewed as "the cornerstone of the present century which is now rapidly approaching the third millennium" (apostolic exhortation *Ecclesia in Africa*, September 14, 1995, 2). The best preparation for the new millennium, consequently, will be "a renewed commitment to apply, as faithfully as possible, the teachings of Vatican II to the life of every individual and of the whole church" (*Tertio Millennio Adveniente* 20). That council is "the great beginning—the Advent as it were—of the journey leading us to the threshold of the third millennium" (encyclical *Ut Unum Sint*, May 25, 1995, 100). The great themes of the council, such as evangelization, religious freedom, ecumenism, interreligious dialogue, and openness to the world, have set the agenda for our time.

The program of evangelization for the final part of the century is set forth in the encyclical *Redemptoris Missio*, which builds upon Paul VI's magnificent apostolic exhortation, *Evangelii Nuntiandi*, issued in 1975, just twenty years ago. John Paul's encyclical begins with the stirring words "The mission of Christ the redeemer, which is entrusted to the Church, is still very far from completion. . . . It is the Spirit who impels us to proclaim the great works of God: 'For if I preach the Gospel, that gives no ground for boasting. For necessity is laid upon me. Woe to me if I do not preach the Gospel'" (1 Cor 9:16). All four gospels, as well as the Acts of the Apostles, make it clear that the Church received from Christ the mission to preach the Gospel to all nations, to the whole world, to every creature. On the eve of the year 2000, the Church must prepare to render an account of its fidelity to this essential charge.

The pope remarks on a variety of factors that make the missionary task especially urgent in our time. New challenges and new opportunities are present. The number of people who do not know Christ and who do not belong to the Church has almost doubled since the close of Vatican II. The traditionally Christian nations of the West are in need of re-evangelization, since they have witnessed a dramatic decline of faith, connected in some ways with false concepts of freedom and with a relativistic view of truth. Many people have lost the sense of God and are drawn into a kind of hedonism that renders them almost impervious to the message of the Gospel. In some parts of the world, secular governments, seeking to protect a national or regional religion, erect barriers against Christian proclamation.

Notwithstanding these grave obstacles, the pope finds grounds to hope for a new springtime of evangelization. Under the dehumanizing pressures of technology and consumerism, many are hungering for spiritual nourishment. New opportunities for proclamation are offered by the rapidity of travel and the abundance of new media of communication. Certain Gospel ideals and values, such as human dignity, peace, solidarity, and freedom, have become part of the patrimony of the whole world. The year 1989 witnessed the collapse of some oppressive regimes that were blocking the spread of the Gospel. Thus the pope can say: "God is opening before the church the horizons of a humanity more fully prepared for the sowing of the Gospel. I sense that the moment has come to commit all of the church's energies to a new evangelization and to the mission *ad gentes*. No believer in Christ, no institution of the church can avoid this supreme duty: to proclaim Christ to all peoples" (*Redemptoris Missio* 3).

Another priority of the Second Vatican Council was ecumenism. As the new millennium approaches, the Church must interrogate itself on its fidelity to this mandate. Jesus at the Last Supper prayed for his disciples "that they may all be one . . . so that the world may believe that thou hast sent me" (Jn 17:21). What account can Christian leaders give to their Master if they have allowed the sign of unity to be defaced by conflict and division? The task of evangelization, so urgent in these closing years of the present century, is gravely impeded by the mutual divisions among Christians. In the words of Vatican II: "This discord openly contradicts the will of Christ, provides a stumbling block to the world and inflicts damage on the most holy cause of proclaiming the good news to every creature" (*Decree on Ecumenism* 1). Reflecting on this text, John Paul II asks: "When nonbelievers meet missionaries who do not agree among themselves, even though they all appeal to Christ, will they be in a position to receive the true message?" (*Ut Unum Sint* 98).

The great jubilee of the year 2000 calls for major celebrations on the part of all Christians, whether Catholic, Protestant, or Orthodox. It would be a scandal if the different churches and Christian communities were unable to come together with a greater show of unity than they have displayed in recent centuries. Glancing over past history, John Paul II notes that the millennium that is about to end is the period in which most of the great separations between Christians have occurred (*Dominum et Vivificantem* 62). The final years of the second millennium, he says, demand "the promotion of fitting ecumenical initiatives so that we can celebrate the Great Jubilee, if not completely united, at least much closer to overcoming the divisions of the second millennium" (*Tertio Millennio Adveniente* 34).

This ecumenical emphasis, always prominent in the teaching of John Paul II, has been intensified in the past year with his apostolic letter *Orientale Lumen*, written to the Catholic Church on relations with the East (May 2, 1995), and with his encyclical letter *Ut Unum Sint* (May 25, 1995). In the first of these documents he pleads with a holy impatience for the day when the churches of the East and West may come together at the Lord's table, confessing the one faith in mutual harmony. He expresses the hope that the arrival of the third millennium may be an occasion for the discovery that these two major branches of Christianity have been walking in close company, perhaps even without knowing it.

The recent encyclical on ecumenism strikes a note of optimism, expressing the pope's intense desire that the year 2000 may see a significant advance along the path to unity, thus fulfilling the call made with such impassioned commitment by the Second Vatican Council. The encyclical contains a detailed exposition of the various means to unity, including theological dialogues and the reception of their results by the respective churches. Mention is also made of the importance of practical cooperation among the churches and the crucial necessity of prayer for unity, since full communion can only be a gift of the Holy Spirit. The new millennium, says the pope, "will be an exceptional occasion, in view of which she [the Church] asks the Lord to increase the unity of all Christians until they reach full communion" (*Ut Unum Sint* 3).

John Paul II does not restrict the significance of the coming millennium to the religious sphere. In his view, it has a salutary potential for the entire human race, even in secular relationships. The popes of the present century, he observes, have accepted their responsibility to defend the values of peace and justice and the principles of international order. Evangelization, if it is to be complete and integral, calls for the safeguarding of human dignity and human rights.

The jubilee, as understood by John Paul II, has secular and social implications that appear prominently in Jesus' proclamation of his mission, as already quoted from Luke's gospel. "Commitment to justice and peace," says the pope, "is a necessary condition for the preparation and celebration of the jubilee" (*Tertio Millennio Adveniente* 51). Reflecting on the Old Testament prescriptions regarding debts, he asks whether the jubilee might not be an appropriate time for "reducing substantially, if not canceling outright, the international debt which seriously threatens the future of many nations."

To illustrate how John Paul II weaves together the religious and the secular aspects of the coming jubilee, it may suffice to recall his address to the United Nations on October 5, 1995. He there commented on the global acceleration of the quest for freedom as one of the outstanding phenomena of our time. The moral dynamics of this universal quest clearly appeared during the nonviolent revolutions of 1989. These uprisings were provoked by the sense of personal dignity that had been ignored and violated by totalitarian regimes. But, as we have learned in the past few years, freedom calls for discipline. To prevent liberty from deteriorating into license or being abused by the arrogance of power, it is necessary to develop a shared awareness of universal human rights and the sense of belonging, as it were, to a "family of nations." The politics of nations, said the pope, can never ignore the transcendent, spiritual dimension of human existence without detriment to the cause of freedom.

In the conclusion of his United Nations address, the pope called attention to the role of the Church in sustaining faith, hope, and love in an age when people are tempted to cynicism, despair, and violence. The antidote to the fear that darkens human existence, he said, must be a common effort to build a civilization of love, founded on the universal values of peace, solidarity, justice, and freedom. "Thus, as we approach the 2,000th anniversary of the birth of Christ, the church asks only to be able to propose respectfully this message of salvation and to be able to promote, in charity and service, the solidarity of the entire human family." On the ground that each and every person has been created in the "image and likeness" of God, the pope went on to maintain that human beings have within them a capacity for wisdom and virtue and are able, with the help of God's grace, "to build in the next century a civilization worthy of the human person, a true culture of freedom. . . . In doing so, we shall see that the tears of this century have prepared the ground of a new springtime of the human spirit" (Address to the United Nations, October 5, 1995, 18).

In his book *Crossing the Threshold of Hope* (1994), John Paul II eloquently explains the role of faith in overcoming the paralyzing effects of fear. Christ alone, he asserts, can give the assurance of God's love that is needed by those who struggle to regenerate contemporary society. "At the end of the second millennium, we need, perhaps more than ever, the words of the risen Christ: 'Be not afraid!'"

Echoing the message of John the Baptist, Advent preachers commonly call for a serious examination of conscience and, if need be, for penance and conversion. The joy of any jubilee, according to John Paul II, must be based on the forgiveness of sins, penance, and reconciliation. Conscious of the sinfulness of her members, the Church does not tire of doing penance. As it presents herself anew to the Lord, the Church must ask itself how much of Christ's message has been heard and implemented in life (Letter to Women, June 29, 1995, 3).

In the spirit of John the Baptist, the pope summons the whole Church to a collective examination of conscience regarding the mistakes and sins of the past millennium. At the head of the list of sins to be reckoned, the pope mentions offenses against ecclesial communion. While repenting the misdeeds that have divided Christians from one another, the Church should with great insistence invoke the Holy Spirit for the grace of unity.

As a second sin requiring corporate penance and conversion, John Paul II mentions the acquiescence given to intolerance and even to violence used in the service of truth (*Tertio Millennio Adveniente* 35). He does not indicate in detail what he has in mind, but one can easily imagine that he is thinking of events such as the Crusades, the wars of religion, and the excesses of the Inquisition. He might also have in mind the Church's compromises with the slavery system and with persecutions of the Jews. Vatican II, in his judgment, has made it clear that freedom of conscience demands the renunciation of any undue pressure to obtain acceptance of religious truth (*Redemptoris Missio* 7, 39).

It will be recalled that in 1979 John Paul II ordered a reexamination of the case of Galileo. After more than a decade of study, the papal commission reported its finding that Galileo's judges, erroneously believing that the Copernican theory conflicted with revealed truth, wrongfully forbade Galileo to teach the theory. The pope in October 1992 delivered an address to the Pontifical Academy of Sciences on the lessons to be derived from the Galileo case. He emphasized the need to distinguish between the proper spheres of theology and science and the responsibility of theologians to keep themselves regularly informed of scientific advances.

Under the rubric of past mistakes calling for connection, it is of great interest to note the statements in the pope's Letter to Women on the eve of the Fourth World Conference on Women at Beijing last September. For many centuries, he observed, the dignity of women had been unacknowledged; they had been relegated to the margins of society and even reduced to servitude. This situation was contrary to the teaching and example of Jesus, who always honored the dignity of women. Because such patterns of behavior have been so heavily ingrained in the cultural heritage, it is difficult to assign culpability, but the pope was prepared to say: "If objective blame, especially in particular historical contexts, has belonged to not just a few members of the church, for this I am truly sorry" (Letter to Women 3). He expressed the wish that, as the Church moves into the new millennium, this regret might be transformed into a new commitment to recognize what he called "the feminine genius."

As is evident from these examples, John Paul II does not wish the Church's examination of conscience to be confined to the past. "On the threshold of the new millennium Christians need to place themselves humbly before the Lord and examine themselves on the responsibility which they too have for the evils of our day" (*Tertio Millennio Adveniente* 36). Among the shadows of our age the pope singles out religious indifference, the loss of the sense of the transcendent, ethical relativism, and the crisis of obedience vis-à-vis the Church's teaching authority. He exhorts Catholics to examine themselves on the fidelity with which they have received the teaching of Vatican II regarding the primacy of the Word of God, the value of the liturgy, the ecclesiology of communion, and openness to dialogue with the world without sacrifice of their courage in witnessing to the truth. In another context the pope declares that the European nations are today obliged to make a serious examination of conscience with regard to the threat of exaggerated nationalism (*Tertio Millennio Adveniente* 27).

In conclusion, I would like to say something about the concrete planning for the coming jubilee year. A schedule has been drawn up on the basis of extensive consultation, including a special consistory of cardinals that met in June 1994. For the period until the end of 1996, John Paul II proposes a phase of remote preparation given to inculcating awareness of the situation and instilling the required attitudes, such as hope, prayerfulness, and sorrow for the sins and mistakes of the past. During this period, or shortly thereafter, the pope expects there to be continental synods for the Americas, Asia, and perhaps Oceania, following along the general lines of the synods already held for Europe and Africa.

The synod for the Americas would concentrate on the new evangelization and on issues of justice, especially with regard to international economic relations. The synod for Asia would deal principally with the challenges to evangelization offered by the encounter with local cultures and with world religions such as Buddhism and Hinduism. The syntax for Oceania, the pope indicates, could contribute to the dialogue between Christianity and the aboriginal monotheistic religions found in that part of the world.

John Paul II lays great stress on the importance of regional churches and their own celebrations of jubilees recalling their distinctive histories. Christian history, as he sees it, may be compared to a single river into which many tributaries pour their waters so as to give joy to the city of God (see Ps 46:4).

Each of the years from 1997 to 1999, constituting the period of proximate preparation, has its own theme. The general movement of the triennium will be from Christ, through the Holy Spirit, to God the Father, but each year will also have a Marian dimension. The year 1997 is to be a year of faith, in which Christians will seek to renew their appreciation of baptism and their relationship to Christ the Son of God. Mary, the Mother of Jesus, will be invoked as a model of faith. In 1998 attention will shift to the sanctifying presence of the Holy Spirit, the sacrament of confirmation, and the theological virtue of hope. Notice will be taken of the signs of hope present in the world of our day and of the Virgin Mary, the spouse of the Holy Spirit, as an exemplar of Christian hope. Finally, the year 1999 will focus on God the Father. It will be the occasion for a more intense celebration of the sacrament of penance, for the practice of charity, and for the building of a civilization of love. Praise will be directed to Mary, the beloved daughter of the Father, under the aspects of her holiness and her love for God and neighbor.

The climactic year, of course, will be the bimillennium itself. The plan is for the celebration to be conducted simultaneously in the Holy Land, in Rome, and in local churches throughout the world. John Paul II hopes for an ecumenical meeting of all Christians, planned in cooperation with representatives of other

Christian traditions, with invitations extended to other religious bodies who might wish to acknowledge the joy shared by the disciples of Christ. The pope speaks of his own intense desire to visit Jerusalem and the Holy Land. "It would be very significant," he writes, "if in the year 2000 it were possible to visit the places on the road taken by the people of God of the Old Covenant, starting from the places associated with Abraham and Moses" (*Tertio Millennio Adveniente* 24). He notes the symbolic potential of places such as Bethlehem, Jerusalem, Mount Sinai, and Damascus for furthering dialogue with Jews and Muslims.

It is too early to judge the impact of this elaborate plan of John Paul II, but it would seem that the first reactions have been positive. Committees have been formed in Rome to consider the historical, theological, and pastoral dimensions of the program. In many dioceses and councils of churches, plans are being laid for local and regional celebrations. The first soundings seem to indicate that other Christian bodies will gladly cooperate with the Catholic Church to give a positive ecumenical tone to the celebrations that might otherwise occur in competitive and antagonistic ways.

The coming jubilee is surely an occasion for joy and gratitude, but it presents dangers that should not be overlooked. If celebrated without recognition of the need for repentance and renewal, the festivals could take on a triumphalistic tone that would embarrass Christians and repel adherents of other faiths. If the ecumenical and interreligious dimensions were neglected, the jubilee could lead to tensions and rivalries among religions and especially among Christian bodies. If exclusively religious in its focus, the bimillennium could be dismissed as empty pageantry by those concerned with the future of humanity on earth.

Great credit is due to the Holy See and to the present pope for the care they have taken to avoid these risks. They have called for penance as a preparation for the celebration, thus precluding undue complacency. Looking beyond the Catholic community, they have made provision for the participation of all Christian groups in ecumenical services. The sensitivities of the Jewish community and of other religious bodies are likewise respected. The emphasis given to peace, solidarity, human rights, and economic justice should provide assurance that the focus will not be too narrowly devotional.

More difficult than the preparation of the plan, of course, will be its execution. Total success is not to be expected, since many will fail to hear and heed the call. Yet in many quarters I seem to sense an attitude of eager expectancy. A jubilee of such magnitude presents rare opportunities, critically important for the future of faith and civilization. In contrast to the first millennium, when faith in Christ was confined to a small area of the globe, Christianity is now a worldwide phenomenon having a vital impact on all sectors of human existence. As the largest branch of Christianity, the Catholic Church has special responsibilities for leadership in the coming jubilee. By their manifest devotion to the Incarnate Lord, Catholics can bear witness to the enduring power of the Word made flesh. By their spirit of ecumenism and their openness to dialogue, they can help to bring all companions and all faiths into friendship and cooperation. By their efforts on behalf of justice in the world they can help to build a society of freedom, solidarity, and peace. To the extent that each of us carries out these imperatives, the year 2000 may mark a new phase in that special presence of the Lord which began in the cave at Bethlehem. Even this side of the end of history, the Advent prayer of Christians, "Come, Lord Jesus," may yet be answered in striking and surprising ways.

23. THE ADVANTAGES OF A CATHOLIC UNIVERSITY

November 26, 2001

(Address given on November 26, 2001, at St. Thomas University, originally called Biscayne College, in Miami, Florida, on the occasion of its fortieth anniversary.)

When the history of American higher education is written, scholars will surely remark on the phenomenal proliferation of Catholic universities since the middle of the twentieth century. To some extent, these universities are still finding their way in relation to the Church and the secular society in which they carry on their mission. I believe that notwithstanding all the problems and difficulties, Catholic universities can be proud of their identity and confident of their future.

The status of Catholic universities is still a subject of public debate in our land. One party to the discussion holds that religion belongs in the Church or the private sector, but not in the university, which is a public institution. At most, they would say, the university should study religion as a phenomenon to be analyzed by purely rational methods. Thinkers of a second school maintain that all points of view, including Catholic Christianity, may be allowed to assert themselves within the university, but that the university itself should remain confessionally neutral. A third group maintains that a university may legitimately dedicate itself to the Catholic intellectual tradition, because that tradition makes a valuable contribution to the life of our religiously pluralistic society. But they would add that other traditions have an equal right to maintain their heritage. Still a fourth school of thought, to which I adhere, asserts that Catholic universities have unique qualifications for the discovery and dissemination of truth, which is the task of every university.

In this very brief presentation I should like to say a few words about why I think that a university not only can but ought to be Catholic if it is to achieve its highest potentiality. In saying this I take inspiration from John Henry Newman and from our present pope, John Paul II. With the help of these authors, I wish to call attention to six major benefits that higher education can receive from being Catholic.

PERSONALISM

Although personalism is not peculiarly Catholic, the dignity of the human person is central to Catholic faith, especially as it has been expressed in and since the Second Vatican Council. Applying this principle to our present theme, one may say that Catholic universities may be expected to recognize the primacy of persons over things, the superiority of being over having, and of spirit over matter (*Ex Corde Ecclesiae* [ECE] 18, Pope John Paul II's 1990 apostolic constitution on Catholic universities). Our modern utilitarian and technological society tends to reduce the individual to the status of a mere instrument, a docile servant of the state or of the firm, an efficient tool in the workforce. Education, however, is more than an acquisition of technical skills. It is cultivation of the students' active powers. A genuinely humanist formation will help them to rise to the full level of their humanity, enabling them to find truth and meaning in their lives. As Newman contended, liberal education is its own end.

A SENSE OF TRADITION

Although all religions have traditions, the Catholic Church has a special affinity with tradition. It has lived by tradition for two thousand years, and has consistently defended the rights of tradition against those who denigrate it. It knows how to preserve the past not as a dead museum piece but as a living memory, enriching the present.

The school by its very nature ought to be a locus of tradition. It passes on to new generations a fund of knowledge and skills that has been built up over time, presenting it in a form appropriate to the current situation. The goal is to enable the young to take advantage of what their elders have learned, rather than having to begin again and, so to speak, "reinvent the wheel." Thanks to their humanistic formation, students should be able to adapt the heritage of the past to the needs of their own day, and in some respects to make progress beyond what was previously known. Catholic institutions, instilling a lively sense of tradition, are especially qualified to form students for this task.

ROOTEDNESS IN THE CULTURE OF THE WEST

The Catholic Church, I would contend, is the principal bearer of the great heritage of wisdom that emerged from the confluence of biblical revelation and Greco-Roman culture. While other cultures have much to offer, none of them, I believe, has equaled Western culture in the fields of literature, philosophy, and science. However that may be, it may be safely said that most American students today can best find their identity in relation to this biblical and classical heritage, which has been foundational for the United States and the whole family of nations to which the United States belongs.

Some are asking today whether education should be multicultural. To the extent that cultures are consonant with authentic Christian values, their diversity is something to be celebrated, not suppressed. An educational institution should respect the various cultures from which the students come and to which they are likely to return. Any given university will take account of all the major streams of culture that are vitally represented in its own student population.

Catholic universities located in other parts of the world, such as Central Asia and the Far East, will have special responsibility to engage in dialogue with non-Western cultures. Without prejudice to other civilizations, Pope John Paul II expresses his deep respect, in particular, for the spiritual traditions of India, from which humanly sound and beneficial elements may be gleaned (*Fides et Ratio* 72). But in carrying out this discernment the Christian will have to make use of the full range of wisdom that has been acquired from Christianity's prior inculturation in the world of Greco-Latin thought.

UNITY OF KNOWLEDGE

It is of the very nature of a university to impart knowledge of many fields. It is good to have courses in the various arts and sciences, even though no individual student will be able to take more than a limited selection. While specializing in certain areas, students should see their fields of specialization in relation to the realms of knowledge that they have not been able to study in detail.

A fourth criterion for Catholic education, therefore, is that it be such as to impart a sense of the unity of knowledge. In the absence of this sense, one could not have a true university but at best a "multiversity." In some schools the struggle for coherence has been abandoned, with the result that the students are disoriented and perplexed. How can the claims of different specialties, they ask, be reconciled and integrated? Reason itself teaches us that there can be no ultimate contradiction between truth and truth. In the Catholic university, the search for a higher synthesis will be kept alive.

THE LIGHT OF FAITH

Christians are convinced that no synthesis of knowledge will be successful without reference to God, the supreme Truth, and to Christ, who is the divine Logos, the center of creation and human history (*Ex Corde Ecclesiae* [ECE] 16). In this season of national and international peril, it needs to be said quite simply that the future of the world will be in danger unless it turns to him who is "the Way, the Truth, and the Life" (ECE 4). A university that neglects the Word of God deprives itself of an important source of truth.

Theology, which studies all reality in the light of divine revelation, has its proper principles and methods, defining it as a distinct branch of knowledge (ECE 29). It should, moreover, interact with the other disciplines by bringing a perspective and orientation not contained in their own methodologies (ECE 19). In the words of Pope John Paul II: "In promoting the integration of knowledge, a specific part of a Catholic university's task is to promote dialogue between faith and reason, so that it can be seen more profoundly how faith and reason bear harmonious witness to the unity of all truth" (ECE 17). The university should be a place in which faith enters into conversation with reason on every level, including historical reason, scientific reason, and philosophical reason.

A SENSE OF MISSION

As they are intellectually formed in the light of faith, students will become aware of moral imperatives and the power of the Gospel for the transformation of human society. Conscious of the gap between what is and what ought to be according to God's design for the world, they will be motivated to bring ethical values and a sense of service into their lives as husbands or wives, parents or children, employers or employees, citizens or statesmen. They will work for peace and justice in the family, the neighborhood, the nation, and the world. By their integrity they will evoke trust and respect not only for themselves but for the tradition within which they stand. They will bring credit upon the religiously oriented education they have received.

For all the reasons I have given, I believe that every university, no matter how excellent it may be, would stand to gain if it stood fully within the Christian and Catholic tradition. Most American Catholic universities, to be sure, fall far short of realizing their promise. For the most part they are relatively small, young, and poorly endowed. But with all their limitations, they are on the right path. Even now they are capable of giving their students an excellent formation as persons, imbuing them with a keen sense of tradition, an appreciation of the biblical and classical heritage, and a capacity to see the bearing of faith upon the whole universe of knowledge and upon every area of human conduct. If students take advantage of the specific strengths of Catholic higher education, they can be proud of their alma mater.

24. CHRIST AMONG THE RELIGIONS

February 4, 2002

(Address originally delivered at Fordham University on November 7, 2001.)

T he relations between the various religions of the world have often been hostile, and in many places they remain so today. When we pick up the daily newspaper, we can hardly avoid reading about conflicts between Jews and Muslims, between Muslims and Hindus, between Hindus and Sikhs, or between Muslims and Baha'is. All of these faiths have at one time or another clashed with Christianity. Christianity, for its part, has also contributed more than its share to interreligious tension and warfare. Christians have persecuted Jews and have fought holy wars against Muslims. Within Christianity there have been internecine wars, especially between Protestants and Catholics, but sometimes also with Eastern Orthodox. Struggles of this kind continue to rage in Northern Ireland, for example, although it would be unfair to describe the Catholic Church as a belligerent in that conflict, since its authorities have disapproved of violence on either side.

The present armed intervention in Afghanistan is sometimes described as a religious war. This interpretation is on the whole false, but it contains a grain of truth. From the American standpoint, there is nothing we are less interested in than a war against Islam. Our own nation is hospitable to Muslims, who constitute well over a million of its inhabitants. They enjoy full freedom of worship throughout North America and Western Europe. A new crusade would gain no support from any major power in the West and would certainly not receive the blessing of Christian religious authorities. Our quarrel with Osama bin Laden has to do only with his politics of violence, which does not seem to be in accord with the tenets of authentic Islam.

From the Arab side, religion is part of the picture, but Muslim extremists such as bin Laden seem to be working for ends that are cultural, political, ethnic, and economic rather than exclusively religious. They resent the power of the United States and its allies, which they perceive as arrogant and brutal. Even more fundamentally, they are repelled by what they perceive as the culture of the West. Their quarrel is not primarily with Christianity as a religion but much more with what they regard as the loss of religion in the West: its excessive individualism, its licentious practice of freedom, its materialism, and its pleasure-loving consumerism. They see this hedonistic culture as a threat, since it exercises a strong seductive power over many young people in the traditionally Islamic societies of Asia, Africa, and other continents.

If this analysis is correct, globalization might be seen as an underlying cause of the conflict in Afghanistan. Modern means of travel and communication bring together cultures that have developed in relative autonomy in different regions of the earth. The encounter produces a kind of culture shock, especially in nations that have not gone through the gradual process of industrialization and modernization that occurred two centuries ago in the West.

Christians of North America and Western Europe have by now grown accustomed to rubbing shoulders with Jews, Muslims, Hindus, Buddhists, and members of practically every other religion that can be named. Where immigration is taking place on a large scale and modern means of communication are generally available, no religion is any longer in a position to claim exclusive domination of a region and shelter its faithful from contact with other faiths. Like it or not, most of us are destined to live in a religiously mixed society that includes people of many faiths and of no faith at all.

FOUR MODELS

For this reason we have to discuss the ways in which different religions can relate to each other. I should therefore like to propose a typology consisting of four possible models: coercion, convergence, pluralism, and tolerance.

The first model, coercion, predominated throughout the greater part of human history. In most periods of history, political authorities have wanted to enforce unity of religion within their respective jurisdictions and to compel the populations of subject peoples to adopt the religion of the conqueror. The Roman Empire for a time accepted religious pluralism, but the emperors soon began to insist that divine honors be paid to themselves. They consequently came to persecute religions like Christianity, which refused such worship. When the empire adopted Christianity as its official religion, the emperors began to enforce Christian orthodoxy and persecute all other religions, including dissident forms of Christianity. The pattern of a single religion for a single state remained normative until early modern times, even after the Reformation. The terrible wars and persecutions of the sixteenth and seventeenth centuries were largely brought about by the assumption that every state must have only one religion, that of its ruler (*cuius regio eius religio*).

In this situation, wars between states frequently became, under another aspect, wars between religions. The Crusades vividly illustrate this fact. Although the Europeans are usually depicted as the aggressors, much of the military action was in fact defensive. The Turks had conquered Syria, North Africa, and large portions of European soil, including Portugal, Spain, and southern France and parts of Italy and Switzerland in the West, and the Balkans, present-day Yugoslavia, and Hungary in the East. The advance of the Turks meant, of course, the extension of

Islam as a religion, and their retreat, more often than not, meant the Christianization of the territories they had lost, as can be seen from fifteenth-century Spain, which expelled all Jews and Muslims who did not convert to Christianity.

In the present situation of the "global village," this coercion model is difficult to maintain. As a result of the bloody "wars of religion," Europe and the United States learned the lesson that the cost is too great. From the perspective of Christian theology, it is indefensible to try to convert people by the sword. Protestants and Catholics alike have learned that adherence to the faith must be a free and uncoerced act. Past efforts to force conversions have served to discredit religion and have contributed to the spread of indifferentism and irreligion.

True, there are still rulers in the world who seek to enforce uniformity of faith. They are both troublesome neighbors and threats to global peace. From a Christian point of view, their coercive policies must be disapproved. In time, I suspect, they will come to recognize that their policies are mistaken. For, as I have said, modern means of travel and communication make it very difficult to prevent the growth of different religious communities in every region of the globe. Although authoritarian governments may resist the penetration of other faiths, as they are doing in some Muslim, Hindu, and Buddhist regions today, the barriers will ultimately be pierced and will crumble. Sooner or later, populations that have been compelled to adopt the religion of their rulers will demand freedom to make conscientious choices and testify to their sincerely held convictions.

In spite of setbacks, the tide of history has been running in favor of religious freedom. The Soviet Union was not able to enforce its atheist ideology beyond the span of seventy years. Religious coercion survives only in nations that have come late to modernity. It is promoted by extremists who sense that desperate measures are needed to save their theocratic vision of the state.

The second model for relating the religions to one another is one of convergence. On the ground that the religious impulse is essentially the same in all peoples, some scholars contend that the religions agree in essentials and that their differences are superficial. In the 1970s John Hick, among others, contended that the religions could agree on the basis of theocentrism, recognizing their differences about the means of salvation as culturally relative. But theocentrism is not a satisfactory platform for dialogue with the many religions that are polytheistic, pantheistic, or atheistic. Even faiths that are clearly theistic, such as Judaism, Islam, and Christianity, are unwilling to surrender their convictions regarding the way to God, whether it be the law of Moses, the Koran, or Jesus Christ.

A number of scholars, abandoning the theocentric idea of religious convergence, have recently turned to what they call the "soteriocentric" model. All religions, they maintain, agree that the purpose of religion is to give salvation or liberation, which they understand in different ways, perhaps because of the variety of cultures. By dialogue about liberation, it is presumed, they could overcome their mutual divisions.

The basic premise of these convergence theories is that all religions, at least in their differentiating features, are human constructions—faltering attempts to articulate the holy and transcendent mystery by which human existence is encompassed. This theory, however, runs counter to the official teaching and historic identity of the religions and meets with resistance on the part of religiously minded people, who contend that their specific faith is true, even that it is divinely revealed. Christians hold that central doctrines of their own faith, such as the Trinity and the Incarnation, belong to revelation and cannot be sacrificed for the sake of achieving some putative reconciliation. Jews adhere passionately to the law of Moses and to rabbinic tradition. Muslims, for their part, regard the Koran as the final revelation of God and look to Muhammad as the greatest and last of the prophets. Soteriology is a point of division, because the religions vehemently disagree about the way to salvation. Soteriocentrism, therefore, is no more promising than theocentrism as a remedy for disunion.

The third model of religious encounter is that of pluralism. By this I mean not simply the fact of religious plurality, but the view that it is a blessing. The contention is that each religion reflects certain aspects of the divine. All are partially true but need to be supplemented and counterbalanced by the elements of truth found in the others. The coexistence of all overcomes the errors and limitations of each taken alone. As the fourth-century rhetorician Symmachus maintained in his debate with St. Ambrose, "It is impossible that so great a mystery should be approached by one road only." This approach has a certain appeal for relativists, who maintain that the human mind cannot attain objective truth, and that religion is an expression of merely subjective feelings. But it will not appeal to orthodox believers, who hold that the doctrines of their religion are objectively and universally true. Christianity stands or falls by the claim that there really are three persons in God and that the second of them, the eternal Son, became incarnate in Jesus Christ. Christians gladly admit that there are elements of truth and goodness in other religions, but they continue to insist that God's revelation in Christ is intended to be transmitted to all peoples. Committed Jews and Muslims likewise regard their religions as divinely revealed and reject any attempt to put all religions on the same level. This negative response does not of course mean that members of different religions have nothing to learn from one another. Christianity has developed over the centuries by entering into contact with a great variety of philosophies and religions, which have enabled Christians to find implications in their own faith that they would not otherwise have recognized. Christianity grows like an organism that takes in food from the environment in which it finds itself and assimilates that food into itself. It does not admit the validity of doctrines and practices that run counter to its own self-understanding. As we shall soon be seeing, dialogue can increase the mutual respect of the different religions, but experience gives no ground for supposing that it leads to the conclusion that all religions are equally good and true. On points where they contradict one another, at least one of them must be wrong.

We turn, then, to the fourth option, which I call toleration. Toleration is not the same thing as approval, although it normally includes a measure of approval. We tolerate things that we find less than acceptable because we find ourselves unable to suppress them or because the suppression would itself be evil. In the eighteenth century, the principle of tolerance—as expressed, for example, in John Locke's famous Letter Concerning Tolerance—came to be generally accepted in many countries of Western Europe. That principle was also fundamental to the American experiment in ordered freedom. From the beginning we had in this nation a great variety of Christian denominations that regarded one another as mistaken. The American political settlement did not require them to approve of each other's doctrines and practices, but it did insist that they avoid any effort to coerce the members of other denominations to agree with them. In the course of time, the religious scene has become increasingly diverse. It contains many more varieties of Christianity than were originally present. In addition, the nation has welcomed to its shores multitudes of Jews, Muslims, Buddhists, and Hindus. With rare exceptions, all of these religious groups live peaceably together, not interfering with one another's teaching, life, and worship. The American experiment has worked well enough to offer a possible model for the global international community that is currently experiencing its birth pangs.

TOLERANCE IN CHURCH TEACHING

Although the term "tolerance" has not been extensively used in Catholic official teaching during the past fifty years, this fourth model, in my opinion, is the one that best coheres with the doctrine of the magisterium. Pius XII, in an important address in

1953 (*Ci Riesce*), stated that in the world community then coming into being, the Catholic Church would not expect to have a privileged position or to be recognized as the established religion. It would ask only that the various religions be allowed full freedom to teach their own beliefs and practice their own faith. The Second Vatican Council in its *Declaration on Non-Christian Religions* and its *Declaration on Religious Freedom* endorsed this model as suitable for individual nation-states.

Vatican II explicitly renounces the use of any kind of coercion, whether physical or moral, in order to bring others into the Catholic fold. It taught that the religious freedom of all citizens and religious communities should be recognized and upheld, even in commonwealths that give special recognition to some one religion (*Declaration on Religious Freedom* 6). For the peace of civil society and the integrity of the religions themselves, it is essential to cultivate an atmosphere of mutual tolerance and respect.

The council has sometimes been misunderstood as though it had adopted the pluralist model, renouncing the exclusive claims of Christianity. But in point of fact, the council insisted on the unique truth of the Catholic faith and on the duty of all persons to seek the true religion and embrace it when found (1).

Vatican II proclaimed a very high Christology. It taught that God had established Christ as the source of salvation for the whole world (*Dogmatic Constitution on the Church* 17) and that he is "the goal of human history, the focal point of the longings of history and civilization, the center of the human race, the joy of every human heart and the answer to all its longings" (*Pastoral Constitution on the Church in the Modern World* 45). The council quoted Paul to the effect that God's intention is "to reestablish all things in Christ, both those in the heavens and those on the earth" (Eph 1:10).

As a consequence of its high Christology, Vatican II took great care to insist on the unique mediatorship of Christ and to emphasize the abiding importance of missionary activity. Acknowledging Christ as the redeemer of the world, the council called on

Christians to disseminate the Gospel as broadly as possible. To be ignorant of the Gospel or to deny it would be to overlook or reject God's greatest gift to humankind. The Church by its intrinsic dynamism tends to expand and take in members from every race and nation. The *Decree on the Church's Missionary Activity* holds that since all human beings have sinned and fallen short of the glory of God, "all have need of Christ as model, master, liberator, savior and giver of life" (8).

As for the non-Christian religions, the council taught that they often contain "seeds of the word" and "rays of that divine truth which enlightens all men," but it did not teach that these religions were revealed, or that they were paths to salvation, or that they were to be acceptable alternatives to Christianity. Judaism, of course, holds a special position among the non-Christian religions, since the faith of Israel is the foundation on which Christianity rests (cf. *Declaration on the Relation of the Church to Non-Christian Religions* 4). The Hebrew Bible is a permanently valid and inspired record of God's revelation to his elect people before the coming of Christ (*Dogmatic Constitution on Divine Revelation* 14).

The council is far from teaching that the other religions are free from error. It declares that "rather often people, deceived by the Evil One, have become caught up in futile reasoning and have exchanged the truth of God for a lie, serving the creature rather than the Creator (cf. Rom 1:21, 25). Consequently, to promote the glory of God and procure the salvation of all such persons, and mindful of the command of the Lord, 'preach the gospel to every creature' (Mk 16:16), the church painstakingly fosters her missionary work" (*Dogmatic Constitution on the Church* 16).

Evangelization, according to the *Decree on Missionary Activity* frees the rites and cultures of the nations "from all taint of evil and restores [them] to Christ as their source, who overthrows the devil's domain and wards off the manifold malice of evil-doing" (9). These sentences imply that the other religions are by no means adequate substitutes for Christianity. The implication is that they may in some respects hinder the salvation of their own adherents. To that extent the council's attitude toward them is one of qualified approval and toleration.

The charge is sometimes made that absolute convictions, such as the claims made for Jesus Christ by the scriptures and the councils, give rise to oppression and violence. I believe that the contrary is true. The leaders in the antislavery movement of the nineteenth century and the civil rights movement of the twentieth century, as well as the great champions of nonviolence, have been, more often than not, men and women of strong religious conviction.

Persons who recognize no moral absolutes lack any solid grounds for defending human rights and human dignity. Anyone who is unsure whether the taking of innocent human life is unconditionally forbidden will be able to make only a weak case against genocide and against the massive slaughter of innocents that occurs in abortion clinics all over the world. It is possible, of course, that a few opponents of abortion may misguidedly murder those who commit abortions, but these killings are rare; they also violate Catholic ethical principles, which forbid individuals to take the law into their own hands.

Christians are tolerant of other religions not in spite of but in part because of their certainty about revelation. Revelation assures them that God made human beings in his own image as free and responsible subjects. It also teaches that faith is by its very nature a free act. Vatican II's *Declaration on Religious Freedom* makes it clear that Christians must respect the right and duty of all persons to seek the truth in matters of religion and to adhere to it when found. Believers must be allowed to profess and practice their religion, provided that in so doing they do not disturb the requirements of just public order.

TOWARD PEACEFUL COEXISTENCE

The posture of tolerance and qualified approval, if it is recipro-cated, opens the way for a variety of strategies that may lead to peaceful and friendly coexistence. First I should like to men-tion the avenue of knowledge. The different religious groups will normally experience a healthy impulse to get to know one another by encountering them in actual life and by obtaining accurate information about them through study and reading. In a religiously diverse society, people should be educated not only in their own faith but also, to some degree, in the faiths of oth-ers with whom they will have to interact. All should be on guard against caricatures based on prejudice or ignorance.

Second, the groups can engage in certain joint programs based on a common recognition of basic moral values. Opportunities arise for people of different faiths to work together for objectives such as the defense of the family, the rights of migrants and ref-ugees, the relief of poverty and hunger, the prevention and cure of disease, the promotion of civil and international peace, and the care of the environment. Religious groups, because of their authority over the consciences of the faithful, can give powerful motivation for humanitarian reform.

Third, the groups can bear common witness regarding the religious and moral convictions that they share in common. Most religions agree on the importance of prayer and worship. They encourage the pursuit of holiness and speak out against socially harmful vices such as anger, theft, dishonesty, sexual promiscu-ity, and drunkenness. In a society that is threatened by selfish-ness and hedonism, the harmonious voices of religious leaders can greatly help to raise the tone of public morality.

On occasion the different groups can unite for interfaith ser-vices of prayer and worship. This fourth expression of qualified approval occurred very dramatically in the days of prayer for peace sponsored by Pope John Paul II in 1986 and 1993. Many interfaith meetings for prayer and silent reflection have been held in New York and other cities since the terrible events of September 11, 2001.

Still another critical need, frequently noted by Pope John Paul II, is the healing of memories. Religion, since it relies heavily on tradition, perpetuates the past experiences of the faith community, including its moments of glory, suffering, and humiliation. Injuries that were inflicted generations or centuries ago continue to rankle and breed hostility. Unless the sources of resentment are honestly faced, they poison the atmosphere, so that men and women living today are unjustly blamed for the real or imagined misdeeds of their ancestors. If friendship is to be restored, the communities should disavow the conduct attributed to their predecessors. They may fittingly apologize for what their forebears may have done and extend forgiveness for the wrongs their own communities have suffered. John Paul II has courageously followed this procedure in his dealings with other Christian churches, with Jews, and with Muslims. Expressions of repentance and forgiveness constitute a fifth category of interreligious action.

Since the Second Vatican Council the Catholic Church has placed strong emphasis on a sixth program, namely, theological dialogue. Paul VI set up a special secretariat, which continues to exist as the Pontifical Council for Interreligious Dialogue. In dialogues of this type the parties explain their beliefs to one another, explore ways in which they can live amicably together, enrich themselves from one another's insights, and seek to narrow the disagreements by finding convergences. Such dialogues have proved extremely useful for improving relations among different Christian communions. They likewise hold great promise for interfaith relations.

Valuable though it be, dialogue is not a panacea. It cannot be expected to overcome all disagreements. After shared insights have been achieved and convergences established, the parties will normally come to recognize that full unity cannot be achieved by dialogue alone. The religions are firmly committed to contradictory positions, which they could not abandon without sacrificing their identity. Although Christians will undoubtedly hope that their partners in the dialogue will come to recognize Christ as Savior of the world, any such result lies beyond the expectations and horizons of dialogue itself. Dialogue is intended to achieve agreements that the parties can achieve within the framework of their defining religious commitments.

It is sometimes said that dialogue is a sign of weakness, since it implies uncertainty about the adequacy of one's own positions. In my opinion dialogue is rather a sign of strength. It takes considerable self-confidence to listen patiently while others tell you why they think you are wrong. Groups that have not reflected deeply on the grounds of their beliefs quite understandably shy away from a dialogue for which they are not prepared.

If dialogue is misused, it can do positive harm. One error would be to make it a platform for proselytization, with the aim of converting the dialogue partner to one's own faith. This would be a distortion of the purpose of dialogue, which differs from missionary proclamation. The opposite error would be to conceal or renounce the convictions of the group to which one belongs, thus raising false expectations. Quite obviously, dialogue teams are not authorized to change the doctrines of their religious communities.

Rightly pursued, however, dialogue is one of the most auspicious paths for the growing encounter of the great religions. It does not have to start with the most sensitive and disputed issues. The parties will generally do better to begin with topics on which there is promise of achieving a significant measure of consensus. Paul VI in his encyclical *Ecclesiam Suam* (1964) suggested that common ideals such as religious freedom, human brotherhood, sound culture, social welfare, and civil order might be taken as themes of interreligious conversation (*colloquium*). It might also be possible to conduct dialogues on some properly religious themes, such as the value of prayer and the nature of mystical experience, which seems to occur in similar ways in different religious traditions. (Authors such as Bede Griffiths and Thomas Merton have described how the experience of mystical prayer can be a bond of union among members of different religious communities.) One could imagine very fruitful dialogues about suffering and happiness, life and death, speech and silence. The most important result of such encounters would be for the participants to get to know and respect one another. Friendship among qualified representatives of different religions could help to overcome some of the accumulated hostility and to restore trust.

In the opening years of the third millennium, interreligious dialogue is not a luxury. Together with the other five strategies I have recommended, it may be required to prevent disastrous collisions between major religious groups. In the present crisis, the religions have a great opportunity to overcome hostility and violence among peoples and to promote mutual esteem and cordial cooperation. But the stakes are high. If the various religious communities refuse to adopt programs of tolerance and to engage in respectful dialogue, there is a serious danger of relapsing into mutual recrimination and hatred. Religion may once again be abused, as has so often happened in the past, to justify conflict and bloodshed. As John Paul II said with reference to the events of September 11, "We must not let what has happened lead to a deepening of divisions. Religion must never be used as a reason for conflict." Religious believers must take the lead in building a world in which all peoples can live together in peace and brotherhood.

25. VATICAN II: THE MYTH AND THE REALITY

February 24, 2003

(Based on lectures given in October 2002 at Loyola University in New Orleans and Georgetown University in Washington, D.C.)

Ｔhe memory of the Second Vatican Council, forty years after the opening of the council, continues to arouse both acclamation and vilification. Its champions, in many cases, see it as having liberated Catholics from a long night of oppression, thus restoring to the people of God their rightful liberties. Its detractors blame it for shattering the unity and order of the Church and introducing an era of contestation and doubt. While reformers caricature the preconciliar Church as tyrannical and obscurantist, traditionalists idealize the preconciliar Church as though it were a lost paradise.

In part, the quarrels are due to a conflict of interpretations. The council documents, like most committee products, reflect some compromises. Four factors make the interpretation especially difficult.

1. The Council Fathers, under the direction of Pope Paul VI, made every effort to achieve unanimity and express the consensus of the whole episcopate, not the ideas of one particular school. For this reason, they sought to harmonize differing views, without excluding any significant minority. In some cases they adopted deliberate ambiguities.

2. Pope John XXIII, in his opening speech on October 11, 1962, declared that although the Church had sometimes condemned errors with the greatest severity, it would best meet the needs of

our time "by demonstrating the validity of her teaching rather than by condemnations." Because the council saw fit to follow this instruction, it did not dwell on the negative implications of its doctrine. Framed so as not to offend any large group, except perhaps atheistic Communism, the documents are markedly irenic.

3. The council occurred at a unique moment of history, when the Western world was swept up in a wave of optimism typified by Pope John XXIII himself. The "new humanism" was confident that if free play were given to human powers and technology, the scourges of poverty, disease, famine, and war could be virtually eliminated. Christians, on this theory, had no good reason for standing apart from the rest of humanity. They should throw in their lot with all the forces making for humanization and progress. Books like *The Secular City* (1964), by Harvey Cox, served as bibles for the new gospel of freedom and creativity. Secular enthusiasts interpreted Vatican II as an invitation for Catholics to jump on the bandwagon.

4. In the postconciliar period, the communications media favored the emphasis on novelty. Progressive theologians were lionized for writing books and articles that seemed to be breaking new barriers and demolishing the old edifice of preconciliar Catholicism.

In this atmosphere, early interpreters of the council suggested that the documents contained revolutionary implications not apparent on the surface. Some propounded the hermeneutical principle that where there are ambiguities in the council documents, these should always be resolved in favor of discontinuity. Others used the device of preferring to follow the "spirit of Vatican II" at the expense of the letter.

Whereas this innovationist hermeneutic of Vatican II was clearly predominant in the literature of the first decade after the council, another school of interpretation began to surface toward the middle 1970s. Such distinguished theologians as Henri de Lubac, S.J., Hans Urs von Balthasar, and Joseph Ratzinger banded together to found a new international review, *Communio,* which was widely viewed as an attempt to offset the progressive Dutch-based journal *Concilium.* Writers for *Communio* preferred to interpret Vatican II with what they called "a hermeneutics of continuity," emphasizing the diachronic solidarity of the council with the whole Catholic tradition.

To overcome polarization and bring about greater consensus, Pope John Paul II convened an extraordinary assembly of the Synod of Bishops in 1985, the twentieth anniversary of the close of the council. This synod in its final report came up with six agreed principles for sound interpretation, which may be paraphrased as follows:

1. Each passage and document of the council must be interpreted in the context of all the others, so that the integral teaching of the council may be rightly grasped.
2. The four constitutions of the council (those on liturgy, Church, revelation, and Church in the modern world) are the hermeneutical key to the other documents—namely, the council's nine decrees and three declarations.
3. The pastoral import of the documents ought not to be separated from, or set in opposition to, their doctrinal content.
4. No opposition may be made between the spirit and the letter of Vatican II.
5. The council must be interpreted in continuity with the great tradition of the Church, including earlier councils.
6. Vatican II should be accepted as illuminating the problems of our own day.

These principles seem to me to be sound. Applying them, I should like to propose twelve points on which I believe that the council has been rather generally misunderstood.

1. It is widely believed that the council taught that non-Christian religions contain revelation and are paths to salvation for their members. A careful examination of the documents,

however, proves the contrary. The council taught that salvation cannot be found in any other name than that of Jesus (Acts 4:12; cf. *Ad Gentes* [AG; *Decree on the Church's Missionary Activity*] 9, and *Gaudium et Spes* [GS; *Pastoral Constitution on the Church in the Modern World*] 10). In solemn language it declared: "This sacred Synod professes its belief that God has made known to mankind the way in which men are to serve him, and thus to be saved in Christ and come to blessedness" (*Dignitatis Humanae* [*Declaration on Religious Freedom*] 1). Without denying that there are truths and values in other religions, the council asserted that these truths and values are commingled with serious errors, and that even the truths have salvific value only to the extent that they are preparations for, or reflections of, the Christian Gospel (*Lumen Gentium* [LG; *Dogmatic Constitution on the Church* 16]; AG 9).

2. Regarding the means by which revelation is transmitted, many theologians have argued that the council gave priority to scripture as the written Word of God, and demoted tradition to the status of a secondary norm, to be tested against the higher norm of scripture.

An impartial reading of Vatican II's *Dei Verbum* (DV), the *Dogmatic Constitution on Revelation,* indicates on the contrary that the council gave a certain priority to tradition. It asserts that the apostles and their successors, the bishops, by their preaching and teaching have faithfully preserved the Word of God. Scripture is an inspired and privileged sedimentation of tradition but not an independent or separable norm. Scripture and tradition together constitute a single indivisible channel of revealed truth, in which neither element could stand without the other (DV 9).

3. A third error relating to revelation is the view that, according to the council, God continues to reveal himself in secular experience through the signs of the times, which therefore provide criteria for interpreting the Gospel. Vatican II, in fact, rejected the idea of continuing revelation. It taught that revelation became complete in Jesus Christ and that no further public revelation is to be expected before the end of time, when Christ

returns in glory (DV 4). In *Gaudium et Spes* the council spoke of the Church's duty to interpret the signs of the times, but it specified that these signs are to be interpreted in the light of the Gospel (GS 4).

4. Turning now to the Church, we can put the question of its necessity. It has become almost a platitude to say that the council, reversing earlier Catholic teaching, taught that the Church is not necessary for salvation. But in reality the council affirmed that faith and baptism are necessary for salvation (Mk 16:16; Jn 3:5), and that, since baptism is the door to the Church, the Church too is necessary. The council went on to say that anyone who knows that the Church is necessary has the obligation to enter it and remain in it as a condition for salvation (LG 14).

Vatican II did, however, face the question whether persons who have no opportunity to hear the Gospel are necessarily lost. It replied that they can be "associated with the paschal mystery" if, with the help of God's grace, they consistently strive to do God's will as it is known to them (GS 22). But because people outside the Church fall frequently into sin and error, the Gospel and the Church could greatly help them on their way to salvation (LG 16).

5. Turning now to the ecumenical problem, we must evaluate the common impression that the council, in stating that the Church of Christ "subsists" in the Roman Catholic communion (LG 8), implied that the former is wider and more inclusive than the latter. Cardinal Ratzinger, rejecting this view, argues that because the Church of Christ has its subsistence in Roman Catholicism, it cannot subsist anywhere else. This reading coheres well with the full teaching of the council. Certain endowments of the Church can, to be sure, exist in other Christian communions, bringing their members into "imperfect communion" with the Catholic Church (*Unitatis Redintegratio* [UR; the *Decree on Ecumenism*] 3). Non-Catholic communities that have a genuine apostolic ministry and a valid Eucharist are properly called churches,

but they should not be reckoned as constituent parts of the one and catholic Church in which the true religion subsists (UR 1).

6. The doctrine of collegiality is frequently misunderstood as though it restricted the powers of the pope, requiring him to establish a consensus of the world's bishops before deciding important issues. Vatican II did indeed affirm that the bishops as a college, when acting together with their head, the pope, enjoy supreme authority, but it affirmed that the pope likewise has supreme authority as successor of Peter and head of the college. The full power of the college is present in the pope alone, who is always free to exercise his primatial office according to the grace given to him. The college, on the other hand, cannot act except when summoned to collegial action by the pope. Its decisions have no efficacy without the pope's approval. Thus the primacy of the pope, as it had been defined by Vatican I, remains intact. His power is in no way limited by that of the episcopal college (LG 22).

7. Passing to another point, we may ask whether the council recognized that theologians and others have a right to dissent from non-infallible teachings of the magisterium. Some Catholic theologians, while admitting that all the faithful are obliged to submit to infallible teaching, contend that faithful Catholics are entitled to reject non-infallible teaching when it conflicts with their private judgment.

Vatican II never mentioned dissent, but by implication rejected it. It stated that even when the pope and the bishops do not speak infallibly, their authoritative teaching is binding, and that the faithful are required to adhere to it with a "religious submission of mind" (LG 25). Vatican II, therefore, cannot be quoted as favoring dissent.

8. Regarding the laity, the council did much to clarify their active role in the worship and mission of the Church and their vocation to refashion secular society according to the norms of the Gospel. At several points Vatican II urged pastors to consult the laity and to listen to them when they speak within

their competence (LG 37; GS 43, 62). But at no point did it suggest that the hierarchy have any obligation to accept the recommendations of the laity with regard to matters pertaining to the pastoral office. While encouraging cooperation with priests, deacons, and laypersons, the council placed the powers of authoritative teaching, sacramental worship, and pastoral government squarely and exclusively in the hands of the hierarchy (*Christus Dominus* [the *Decree on the Bishops' Pastoral Office in the Church*] 30).

9. It is often said that with Vatican II the Church, reversing its earlier position, acknowledged marriage as a vocation no less blessed than celibacy. The council wrote eloquently of the sacrament of matrimony as a sacred bond mirroring the union between Christ and the Church (GS 48), but it also reaffirmed the teaching of Trent that it is better and more blessed to remain in virginity or celibacy than to be joined in matrimony—a doctrine that Trent traced back to Jesus (Mt 19:11–12) and to Paul (1 Cor 7:25–26, 38, 40). In *Optatam Totius* (OT), the *Decree on Priestly Formation*, Vatican II declared that seminarians "should acquire a right understanding of the duties and dignity of Christian marriage, as representing the love between Christ and his Church (cf. Eph 5:22–33). They should, however, realize the greater excellence of virginity consecrated to Christ, so that by a maturely considered and magnanimous free choice they may consecrate themselves to the Lord by an entire dedication of body and mind" (OT 10). If this passage had been better understood and more energetically taught, the present crisis of vocations to the priestly and religious life might be less severe.

10. Opponents of Paul VI's encyclical *Humanae Vitae* (1968) make much of the fact that Vatican II was silent on the morality of contraception. The council did not explicitly condemn contraception because the pope had reserved this question to a special commission outside the council. But after declaring that the full sense of mutual self-giving and human procreation must be preserved in marital intercourse, the council declared: "Such a goal cannot be achieved unless the virtue of conjugal chastity is

sincerely practiced. Relying on these principles, sons and daughters of the church may not undertake methods of regulating procreation which are found blameworthy by the teaching authority of the church in its unfolding of the divine law" (GS 51). At this point the Fathers inserted footnotes referring to documents of Pius XI and Pius XII forbidding contraception. If this passage had been written after *Humanae Vitae*, no revision would have been needed except the addition of a reference to that document in the footnote.

11. The council's teaching on religious freedom has been poorly understood. It is widely believed that the council recognized that members of non-Catholic and non-Christian religious bodies have a right to believe as they do and to propagate their beliefs freely. But the council declared no such thing. In its *Declaration on Religious Freedom* it rejected coercion by the state in the area of religion, but it did not set all religions on the same level. The "one true religion," it stated, "subsists in the Catholic and apostolic church to which the Lord Jesus committed the duty of spreading it abroad among all men" (UR 1). Other religions and churches do not have the same mandate. The late John Courtney Murray, S.J., stated in his commentary: "Neither the declaration nor the American Constitution affirms that a man has a right to believe what is false or to do what is wrong. This would make moral nonsense. Neither error nor evil can be the object of a right, only what is true and good. It is, however, true and good that a man should enjoy freedom from coercion in matters religious."

12. Turning in conclusion to the liturgy, I shall limit myself to one question. Vatican II is frequently praised or blamed for having authorized the translation of the Latin liturgy into the vernacular. But the matter is not so simple. In *Sacrosactum Concilium* (SC), its *Constitution on the Liturgy* (1963), the council declared: "The use of the Latin language is to be preserved in the Latin rite, except where a particular law might indicate otherwise" (SC 36.1). In the following two paragraphs the constitution went on to

say that competent local ecclesiastical authorities may determine that certain readings, instructions, prayers, and chants be translated into the mother tongue of the people. The Council Fathers would not have anticipated that in the space of a few years the Latin language would almost totally disappear. It would be well if Catholics could be familiar with the Mass in Latin, the official language of the Roman rite. But since there are sound pastoral reasons for the vernacular, faithful translations of high quality should be provided. We may hope that such translations are in the making.

Because the hermeneutics of discontinuity has prevailed in countries like our own, the efforts of the Holy See to clarify the documents have regularly been attacked as retrenchments. The Congregation for the Doctrine of the Faith was denounced for its declaration on infallibility, *Mysterium Ecclesiae* (1973), for the new profession of faith issued in 1989, for its ecclesiology of communion in *Communionis Notio* (1991), and for its document on Christ and the Church, *Dominus Iesus* (2000). The Roman document on the collaboration of the laity in the sacred ministry (1997) was angrily dismissed, as was, in some quarters, John Paul II's apostolic constitution *Apostolos Suos*, on the status and authority of episcopal conferences (1998). In each of these cases there was a clamor of protest, but the critics did not convincingly show that the official teaching had departed from the teaching of Vatican II, interpreted according to the principles set forth in the Extraordinary Synod of 1985.

I am not seeking in this brief article to defend the teaching of Vatican II on points that someone or other might wish to challenge. My authority could not add anything to that of the council, which spoke with the promised assistance of the Holy Spirit. I can say only that I find the teaching of Vatican II very solid, carefully nuanced, and sufficiently flexible to meet the needs of our own time and place. The artful blending of majority and minority perspectives in the council documents should have forestalled the unilateral interpretations. There is no reason today why Vatican II should be a bone of contention among Catholics. History, of course, does not stop. Just as Vatican II made important changes reflecting new biblical studies, the liturgical movement, and the ecumenical movement, we may expect future developments in doctrine and polity. Progress must be made, but progress always depends upon an acceptance of prior achievements so that it is not necessary to begin each time from the beginning.

26. JOHN PAUL II AND THE MYSTERY OF THE HUMAN PERSON

February 2, 2004

(Address originally delivered at Fordham University on October 21, 2003.)

As the literary output of Pope John Paul II has accumulated, expanding almost beyond the assimilative powers of any one reader, and as he celebrates the silver jubilee of his pontificate, I have been asking myself, as I am sure that many others have: What lies at the very heart of his message? Is there some one concept that could serve as a key to unlock what is distinctive to this pope as a thinker? My thesis will be the mystery of the human person. As pope he is of course bound to the whole dogmatic heritage of the Church, but he presents it in a distinctive way, with his own emphases, which are in line with his philosophical personalism.

I. YEARS AS PROFESSOR AND BISHOP

In his early years as a professor of ethics at the University of Lublin in Poland, Karol Wojtyla, the future Pope John Paul II, like other members of the philosophical faculty, identified himself as a Thomist. While enthusiastically affirming the teaching of Thomas Aquinas on most points, he took note of one weakness. St. Thomas paid too little attention to the human person as experienced from within. In a paper on "Thomistic Personalism" delivered in 1961 he declared:

When it comes to analyzing consciousness and self-consciousness—there seems to be no place for it in St. Thomas' objectivistic view of reality. In any case, that in which the person's
subjectivity is most apparent is presented by St. Thomas in an
exclusively—or almost exclusively—objective way. He shows
us the particular faculties, both spiritual and sensory, thanks
to which the whole of human consciousness and self-consciousness—the human personality in the psychological and
moral sense—takes shape, but that is also where he stops. Thus
St. Thomas gives us an excellent view of the objective existence
and activity of the person, but it would be difficult to speak in
his view of the lived experiences of the person.

Wojtyla was satisfied that St. Thomas correctly situated the
human person in terms of the general categories of being, as an
individual subsisting in an intellectual nature. But he wished to
enrich Thomas's doctrine of the person by reference to our experience of ourselves as unique ineffable subjects. Each person is an
"I," an original source of free and responsible activity.

Wojtyla's experience as a young bishop at the Second Vatican Council confirmed and deepened his personalism. He was
particularly involved in writing the *Pastoral Constitution on the
Church in the Modern World* (*Gaudium et Spes*), which speaks of
"the exalted dignity proper to the human person" and of universal, inviolable human rights (GS 26). In another of John Paul's
favorite passages, *Gaudium et Spes* states that human beings are
the only creatures that God wills for their own sake, and adds
that they cannot rise to their full stature except through a disinterested gift of self (GS 24).

Bishop Wojtyla enthusiastically accepted the council's teaching that the human person is "ex-centric" rather than egocen-
tric. Paradoxically, we cannot fulfill ourselves except through
transcending ourselves and giving ourselves in love toward others. Sometimes John Paul II calls this the "law of the gift." He
thus provides an anthropological grounding for the paradoxical

sayings of Jesus in the gospels about how we can find true life by dying for his sake and unintentionally find spiritual death by clinging selfishly to life.

At Vatican II Wojtyla entered vigorously into the debates on religious freedom. The council opened its declaration on that subject with sentences that could almost have come from the pen of Bishop Wojtyla, had he been one of the authors: "A sense of the dignity of the human person has been impressing itself more and more deeply on the consciousness of contemporary man. And the demand is increasingly made that men should act of their own judgment, enjoying and making use of a responsible freedom, not driven by coercion but motivated by a sense of duty" (*Dignitatis Humanae* 1).

At the council and many times since, John Paul II has quoted from John 8:32: "You will know the truth, and the truth will make you free" (e.g., *Redemptor Hominis* 12; *Veritatis Splendor* [VS] 34, 87). Throughout his pontificate he has never ceased to be a firm champion of human freedom, including religious freedom. He is on principle opposed to physical and moral coercion as infringements of human dignity.

While glorying in freedom, the pope insists that it is not an end in itself but a means of personally adhering to the true good, as perceived by a judgment of conscience. "Authentic freedom," he writes, "is never freedom 'from' the truth but always freedom 'in' the truth" (VS 64). When freedom is abused, it diminishes itself, falling into chains. As he told the General Assembly of the United Nations in 1995, "Detached from the truth about the human person, freedom deteriorates into license in the lives of individuals, and in political life it becomes the caprice of the most powerful and the arrogance of power. Far from being a limitation upon freedom or a threat to it, reference to the truth about the human person—a truth universally knowable through the moral law written on the hearts of all—is, in fact, the guarantor of freedom's future."

The pope is quite aware that this concept of freedom is not widely accepted and understood. "The essential bond between Truth, the Good, and Freedom has been largely lost sight of in present-day culture" (VS 84). Libertarianism erroneously severs the bonds between freedom and responsibility. Because freedom is inevitably linked with responsibility, we are accountable for the use we make of it.

In his continuing struggle against Marxism in Poland after the Second Vatican Council, Cardinal Wojtyla identified the doctrine of the person as the Achilles' heel of the Communist regime. He decided to base his opposition on that plank. In 1968 he wrote to his Jesuit friend, the future Cardinal Henri de Lubac:

> I devote my very rare free moments to a work that is close to my heart and devoted to the metaphysical significance and the mystery of the PERSON. It seems to me that the debate today is being played on that level. The evil of our times consists in the first place in a kind of degradation, indeed in a pulverization, of the fundamental uniqueness of each human person. This evil is even much more of the metaphysical than of the moral order. To this disintegration, planned at times by atheistic ideologies, we must oppose, rather than sterile polemics, a kind of "recapitulation" of the mystery of the person.

As pope, John Paul II would continue to insist that the extraordinary brutality of the twentieth century was due to an unwillingness to recognize the inherent value of the human person, who is made in the image and likeness of God, who confers upon it inalienable rights that can neither be bestowed nor withdrawn by any human power. "The human person," he proclaims, "receives from God its essential dignity and with it the capacity to transcend every social order so as to move toward truth and goodness" (*Centesimus Annus* 38.1).

In *The Acting Person*, a work first published in Polish in 1969 before he became pope, Cardinal Wojtyla expounded a theory of the person as a self-determining agent that realizes itself through free and responsible action. Activity is not something strictly other than the person; it is the person coming to expression and constituting itself. Persons, moreover, are essentially social and oriented to life in community. They achieve themselves as persons by interaction, giving to others and receiving from them in turn. To reconcile the good of the community with that of its individual members, Wojtyla proposed a theory of participation. All must contribute to the common good, which then redounds to the benefit of the individual members. This teaching on participation and the common good contains an implicit critique not only of Marxist collectivism but also of libertarian individualism and anarchist alienation.

II. THEMES OF HIS PAPACY

Since becoming pope, John Paul II has used personalism as a lens through which to reinterpret much of the Catholic tradition. He unhesitatingly embraces all the dogmas of the Church, but expounds them with a personalist slant. As a first example of this personalism one might select the pope's conception of the Christian life itself. In his closing homily at World Youth Day in August 2000, the pope told his hearers: "It is important to realize that among the many questions surfacing in your minds, the decisive ones are not about 'what.' The basic question is 'who': to whom am I to go? whom am I to follow? to whom should I entrust my life?" In another message to youth he declared: "Christianity is not an opinion and does not consist of empty words. Christianity is Christ! It is a Person."

In his encyclical on the theology of missionary activity, *Redemptoris Missio*, John Paul speaks of the kingdom in personalist terms. "The kingdom of God," he writes, "is not a concept, a doctrine, or a program subject to free interpretation, but it is before all else a person with the face and name of Jesus of Nazareth, the image of the invisible God" (RM 18). The face of Jesus is for this pope almost a synonym for the person. His apostolic constitution on the Church in America begins with the stirring chapter "On the Encounter with the Living Christ." In his program for the third millennium, *Novo Millennio Ineunte* (NMI), he declares that the Church's task is to make the face of Christ shine in every historical period, a task that requires that we ourselves first contemplate his face (NMI 16). The ancient longing of the psalmist to see the face of the Lord (Ps 27:8) is surpassingly fulfilled in Christian contemplation of the face of Jesus (NMI 23). The pope's apostolic letter on the Rosary speaks at length of contemplating Jesus, as it were, through the eyes of Mary.

Personalism permeates the ecclesiology of John Paul II. "The Church," he teaches, "wishes to serve this single end: that each person may be able to find Christ, in order that Christ may walk with each person the path of life" (*Redemptor Hominis* [RH] 13.1). He goes on to describe the Church as "the community of disciples, each of whom in a different way—at times not very consciously and consistently—is following Christ. This shows also the deeply 'personal' aspect and dimension of this society" (RH 21). The pope often asserts that the ultimate reality and model of the Church is the divine communion of persons realized eternally in the Holy Trinity (see his *Sources of Renewal: The Implementation of Vatican II* [1979], 121).

In various documents John Paul II exhorts us to find the face of Jesus not only in the gospels but also in the sacraments. "The risen Jesus accompanies us on our way and enables us to recognize him, as the disciples of Emmaus did, 'in the breaking of the bread' (Lk 24:35)" (NMI 59). John Paul II's recent encyclical on the Eucharist, *Ecclesia de Eucharistia* (EE), has the same personalistic dimension. The Eucharist, he says, forms the Church because it brings the baptized into full communion and friendship with Christ. When we receive him devoutly in Holy Communion, he abides in us even as we abide in him (EE 22). The encyclical ends by recalling that the bread we receive is the Shepherd who feeds us. It quotes the eucharistic hymn of Thomas Aquinas: *"Bone pastor, paths vere,"* "Come then, good Shepherd, bread divine" (EE 62).

A profound personalism undergirds Pope John Paul's theology of ecumenism and interreligious relations. "If prayer is the soul of the ecumenical movement and of its yearning for unity," he writes in his encyclical on ecumenism, "it is the basis and support for everything the council defines as 'dialogue.' This definition is certainly not unrelated to today's personalist way of thinking. The capacity for dialogue is rooted in the nature of the person and his dignity. . . . Although the concept of 'dialogue' might appear to give priority to the cognitive dimension (dia-logos), all dialogue implies a global, existential dimension. It involves the human subject in his or her entirety; dialogue between communities involves in a particular way the subjectivity of each. . . . Dialogue is not simply an exchange of ideas. In some way it is always an 'exchange of gifts'" (*Ut Unum Sint* 28). A little later he asserts: "Dialogue does not extend exclusively to matters of doctrine but engages the whole person; it is also a dialogue of love" (47).

These statements on ecumenical dialogue apply analogously to interreligious dialogue. In his encyclical on missionary activity, John Paul II teaches that dialogue is an essential part of the Church's evangelizing mission. Christian proclamation and dialogue are not opposed to each other but are inextricably interlinked (RM 55).

The personalist theme shows up almost everywhere in the teaching of this pope. Think, for example, of his apostolic constitution on Catholic higher education, *Ex Corde Ecclesiae* (ECE). Because of its essential connection with Christ as the way, the truth, and the life, the Catholic university is imbued with a kind of universal humanism (ECE 4). It enables people to rise to the full measure of their humanity, created in the image of God and renewed in Christ and his Spirit (ECE 5). Quoting from his UNESCO address of 1980 and Vatican II's *Gravissimum Educationis* (10), the pope adds:

It is essential that we be convinced of the priority of the ethical over the technical, of the primacy of the person over things, of the superiority of the spirit over matter. The cause of the human person will only be served if knowledge is joined to conscience. Men and women of science will truly aid humanity only if they preserve "the sense of the transcendence of the human person over the world and of God over the human person." (ECE 18)

Personalism also permeates the pope's teaching on social matters. In the first of his social encyclicals, *Laborem Exercens* (LE), he expounds a highly original theology of work, based on the relationship between the person and activity. Human beings, he asserts, are called to participate in God's own creative activity by productive labor. The pope censures economism as the error of "considering labor solely according to its economic purpose" (LE 13.3). Since workers are persons, they are of more value than their products. Through their labor they should be able to transform nature, making it serve as a more fitting habitation for humankind, and at the same time perfect themselves as persons rather than suffer degradation. To the extent that labor is onerous and painful, this may be seen as a just penalty for human sin and may be spiritually fruitful when patiently accepted and united to the sufferings of Christ (LE 27).

Some commentators thought that *Laborem Exercens* was anticapitalist and that it advocated a kind of socialism, not doctrinaire or ideological but moral. But this interpretation cannot stand in view of the pope's other social encyclicals, which call for a free participatory society. His encyclical on economic development, *Sollicitudo Rei Socialis* (SRS), illustrates this position. Building on notions already sketched in *Laborem Exercens*, the pope defines solidarity as a virtue, whereby people firmly commit themselves not to exploit others but to work for their good and even to "lose themselves" for the sake of others. The virtue of solidarity applies analogously to corporations and nations, which must responsibly contribute to the general good of society and of humanity as a whole (SRS 38–40).

The theme of development provides John Paul with an occasion to speak again of personal initiative and participation. "Development," he states, "demands above all a spirit of initiative on the part of the countries which need it. Each of them must act in accordance with its own responsibilities, not expecting everything from the more favored countries. . . . Each must discover and use to the best advantage its own area of freedom" (SRS 44). While opposing all kinds of exploitation of the poor and marginalized, the pope affirms the right of human initiative in undertaking new economic ventures.

The pope's experience of living under a Marxist regime in Poland turned him against the welfare state. The controlled economy, he maintains, "diminishes, or in practice absolutely destroys, the spirit of initiative, that is to say, the creative subjectivity of the person" (SRS 15.2). The notion of creative subjectivity moves to center stage in John Paul II's third social encyclical, *Centesimus Annus*. "The free market economy," it states, "is the most efficient instrument for utilizing resources and effectively responding to needs" (34.1). At one point the pope pointedly asks whether formerly Communist nations seeking to rebuild their economies should be advised to embrace capitalism. His answer is a carefully qualified yes. He is in favor of the business economy, the market economy, the free economy, but he is convinced that the energies unleashed by the market need to be contained within a strong juridical framework and a public moral culture so that the economy is kept in service to the common good (42).

Whereas his predecessors had tended to look on wealth as an accumulation of material possessions, John Paul II as a personalist adds a new factor. He points out that the primary source of wealth today is the human spirit with its fund of knowledge and its creative capacities (32). Wealth, therefore, consists more in what we are than in what we have.

III. TENSIONS WITH PREVIOUS TRADITION

I could say a great deal more about the pope's personalism as illustrated, for example, in his concept of the priest as acting "in the person of Christ" in consecrating the host and chalice at the altar and in giving absolution in the sacrament of penance, which he refers to as "the tribunal of mercy." But the examples already adduced should probably suffice to establish my thesis about the importance of the personalist perspective in the thought of John Paul II. But before concluding, I should like to reflect on several points at which this perspective stands in tension with previous Catholic tradition.

1. *Natural Theology.* At least since the time of Thomas Aquinas, the Catholic tradition has insisted that the existence of the one personal God, creator and goal of all things, can be established by human reason on the basis of things seen. The standard arguments have been based on the principle of causality, contingency, the degrees of perfection, and the principle of finality. The present pope nowhere rejects these arguments, but he is curiously silent about them. Instead he takes his point of departure from the longings of the human heart for personal communion with others and with the divine. For personalist philosophers such as Martin Buber and Emmanuel Levinas, he writes, "The path passes not so much through being and existence [as in St. Thomas] as through people and their meeting each other" in coexistence and dialogue. We encounter God as the ultimate Thou. This approach is highly suggestive, but the pope does not develop it in detail. And so we are left with questions such as these: Can a rigorous and convincing proof be erected on a personalist foundation? If so, is it to be preferred to the traditional ontological and cosmological arguments? Have these other arguments been exposed as deficient? I believe that the thought of John Paul II can be integrated with the tradition.

2. *Natural Law.* When he writes on natural law, the present pope speaks more of the human person than of human nature.

As Janet Smith points out, he wishes to integrate the natural law into his personalist framework, thus avoiding the charge of "biologism" sometimes directed against standard presentations. "The true meaning of the natural law," says the pope, is that "it refers to man's proper and primordial nature, the 'nature of the human person,' which is the person himself" (VS 50.1).

The Oxford professor Oliver O'Donovan objects that the pope seems overindebted to the idealist tradition, which "understands the rationality of the moral law as something grounded in the human mind." But in his work as a professor, Karol Wojtyla anticipated this objection and sought to answer it. In an essay on "The Human Person and Natural Law," he firmly rejected the view of Kant and the idealists, who would allow reason to impose its own categories on reality. For Wojtyla, reason discerns and affirms an objective order of reality and value that is prior to reason itself. The freedom of the human person is not to be understood indeterministically, as though it meant emancipation from all constraints. Although the mind must conform to the real order, law as a moral obligation is not something merely mechanical or biological. It presupposes a subject with personal consciousness.

3. *Contraception.* The question of natural law comes up concretely in the pope's writings on contraception. Following Pius XI and Pius XII, Paul VI in his encyclical *Humanae Vitae* (HV) argued primarily from natural law; contending that contraception is intrinsically evil because the generative faculties are intrinsically ordered toward the raising up of life (HV 13). But the present pope, in his various writings on the subject, says nothing about the intrinsic ordering of the faculties. He speaks of sexual union as a tangible expression of love between a man and a woman who generously and unreservedly give themselves to each other. Contraception, he maintains, is "a falsification of the inner meaning of conjugal love," since it turns sexuality into a means of hedonistic satisfaction (*Familiaris Consortio* 32.4). Paul VI in *Humanae Vitae* had already spoken of conjugal love as a

reciprocal personal gift of self and had warned that the practice of contraception could easily lead to the lowering of the partners into mere instruments of selfish enjoyment (HV 8, 17). Some authors contend that if Paul VI had more consistently followed the personalist rather than the legalist approach, his condemnation of contraception would have been more warmly received. The question therefore arises: does John Paul II intend to correct Paul VI by substituting a superior argument, or does he mean to leave intact all that Paul VI said about the ontological dimension of the moral law, adding only a further reflection on the subjective or psychological dimension? I suspect that he intends to support the tradition, not to supersede it. But he wants to induce people to be open to life from a motive of love, not just as a matter of submitting to law.

4. *Death Penalty.* In a McGinley lecture several years ago, I spoke at some length of the pope's views on the death penalty. Although he does not hold that the death penalty is intrinsically evil, his deep respect for human life inclines him to reject capital punishment in practice. He allows for it when there is no other way to defend society against the criminal, but he also holds that in advanced societies today there are alternatives more in accord with human dignity. When convicts on death row are about to be executed, the pope regularly sends messages to governors asking them to grant clemency.

Earlier official teaching, up through the pontificate of Pius XII, consistently supported capital punishment. Catholic moral theologians regularly quoted St. Paul to the effect that secular rulers do not bear the sword in vain; they are God's ministers or instruments in executing his wrath upon wrongdoers (Rom 13:4). Thus the authority of the state to put criminals to death does not conflict with the maxim that God alone is the master of life. But John Paul II, to the best of my knowledge, never quotes this text. Why not, I wonder. Does he believe that governments in the modern democratic society still rule with divine authority or that they enjoy only the authority given them by consensus of the governed? Can retributive punishment be a valid reason for the death penalty? Some Catholics interpret John Paul II as opposing the mainstream Catholic tradition and therefore as perhaps teaching unsound doctrine. Personally I am not convinced that he wishes to break with that tradition. In my earlier McGinley lecture I contended that his statements can be read in a way compatible with the tradition on the death penalty.

5. *Just War.* Similar issues arise with respect to just war. John Paul II, while denying that he is a pacifist, deplores military action as a failure for humanity. In the encyclical *Centesimus Annus* he called attention to the success of nonviolent resistance in bringing about the overthrow of Communism in Eastern Europe. He then pleaded eloquently for a world order in which the need for war would be eliminated. "Never again war," he writes, "which destroys the lives of innocent people, teaches how to kill, throws into upheaval even the lives of those who do the killing and leaves behind a trail of resentment and hatred. Just as the time has finally come when in individual states a system of private vendetta and reprisal has given way to the rule of law, so too a similar step forward is now urgently needed in the international community" (CA 52.1).

In his World Peace Day message of January 1, 2002, John Paul II declared that there is no peace without justice and no justice without forgiveness. Does he mean that the pursuit of justice and forgiveness ought to banish all thought of war? Some astute critics believe that the pope is preparing the way for a doctrinal development that would greatly restrict the conditions of a just war. Is he discarding the just war tradition in favor of what George Weigel calls "a species of functional or de facto pacifism"?

Personalism undoubtedly favors the use of persuasion rather than force. It makes for a reluctance to admit that negotiation can at a certain point become futile. But realism may sometimes require the use of military force. The pope has several times countenanced what is called "humanitarian intervention" to put an end to bloody massacres (e.g., in Rwanda, East Timor, and

Bosnia). He made no objection to the American military action in Afghanistan in 2002. In essentials, I suspect, the classical just war doctrine is still intact, but new and difficult mediating principles are needed, especially in cases where the belligerents are not sovereign states with mercenary troops but factions or terrorist organizations.

6. *Social Order.* I have already commented on the social and economic teaching of the present pope. Michael Novak sees this teaching, especially in *Centesimus Annus*, as supplying the rationale needed for building a new order of society. The key concepts in this new synthesis, Novak finds, are those of the acting person, the right to personal economic initiative, the virtues associated with entrepreneurship, and human creativity grounded in the imago Dei implanted in every woman and man by the Creator himself.

Not all commentators share Novak's enthusiasm. James Hug, S.J., for example, ruefully writes of *Centesimus Annus*, "Some of the language suggests that U.S. neoconservatives helped to shape its content." He looks forward to the day when he and "the progressive segment of the church justice community" will be able to have comparable input into papal social teaching.

These varying reactions leave us with the question, Is the social teaching of the present pope a passing deviation or a permanent shift? I would hazard the opinion that his personalist slant will continue to enrich Catholic political and economic theory for the foreseeable future.

7. *Kingship of Christ.* In his talks and writings, Pope John Paul II speaks frequently of Christ's threefold office as prophet, priest, and king. While he elaborates on the first two members of this triad, he has relatively less to say about Christ's kingly office. The Feast of Christ the King was instituted by Pius XI in 1925 to make it clear that Christ "holds all nations under his sway" (*Quas Primas* [QP] 20). "Nations," wrote Pius XI, "will be reminded by the annual celebration of this feast that not only individuals but

also *rulers and princes are bound to give public honor and obedience to Christ"* (QP 32, italics supplied).

John Paul II, by contrast, speaks of Christ's lordship as a triumph of humble submission and of his kingdom as a "kingdom of love and service." He says relatively little about Christ as lawmaker and judge, perhaps because these themes fit less well into his personalist scheme. The Second Vatican Council's *Declaration on Religious Freedom*, with its accent on the mutual independence of Church and state, has made it more difficult to speak with the boldness of Pius XI. But we should not allow ourselves to forget that Christ, who lived humbly as a servant in our midst, has been crowned with glory and that he reigns as sovereign Lord at the right hand of the Father.

8. *Last Judgment.* John Paul II of course accepts the article of the creed that Christ "will come again to judge the living and the dead." But he quotes by preference from the fourth gospel that "God sent the Son into the world, not to condemn the world, but that the world might be saved through him" (Jn 3:17). "Only those who will have rejected the salvation offered by God in his boundless mercy," he writes, "will be condemned, because they will have condemned themselves." A little later he adds that eternal punishment is not to be attributed to God's initiative, because in his merciful love God can only desire the salvation of the human beings he has created.

Damnation, according to the pope, means definitive separation from God "freely chosen by the human person and confirmed with death." Paraphrasing the parable of the sheep and goats, he says that the Lord Jesus will come to "question" us when we appear before him. But in the parable itself, the Son of Man actually sentences some to hell with the words: "Depart from me, you cursed, into the eternal fire that has been prepared for the devil and his angels" (Mt 25:41). The shift in imagery betrays the pope's reluctance to speak of Christ as judge.

9. *Purgatory.* The Catholic tradition has depicted purgatory as a place where the debt of temporal punishment for forgiven sins

is paid. The classical proof text from scripture (2 Mc 12:41–45) speaks of sacrifices being offered to atone for the sins of slain Jewish soldiers. The Second Council of Lyons taught that the souls in purgatory undergo cleansing punishments. Paul VI in 1967 reiterated the doctrine that even after sins have been remitted, a debt of expiation may remain to be paid in purgatory. But John Paul II, in texts familiar to me, makes no mention of punishment or expiation in purgatory. Instead he speaks of it only as a state of "purification" or cleansing, preparing the soul to enter into the fullness of eternal life.

Here, as in the case of hell, we must ask, does the personalism of John Paul II incline him to neglect or minimize the penal aspects? If so, is he simply making a pastoral adaptation on the ground that purgatory can better be understood, or be more ecumenically acceptable, if no mention is made of the punitive dimension? Or is he introducing a new development in which God will no longer be seen as punishing? I am inclined to think that the connection between sin and punishment is so deeply ingrained in scripture and tradition that it will never be eliminated from Catholic teaching.

Pope John Paul II is not a man of one idea. As I have said, he accepts the whole dogmatic heritage of the Church. In his philosophy he combines personalist phenomenology with a strong Thomistic metaphysics. He therefore has many resources with which to address the complex questions we have been considering.

Personalism has its clearest applications in the realm of privacy and one-to-one relations. It is crucial in individual self-realization and in marriage and family life—themes on which John Paul II has written luminously. More remarkably, he has found ways of extending personalism to deal with political and economic issues, drawing on his conceptions of human action, personal participation, and free initiative. Although personalism cannot be an adequate tool for handling the larger issues of law and order, war and peace, John Paul II has injected important new considerations into the fields of business, jurisprudence, political science, and international relations.

Theologically, likewise, the pope is a personalist. He writes movingly of the desire for God inscribed in the human heart. He dwells joyfully on the one-to-one relation between the individual believer and Jesus Christ, mediated through the scriptures, the sacraments, and the Church. His concentration on God's amazing love and mercy is a welcome antidote to pessimistic preachers who have portrayed God as a demanding master and a rigorous judge. But, as John Paul would recognize, God's love cannot be played off against his justice. The pope knows well that the love of God cannot exist without obedience to God's commandments and that persons who reject God's love must reckon with his justice.

John Paul II, however, shies away from threatening words. Fear, in his view, diminishes the scope of freedom and makes only a poor Christian. He holds up the more perfect motives of hope, trust, and love as grounds for joyful adherence to the Lord. Amid all the anger and turmoil of our times, John Paul II stands as a beacon of hope. With calm insistence he stands by the theme of his inaugural homily: "Do not be afraid. . . . Open wide the doors to Christ. He alone has the words of life, yes, of eternal life."

27. A EUCHARISTIC CHURCH

December 20, 2004

(Lecture delivered on November 10, 2004.)

Karol Wojtyla has always had a deep eucharistic piety. In 2003 he released his most recent encyclical, *Ecclesia de Eucharistia*, emphasizing the bonds between the Eucharist and the Church. Last spring he announced the beginning of a eucharistic year, which began on October 7 and will culminate at the meeting of the Synod of Bishops in October 2005. The theme for that assembly will be "The Eucharist: Source and Summit of the Life and Mission of the Church." This is therefore a good time to look at the eucharistic ecclesiology of John Paul II.

In the course of his encyclical, the pope quotes, without attribution, a statement of Cardinal Henri de Lubac, S.J.: "The Eucharist builds the church and the church makes the Eucharist." Each was founded by Christ with a view to the other. Unless there was a Church, there would be no one to celebrate the Eucharist, but unless there were a Eucharist, the Church would lack the supreme source of its vitality.

The Church renews itself by continually returning to the sources of its own life. By immersing itself in the Eucharist, it takes on the characteristics of that great mystery of faith. Because the greater assimilates the lesser, the usual law of eating is reversed. In a famous passage, Augustine depicts Christ saying, "I am your food, but instead of my being changed into you, it is you who will be transformed into me."

This transformation means concretely that the ideas, attitudes, and sentiments of pastors and faithful are remolded in the likeness of those of Jesus Christ as he gives himself to us in loving obedience to his Father's command. In this way the Church becomes eucharistic.

One of the most original and interesting points in the encyclical is the observation that the Eucharist has the four attributes that we apply to the Church in the Nicene-Constantinopolitan Creed: one, holy, catholic, and apostolic (EE 26). Although the pope develops only the last of these attributes, apostolicity, all four ecclesial marks may be found in the Eucharist.

HOLY

Holiness is not just moral rectitude, though it certainly includes this. The Israelites of old were profoundly aware that God was the exemplar and source of all holiness. For any creature to become holy, God must bring it into a union with himself. By adopting Israel, God made it a holy nation set apart and consecrated to his service. In the New Testament we learn that the all-holy God, by an almost incredible act of condescension, appears in the flesh. Jesus Christ, the holy one of God, comes on a mission to save and sanctify the world.

Christ founded the Church as the people of God of the New Testament. The First Letter of Peter reminds its readers: "You are a chosen race, a royal priesthood, a holy nation, God's own people" (1 Pt 2:9). The Letter to the Ephesians depicts the Church as the fruit of Christ's loving sacrifice. "He loved the church and gave himself up for it, that he might sanctify it, having cleansed it by the washing of water with the word, that he might present the church to himself in splendor, without spot or wrinkle or any such thing, that she might be holy and without blemish" (Eph 5:25–27).

As we know from the creed, the Church is always holy. It is holy in its divine head, Jesus Christ, to whom we sing in the

Gloria, "You alone are holy." It is holy in the doctrines taught by the Lord and in the sacraments by which he remains present with his people. All the sacraments are holy and have power to sanctify, but the Eucharist is "most holy," because in it Christ himself is substantially present, performing his supreme redemptive act. Thomas Aquinas wrote, in a frequently quoted passage, that the Eucharist contains the entire spiritual wealth of the Church.

The holiness of the Eucharist demands that those who receive the sacrament do so with great reverence, lest they defile what is holy. The Church at all times bears in mind the warning of St. Paul, "Whoever eats of the bread or drinks of the cup unworthily is guilty of profaning the body and blood of the Lord" (1 Cor 11:27). Conversely, those who become Christ's members by feeding on his body take on new obligations. It would be a profanation, Paul tells us, for them to enter into sexual union with prostitutes (1 Cor 6:15–17). Pope John Paul in his encyclical reminds the faithful that they should not receive Communion if they have committed serious sin and have not been absolved in the sacrament of Penance (EE 36).

To be made holy by the Eucharist, it does not suffice for us to be physically present at holy Mass or to receive Communion physically. We must participate personally by reverently hearing the Word of God and sharing in the mind of the Church as it worships. The congregation is called to join in the Church's self-offering, entering in spirit into Christ's own redemptive work (*Lumen Gentium* 11).

Eucharistic holiness is never merely individual; it is ecclesial. The more closely the faithful are conjoined to Christ, the more intimately are they united to one another in his body. The attribute of holiness therefore leads directly into that of unity.

ONE

The Church is one for a variety of reasons. The Lord founded it with a single mission and a single system of government, under the visible headship of Peter and his successors. It is held together by its scripture, its creeds, and its sacraments, and by the Holy Spirit, who is at work in the hearts and minds of the faithful.

The holy Eucharist stands out as one of the most important instruments and signs of unity. Although Masses are celebrated in many different times and places, each alone and all together constitute one and the same sacrifice, that of Christ on the Cross. Each Mass "re-presents" the sacrifice of Calvary, making it present once again. The Eucharist therefore possesses a mysterious unity that is not paralleled by anything else in history. By participating in the eucharistic sacrifice and receiving Holy Communion, we are drawn into mystical fellowship with one another in Christ.

Paul says in the First Letter to the Corinthians that the Church is one body because its members partake of the one bread, which is Christ the Lord (1 Cor 10:17). The Fathers of the Church were keenly conscious of this unitive power. Many of them, including John Chrysostom, dwell on the symbolism of the bread and wine, which suggest how many things can be fused into unity, as many individuals are in the Church. The loaf is made up of many grains of wheat; the chalice is made up from the juice of many grapes.

The Didache of the Twelve Apostles, written about the end of the first century, contains the petition: "As this piece [of bread] was scattered over the hills and then was brought together and made one, so let your church be brought together from the ends of the earth into your kingdom." In the Eucharistic Prayer 3 we ask that "we who are nourished by Christ's body and blood may become one body, one spirit" in him.

Thomas Aquinas calls the Eucharist the "sacrament of ecclesiastical unity" and the "sacrament of the unity of the Mystical Body." He also quotes St. Augustine, who calls it "the sign of unity and the bond of charity."

For the Eucharist to function as a sacrament of unity, a measure of unity must already exist among those who partake of it.

They must not only be baptized but must be one among themselves. They must have a will to be in unity and peace with the whole Church. If anyone were to receive this sacrament of unity while intending to remain apart from the body and its visible head, in a situation of heresy or schism, the meaning of the action would be contradicted by the contrary disposition. It would be wrong for anyone to say, "I do not want to belong to your community, but I want to receive Communion with you." Nor could they properly say, "I do not accept your pastors and doctrines, but I want to partake of your sacraments."

As the preeminent sacrament of unity, the Eucharist ordinarily presupposes that the participants are in full ecclesial communion with one another. Communion is normally reserved to Catholics but, as the pope notes toward the end of his encyclical, there are exceptional circumstances in which baptized Christians belonging to other communities may be admitted for the occasion to Holy Communion (EE 45).

CATHOLIC

The question of unity leads directly to another. Unity among whom? Or among what? The mystery of the Eucharist helps us to answer these questions and in so doing points to the catholicity of the Church. In instituting the sacrament, the Lord had an absolutely universal vision, embracing all peoples of all times and, it would seem, the whole cosmos. He speaks of his blood poured out not only "for you" but also "for the many," in the sense of all.

In the first place, the redemptive sacrifice of Christ extends to those who believe, but through their prayers and evangelizing efforts the power of the sacramental sacrifice reaches out to the whole human community. Jesus is the savior of the world (*Salvator Mundi*). The Eucharist is an acceptable sacrifice that "brings salvation to the whole world," as we say in the fourth eucharistic prayer.

The pope's recent encyclical speaks of the "cosmic" character of the Eucharist. The natural elements, transformed by human hands into bread and wine, are further transmuted into the glorified body and blood of Christ. Celebrated on the altar of the world, the Eucharist unites heaven and earth. "It embraces all creation. The Son of God became man in order to restore all creation, in one supreme act of praise, to the One who made it from nothing" (EE 8).

The Church of the first centuries was acutely conscious of the Eucharist as a bond among churches. In the Diocese of Rome there was a practice of sending a fragment of the consecrated host from the bishop's church to outlying parish churches to signify the unity between the Eucharist celebrated by the presbyters and his own. When bishops came on visits, the local bishop would often invite them to concelebrate with him. The faithful of such churches received eucharistic hospitality as a sign of communion. The refusal to recognize a church led inevitably to a refusal to participate in its eucharistic celebrations or to let its members participate in one's own Eucharist. The eucharistic prayers of the Roman Missal make it clear that every legitimate Eucharist is celebrated in union with the whole body of bishops and the pope, for otherwise it would be deficient in catholicity. A Eucharist celebrated in separation from the college of bishops and the faithful of their churches would lack the attribute of catholicity.

APOSTOLIC

As may be seen from the last few sentences, the catholicity of the Eucharist is closely bound up with its fourth attribute, apostolicity. The doctrine derives from Christian antiquity, which recognized that the Eucharist could not be validly celebrated except by a priest ordained by a bishop who stood in the apostolic succession.

Apostolicity expresses the fact that the Church at the Eucharist, as elsewhere, is a hierarchical community under the supervision of leaders authorized and empowered to act in the name of Christ. Apostolicity also links each and all of the bishops historically with the Twelve as the source of their powers. Jesus at the Last Supper entrusted the Eucharist to the Twelve, who were his table companions, commanding them to do in commemoration of him what he was then doing.

Explaining the apostolicity of the Eucharist, Pope John Paul II asserts that the ministry of a validly ordained priest links the Eucharist historically to the sacrifice of the Cross and to the Last Supper (EE 29). Any eucharistic celebration requires as a condition of its validity the presidency of a bishop or a priest who acts in the person of Christ (EE 32). There can be no such thing as a lay Eucharist or priestless Mass. Deacons and others may, under certain conditions, conduct a service of the Word, followed by a Communion service; but care should be taken to make it clear that this is not a Mass, a Eucharist, because the sacrifice cannot be offered without a priest. Those who preside at such services have a responsibility to create in the congregation a hunger for the Eucharist and to make them conscious of the importance of priestly vocations. The local community has a responsibility to foster vocations so that the people will not be left without the priceless gift of the Eucharist.

THE CHURCH'S NEED OF RENEWAL

We enter upon this eucharistic year with a deep consciousness that the Church is in dire need of renewal. Although it remains irrevocably holy in its divine head and in its apostolic heritage of faith, sacraments, and ministry, the Church is sinful in its members and in constant need of being purified. Many of the faithful are ignorant of its teachings; some few defiantly reject them. Even the clergy are not exempt from grave and scandalous sins, as we have learned all too well in recent years. The Church can be renewed only by turning with ardent love to its eucharistic

Lord, asking to be fed on the Bread of Angels and refreshed from the wellsprings of salvation.

Imperfect in holiness, the Church is likewise feeble in its unity. It suffers from tensions among national and ethnic groups and from ideological conflicts between different factions. At the table of the Lord, all these differences can be taken up into a higher unity. The worshipers become like grains in a single loaf, drops in one chalice.

To be Catholic is often a mere label that we use without any realization of what catholicity involves. We use it to justify our particularism over and against others. But our horizons are too narrow. The Eucharist can enable us to rise above this timid and inward-looking mentality. It will inflame us with Christ's loving desire to share the joy of the saints with all the world. As the first fruits of the new creation, the Eucharist can make us look forward in hope to the new heavens and the new earth.

Apostolicity is also difficult to maintain. In spite of our faith, we run the risk of being cut off from the vine that gives true life. The prevalent secular and democratic culture tricks us into imagining that we can produce whatever we need for our salvation. But the Eucharist reminds us that grace and salvation come from on high and that they are channeled through Christ and the apostles. We must humbly receive redemption through disciples commissioned to speak and act in the person of Christ. The Church is most of all itself when it gathers in worship around its apostolic leaders, who maintain communion with one another and with their predecessors in the faith. Through the Eucharist celebrated in this way, Christ assembles his flock: one, holy, catholic, and apostolic.

28. WHAT DISTINGUISHES THE JESUITS?

January 15–22, 2007

(Lecture delivered on November 9, 2006.)

This lecture is intended to complete a series of four on the Jesuit founders whose jubilees are being celebrated this year. At Fordham we have had in 2006 one lecture on St. Ignatius, one on Peter Faber, one on Francis Xavier, and now, to complete the series, a lecture on the Ignatian charism today.

The notion of the Ignatian charism requires some explanation. A charism is a gift of grace, conferred not for one's personal sanctification but for the benefit of others. St. Paul has a famous list of charisms in the twelfth chapter of the First Letter to the Corinthians. They include the gifts of prophecy, speech, miracle-working, and the interpretation of tongues. If these are charisms bestowed on some members of the Church, what charisms, if any, are given to St. Ignatius of Loyola? Who are the beneficiaries? Are these charisms still bestowed today? And if so, who are the recipients?

In what follows I shall speak principally of the gifts that St. Ignatius possessed in an eminent way and that he expected to be applied and handed down with God's help in the society he founded.

The life of St. Ignatius was remarkably focused. Beginning with his long convalescence at Loyola after being wounded at Pamplona in 1521, he was led by God through a series of stages culminating in the foundation and organization of the Society of Jesus. Although the society, when first officially established in 1540, had only ten members, including the inner circle of the three whose anniversaries we celebrate this year, all ten recognized without a shadow of doubt that the true founder of the Society of Jesus, under God, was none other than Ignatius. He was endowed with an extraordinary gift—charism, one may say—of leadership. His primary achievement was the founding of a new religious order in many ways quite unlike any order that had previously existed. It was an order of men vowed to live in the midst of the world with their eyes continually focused on God, on Jesus Christ, and on the needs of the Church.

These three foci of the Ignatian vision are compactly expressed in the bull of Pope Paul III in 1540, confirmed by a similar bull of Julius III in 1550. Both these documents quoted in full the Formula of the Institute composed by Ignatius himself. The formula begins with these lapidary words: "Whoever desires to serve as a soldier of God beneath the banner of the cross in our Society, which we desire to be designated by the name of Jesus, and to serve the Lord alone and the Church his Spouse, under the Roman pontiff, the vicar of Christ on earth, should, after a vow of perpetual chastity, poverty, and obedience, keep the following in mind."

FOCUSING ON GOD

The first feature of the Jesuit in this description is to be a soldier of God. Anyone who enters the society, says the formula, must "first of all keep before his eyes God and then the nature of this Institute which he has embraced and which is, so to speak, a pathway to God." According to his custom, Ignatius here distinguishes between the means and the end. The end for which the Jesuit order exists is the greater glory of God. In the constitutions he composed for the society, Ignatius repeats the formula *"ad maiorem Dei gloriam"* in the same or similar words 376 times. Because God is God, he deserves all the praise and service we can give him. The use of the comparative "greater" (*maiorem*) is significant. It signifies the desire to excel, to seek ever more (*magis*). What we have done and are presently doing is never enough.

FOLLOWING JESUS CHRIST

The life of the Jesuit according to the institute is in the second place centered on Jesus Christ, who is, in the phrase of St. Ignatius, the way that leads to life. The Formula of the Institute specifies that the society is to be designated by the name of Jesus. St. Ignatius never thought of himself as the head of the Jesuits. He wanted only to be a companion in the following of Jesus, the true head of the society.

St. Ignatius received a remarkable grace while praying at the chapel of La Storta, just outside Rome, in October 1537, together with Peter Faber and Diego Laínez. He was, as he declares, "very specially visited by the Lord," whom he saw carrying his cross on his shoulder in the presence of his Father, who said to Ignatius, "I want you to serve us." From that moment forth, St. Ignatius never doubted that the Father had placed him with the Son; he insisted adamantly that the new congregation ought to be called the Society of Jesus.

Already in the meditation on the Two Standards in the Spiritual Exercises, written some years earlier, Ignatius had the retreatant ask for the grace to be received under the standard of Christ. And so in the Formula of the Institute he has those entering the society express the desire to fight under the banner of the Cross. This is a commitment to struggle ceaselessly against great odds and to fight bravely, not heeding the wounds, imitating the example of Christ who embraced the Cross to accomplish our redemption.

SERVING THE CHURCH

The third component is the ecclesial. Totally and unequivocally a man of the Church, Ignatius writes in the Formula of the Institute that the prospective Jesuit must be resolved to serve "the Lord alone and the Church his spouse." Here we may detect an echo of Ignatius's famous "Rules for Thinking with the Church," at the conclusion of the Spiritual Exercises, where he refuses to admit any discrepancy between the service of Christ and the Church. "I must be convinced," he writes, "that in Christ our Lord, the bridegroom, and in His spouse the Church, only one Spirit holds sway, which governs and rules for the salvation of souls." The hierarchical and Roman Church, he says, is "the true Spouse of Christ our Lord, our holy Mother."

St. Ignatius's allegiance is not to some abstract idea of the Church, but to the Church as it concretely exists on earth, with the Roman pontiff at its summit. The popes of St. Ignatius's day may not have been the holiest and the wisest of men, but he looked upon them with the eyes of faith and saw in each of them the vicar of Christ for the teaching and government of the universal Church. As early as 1534, when the original seven companions took their vows at Montmartre, they had the idea of placing themselves at the disposal of the pope, asking him to assign them to the missions he considered most pressing. After the papal approval of the institute in 1540, Ignatius established himself at Rome, where he spent the rest of his life in order to be accessible to the pope.

As yet I have stated the goal of the Society of Jesus in only the most general terms—the glory of God, the service of Christ, and availability to the pope. Ignatius still had to specify what kind of service his order would be prepared to offer. This too is mentioned in the Formula of the Institute. In the sentence following the one I have quoted, St. Ignatius writes: Whoever wishes to enter should know that he is asking to be "a member of a Society founded chiefly for this purpose: to strive especially for the defense and propagation of the faith and for the progress of souls in Christian life and doctrine." And then he mentions various means whereby these goals are to be achieved: "public preaching, other ministries of the word of God, spiritual exercises, education in Christianity, hearing confessions, and administering other sacraments." And then in the next sentence the formula speaks of certain works of charity: reconciling the estranged, ministering to persons in prisons and hospitals, and similar services.

TEN SHINING FEATURES OF THE SOCIETY OF JESUS

A number of attempts have been made in recent years to gather up certain principles that shine through the writings of St. Ignatius and are envisaged as permanent features of the society he founded. Any such list presupposes, of course, the common elements of all religious orders in the Catholic Church, including the faithful observance of the usual vows of religion: poverty, chastity, and obedience. The following ten features may serve as a summary of what is more specific to the spirit of St. Ignatius.

1. Dedication to the glory of God, the "ever greater God," whom we can never praise and serve enough. This gives the Jesuit a kind of holy restlessness, a ceaseless effort to do better, to achieve the more or, in Latin, the *magis*. Ignatius may be said to have been a God-intoxicated man in the sense that he made "the greater glory of God" the supreme norm of every action, great or small.

2. Personal love for Jesus Christ and a desire to be counted among his close companions. Repeatedly in the Exercises Jesuits pray to know Christ more clearly, to love him more dearly, and to follow him more nearly. Preaching in the towns of Italy, the first companions deliberately imitated the style of life of the disciples whom Jesus had sent forth to evangelize the towns of Galilee.

3. To labor with, in, and for the Church, thinking at all times with the Church in obedience to its pastors. Throughout the constitutions, Ignatius insists on the teaching of the doctrine

that is "safer and more approved," so that students may learn the "more solid and safe doctrine."

4. Availability. To be at the disposal of the Church, available to labor in any place, for the sake of the greater and more universal good. Regarding the society as the spiritual militia of the pope, St. Ignatius sees the whole world, so to speak, as his field of operations. Inspired by this cosmic vision, he admits no divisions based on national frontiers and ethnic ties.

5. Mutual union. Jesuits are to see themselves as parts of a body bound together by a communion of minds and hearts. In the constitutions St. Ignatius asserted that the society could not attain its ends unless its members were united by deep affection among themselves and with the head. Many authors quote in this connection the term used by Ignatius of his first companions: "friends in the Lord."

6. Preference for spiritual and priestly ministries. The Jesuits are a priestly order, all of whose professed members must be ordained, although the cooperation of spiritual and lay coadjutors is highly valued. In the choice of ministries, Ignatius writes, "spiritual goods ought to be preferred to bodily," since they are more conducive to the "ultimate and supernatural end."

7. Discernment. Ignatius was a master of the practical life and the art of decision-making. He distinguished carefully between ends and means, choosing the means best suited to achieve the end in view. In the use of means he consistently applied the principle "*tantum . . . quantum,*" meaning "as much as helps," but not more. In this connection he teaches the discipline of indifference in the sense of detachment from anything that is not to be sought for its own sake.

8. Adaptability. Ignatius always paid close attention to the times, places, and persons with which he was dealing. He took care to frame general laws in such a way as to allow for flexibility in application.

9. Respect for human and natural capacities. Although Igna-
    tius relied primarily on spiritual means, such as divine grace,
    prayer, and sacramental ministry, he took account of natural
    abilities, learning, culture, and manners as gifts to be used
    for the service and glory of God. For this reason he showed a
    keen interest in education.

10. An original synthesis of the active and the contemplative life.
    Jerome Nadal (1507–80) spoke of the Jesuit practice "of seek-
    ing a perfection in our prayer and spiritual exercises in order
    to help our neighbor, and by means of that help of neighbor
    acquiring yet more perfection in prayer, in order to help our
    neighbor even more." According to Nadal, it is a special grace
    of the whole society to be contemplative not only in moments
    of withdrawal but also in the midst of action, thus "seeking
    God in all things."

WISDOM FROM RECENT POPES

In view of my assignment to speak of the Ignatian charism today,
I shall shift immediately to the twentieth century and to the
years since the Second Vatican Council. The popes, as the highest
superiors of all Jesuits, have given us wise directives regarding
the application of our Jesuit charism to the needs of the day. They
have addressed each of the four general congregations held since
1965. On the theory that the charism of the society is correlative
with its mission, I shall particularly examine the injunctions of
recent popes.

Addressing the thirty-first General Congregation on May 7,
1966, Pope Paul VI congratulated the society for being "the legion
ever faithful to the task of protecting the Catholic faith and the
Apostolic See." He took the occasion to charge the Jesuits with
a new mission: to make a "stout, united stand against atheism,"
which was rapidly spreading at the time, "frequently masquer-
ading as cultural, scientific, or social progress."

In an address to the second session of the same congregation on November 16, 1966, Paul VI raised questions about whether some Jesuits were accepting naturalistic norms for their apostolate and weakening in that traditional loyalty to the Holy See that had been so dear to St. Ignatius. In its *Decree on the Mission of the Society Today* General Congregation 31 accepted the mandate to confront atheism and offered the society completely to the Church under the direction of the pope. In his address to the thirty-second General Congregation on December 3, 1974, Pope Paul VI referred to the "vocation and charism proper to Jesuits," transmitted by an unbroken tradition, which includes conformity to the will of God and that of the Church. In a valuable analysis, he reminded Jesuits of their fourfold vocation: to be religious, to be apostolic, to be priests, and to be united with the bishop of Rome. He admonished them not to be seduced by the dazzling perspective of worldly humanism and the pursuit of novelty for its own sake. In subsequent correspondence he renewed his earlier warnings that the Society of Jesus should retain its religious and priestly character and avoid ways of action more appropriate to secular institutes and lay movements. The role of ordained Jesuits, he said, should be clearly distinct from the role of laity.

In response, the thirty-second General Congregation strongly reaffirmed the society's reverence and loyalty to the Holy See and to the magisterium of the Church. It underlined the sacerdotal (or priestly) character of the society, while recognizing the value of the contribution of lay coadjutors.

Pope John Paul II, on September 2, 1983, delivered a homily to the thirty-third General Congregation. The Ignatian spirit, he said, is a special charism that makes the Society of Jesus a privileged instrument of the Church's action at all levels. After repeating the mandate of Paul VI to resist atheism, he spoke of the danger of confusing the tasks proper to priests with those of the laity. "Intimate knowledge, strong love, and closer following of the Lord," he said, "are the soul of your vocation."

John Paul II, in his allocution to General Congregation 34 on January 5, 1995, spoke of the singular charism of fidelity to the successor of Peter, which marks out the Society of Jesus as being "totally and without reservation of the Church, in the Church, and for the Church." The charism of the society, he said, should make Jesuits witnesses to the primacy of God and his will, which points to the primacy of spirituality and prayer. He asked that Jesuits, seeking to follow the leadership of St. Francis Xavier in missionary evangelization, be in the forefront of the new evangelization, promoting a deep interior relationship with Jesus Christ, the first evangelizer. In their universities, His Holiness said, Jesuits should teach clear, solid, organic knowledge of Catholic doctrine. They should be very attentive not to confuse their students by questionable teachings, at variance with the Church's doctrine on faith and morals.

Benedict XVI, in a speech of April 22, 2006, celebrating the current jubilee year, exhorted the society to continue in its tradition of imparting solid training in philosophy and theology as a basis for dialogue with modern culture. The Society of Jesus, he said, enjoys an extraordinary legacy in the holiness of St. Ignatius, the missionary zeal of Francis Xavier, and the apostolate of Peter Faber among leaders of the Reformation. In many of his addresses this pope has aligned himself with Paul VI and John Paul II by insisting that the primary and indispensable task of the priest is to be an expert in the spiritual life and a witness to the truth of revelation. The promotion of justice in society, he believes, is primarily a responsibility of the laity.

CHALLENGES: IGNATIUS'S DAY AND OUR DAY

The challenges of our day are certainly different from those of the sixteenth century, but they are, I believe, analogous, and for this reason, I would contend, the society is well positioned to deal with them. Its charism is by no means outdated. The sixteenth century, like our own, was a time of rapid and radical cultural

change. That time witnessed the rise of anthropocentric humanism, the birth of the secular state, and the autonomy of the social
and physical sciences. Jesuits who have studied their own tradition have stellar examples of scholars who equipped themselves
to enter into these new fields and show the coherence between
the new learning and the Catholic heritage of faith. We have
only to think of the economic and legal philosophy of Luis de
Molina (1535–1600) and Juan de Lugo (1583–1660), the astronom-
ical achievements of Christopher Clavius (1537–1612), the atomic
theories of Roger Boscovich (1711–87), and so many other great
Jesuit thinkers of the past. They spoke incisively to the problems
of their day, building bridges between faith and reason, between
theology and science. In our day some Jesuits are venturing into
questions concerning cosmic and human origins and into complex problems of biochemistry and genetic engineering, all of
which are so vital for the future of faith and morals.

The sixteenth century had early experiences of globalization. It was the great age of discovery. Jesuits, eager to evangelize the whole world, were leaders in the missionary apostolate
to the Americas, to parts of Africa, to India and the Far East.
They not only sent missionaries but also trained them to present
the Gospel in a manner suited to the cultures of various peoples. Francis Xavier (1506–22) is the most famous, but he was by
no means alone. Matteo Ricci (1552–1610) and Robert de Nobili
(1577–1656) are only two of dozens of outstanding missionaries
who preached the Gospel in an inculturated form, inspired by
the principles of St. Ignatius.

Proclamation in an accommodated style is not less needed
today than in the past. The fields are white for the harvest, but
the laborers are few. Who can better fill the urgent demand for
priests to proclaim the Gospel and administer the sacraments in
continents like Africa, where conversions to Christianity are so
numerous and so rapid? Jesuits in the young churches, if they
are well trained, can take up the task left to them by foreign
missionaries.

The age of Ignatius was no stranger to the clash of civilizations. The Muslim world and the Christian world were engaged in incessant warfare. Jews were being mistreated and persecuted in many countries. Jesuit missionaries encountered fierce opposition from religious leaders in practically every country they evangelized. In the course of time, they became leaders in interreligious dialogue. Missionaries learned to respect the good things in native cultures while sifting out the chaff. That is still a task of great urgency today. Jesuits have in their tradition rich resources for learning how and how not to deal with non-Christian religions. Bloody conflict and useless provocation must be avoided, while, on the other hand, Christians must frankly oppose elements in every religion and every culture that promote superstition or injustice.

The sixteenth century saw the division of Western Christianity between the Protestant nations of northern Europe and the Catholic nations of the south. The Jesuits, few though they were in number, accomplished great things by their energy and heroism. Peter Faber (1506–46) did extraordinary work to stem the tide of heresy in Germany and the Low Countries. He inspired Peter Canisius (1521–97) and a host of others to go forward in his footsteps. One wonders what the Jesuits of those days would have done if they were alive today to see the defection of so many Latino Catholics from the Church in the United States and in Central and South America. The need is evident; the principles are clear; but there are all too few talented candidates to take up the task.

Centralization of the Church was imperative in the days of St. Ignatius. He himself clearly perceived the need for the papacy as the headquarters of the universal Church. He saw that Catholicism must be universal and that nationalism and ethnocentrism could have no place in it. He founded a society made up of Spaniards, Portuguese, Frenchmen, Germans, Italians, Englishmen, and many others who worked together in an undivided apostolate under the direction of a single general superior. One of the great blessings of the Society of Jesus, today as in the past, is its worldwide horizon. Jesuits are "friends in the Lord" undivided by distinctions of nationality, ethnic origin, or social class.

A great weakness of the Church in the Europe of St. Ignatius's day was ignorance of the faith. Many priests were barely literate, and the laity in some countries did not know the basic elements of the creed. Rather than complain and denounce, Ignatius preferred to build. Popular education, he perceived, was on the rise. Taking advantage of the new desire for learning, Ignatius quickly set about founding schools, colleges, and seminaries. The educational efforts of the Jesuits in the past count among their greatest services to the Church. These educational institutions, I believe, are still among the major blessings that the Society of Jesus offers to the Church and to the culture at large.

Jesuits in the past have entered deeply into the intellectual apostolate. Many were leaders in practical sciences such as political theory. They can look back on a great tradition extending from Francisco Suárez in the sixteenth century to John Courtney Murray in the twentieth. Nothing suggests that this type of research has lost its relevance. The Church needs loyal and devoted scholars who will carry this type of reflection further, in view of new and developing situations. Here again the society has much to contribute if sufficient numbers will hear the call.

In the sixteenth century, the Society of Jesus was at the vanguard of the Church in dealing with the problems posed by the Protestant Reformation, by the new science, and by access to new continents that had been beyond the awareness of Europeans in the past. Today the Church is confronted with mounting secularism, with new advances in technology, and growing globalization and an attending clash of cultures. If anyone should ask whether these developments render the Ignatian charisms obsolete, I would reply with an emphatic no.

The society can be abreast of the times if it adheres to its original purpose and ideals. The term "Jesuit" is often misunderstood. Not to mention enemies for whom Jesuit is a term of opprobrium, friends of the society sometimes identify the term with independence of thought and corporate pride, both of which St. Ignatius deplored. Others reduce the Jesuit trademark to a matter of educational techniques, such as the personal care of students, concern for the whole person, rigor in thought, and eloquence in expression. These qualities are estimable and have a basis in the teaching of St. Ignatius. But they omit any consideration of the fact that the Society of Jesus is an order of vowed religious in the Catholic Church. They are bound by special allegiance to the pope, the bishop of Rome. And above all, it needs to be mentioned that the Society of Jesus is primarily about a person: Jesus, the redeemer of the world. If the society were to lose its special devotion to the Lord (which, I firmly trust, will never happen), it would indeed be obsolete. It would be like salt that had lost its savor.

EVANGELIZING THE WORLD

The greatest need of the Society of Jesus, I believe, is to be able to project a clearer vision of its purpose. Its members are engaged in such diverse activities that its unity is obscured. In this respect the recent popes have rendered great assistance. Paul VI helpfully reminded Jesuits that they are a religious order, not a secular institute; that they are a priestly order, not a lay association; that they are apostolic, not monastic; and that they are bound to obedience to the pope, not wholly self-directed. Pope John Paul II, in directing Jesuits to engage in the new evangelization, identified a focus that perfectly matches the founding idea of the society. Ignatius was adamant in insisting that it be named for Jesus, its true head. The Spiritual Exercises are centered on the gospels. Evangelization is exactly what the first Jesuits did as they conducted missions in the towns of Italy. They lived lives of evangelical poverty. Evangelization was the sum and substance of what St. Francis Xavier accomplished in his arduous missionary journeys. And evangelization is at the heart of all Jesuit apostolates

in teaching, in research, in spirituality, and in the social apostolate. Evangelization, moreover, is what the world most sorely
needs today. The figure of Jesus Christ in the gospels has not lost
its attraction. Who should be better qualified to present that figure today than members of the society that bears his name?

29. A LIFE IN THEOLOGY

April 21, 2008

(Lecture originally given on April 1, 2008.)

I t is a matter of surprise that I have occupied the Laurence J. McGinley Chair in Religion and Society for twenty years. When I reached the statutory retirement age at the Catholic University of America in 1988, I received several academic offers. As a Jesuit, I consulted my provincial superior as to which I should accept, and he replied that I should await an offer from Fordham that was still in the making. In another month I received a letter from Joseph A. O'Hare, S.J., the president of Fordham, inviting me to be the first holder of this new professorship named for the president emeritus, Laurence J. McGinley, S.J. Fr. O'Hare gave me a choice of accepting for two years or for one year renewable. Being of a cautious nature, I opted for the second alternative. As it turned out, there was no limit on the number of possible renewals, which have cordially been extended both by Fr. O'Hare and by his successor Fr. Joseph McShane, and so here I am, twenty years later, still sitting on the metaphorical chair.

Why, then, a farewell? Why not thirty or forty years on this blissful seat? In this life, unfortunately, all good things must come to an end. I was already making serious preparations to resign when I began to be stricken with a succession of health problems, all resulting from a bout of polio dating from 1945, when I was a naval officer in World War II. Until at least the year 2000 it seemed that I had pretty well overcome the disabilities, but the aftereffects began to manifest themselves in recent years, and in the past year they have become so acute as to prevent me from doing the teaching, lecturing, and writing that my duties here at Fordham require. Divine providence, which has graciously guided my career throughout these many years, is giving clear signs that it is time to move on and make way for a younger and healthier successor.

Among the principal responsibilities attached to the McGinley Chair are the semiannual public lectures that I have been delivering since the fall of 1988. This lecture ought by rights to be the fortieth, but because I had to miss one lecture back in 1994, there are only thirty-nine. The first thirty-eight have been gathered into a book just published by Fordham University Press. The book will probably be the most substantial, if not the sole, memorial of my tenure of the McGinley Chair.

SELECTION OF TOPICS

All told, I have given hundreds of lectures on a great variety of themes during the past twenty years, but the McGinley lectures belong in a category by themselves. I have given them my closest attention to make sure of having in each case a publishable text. Whereas in other cases the theme has usually been set by the persons issuing the invitation, almost all the topics and titles of the McGinley lectures are my own.

The designation of my professorship—religion and society—leaves open a very wide field of choice, ranging from the religious to the secular, from ecclesiastical doctrine to social analysis. I have spoken on strictly theological themes such as the sacrifice of the Cross, the real presence of Christ in the Eucharist, and heaven and hell. But also, gravitating toward the societal pole, I have talked of secular themes such as politics, human rights, and the death penalty.

In the selection of topics I have followed three criteria.

First of all, I wanted all the topics to have at least a theological dimension. A theologian is what I am, and I work within the Catholic tradition, which is my home. Although I try not to display ignorance of fields such as philosophy, history, literature, and sociology, insofar as they are relevant to my inquiry, I claim competence only in theology.

In the second place, I attempted to concentrate on themes that were matters of debate among Catholic theologians. These lectures are not a simple exercise in catechesis or Christian doctrine. In every instance, I suspect, a controversy is being addressed, or at least lurks in the background. My intention is to give an informed judgment as to which positions are sound and which should be rejected.

Third, I have tried to choose topics of general interest not reserved to a small clique of specialists. For these lectures are public. I make an effort to avoid theological jargon and to speak a language that all educated Christians can understand. I recognize the necessity of using technical terms for discussing recondite questions, and even in these lectures I borrow from the Church councils terms such as "substantial presence" and "subsisting in," but I hope I have made these terms generally intelligible. Theologians are sometimes tempted to display their erudition by adopting the most recent coinages of sophisticated European intellectuals even when the terminology serves more to obscure than to clarify their message.

As I glance over the titles of my McGinley lectures, I have the impression that they form a solid collection dealing with major theological and social issues inherited from the Second Vatican Council and still under discussion today. I dare to hope that the opinions I have proposed and defended are true and persuasive. The faith that underlies them is not true today and false tomorrow; its teachings are permanent and universal.

A certain number of these McGinley lectures, I acknowledge, are linked with events now past, such as the advent of the third millennium. Pope John Paul II, however, used the great jubilee as a teaching moment to impress on the faithful ideas that should guide them, and us, at all times. The teaching ministry of that extraordinary pope until his death in 2005 gave me much necessary guidance.

LISTENING AND LEARNING BEFORE SPEAKING

I cannot claim that these lectures are unified by a single method. In each case the method has to be adapted to the topic. But in general I have begun my investigation by asking what others, especially authoritative voices, have had to say about pertinent questions. I want to learn before I speak. If all the witnesses agree, and if there are no unanswered objections, it will be sufficient to note the consensus. But because I have deliberately selected controversial topics, I have generally found both agreements and disagreements. After ascertaining the spectrum of opinions, I search out the best arguments in favor of each major position. To present and classify the existing opinions is, I take it, a service to theology, but I think it necessary also to criticize views that are inadequate. Feeling a responsibility to reach a judgment, I draw conclusions that bring me into conflict with some of my colleagues. In my conclusions I try to incorporate the valid insights of all parties to the discussion, rather than perpetuate a one-sided view that is partial and incomplete. I think of myself as a moderate trying to make peace between opposed schools of thought. While doing so, however, I insist on logical consistency. Unlike certain relativists of our time, I abhor mixtures of contradictions.

I mentioned above that I speak as a theologian. By that term I mean that I draw conclusions from what I believe as a Catholic Christian. The Church teaches, and I firmly believe, that the Son of God became man some two thousand years ago, died to redeem us, and rose for the sake of our salvation. Christ the Redeemer, who has given the fullness of revelation, has also made provision for the revelation to be kept alive in the Church without corruption or dilution. These basic teachings of our faith, held in common by all believers, are presupposed by Catholic theology. The faith takes nothing away from what I can know by my native reasoning powers, but it adds a vast new light coming from on high.

In my lectures, then, I have made continual use of Christian revelation as conveyed through holy scripture and Catholic tradition. I am reluctant to say anything that runs against these sacred sources on the pretext that we have superior insight today. Respect for the deposit of faith should not be called conservatism in the pejorative sense but a simple loyalty to the Word of God. When in these lectures I affirm that Jesus sacrificed himself on the Cross, or that he makes himself substantially present in the Eucharist, or that the gate to salvation is a narrow one, or that priestly ordination is reserved to men, or that capital punishment is sometimes warranted, in each case I am willingly adhering to the testimony of scripture and perennial Catholic tradition.

These lectures, I hope, make it clear that tradition is a developing thing because the Church lives in history. Tradition develops in fidelity to its own deepest principles, as this set of lectures illustrates, for instance, with reference to religious freedom and Mariology. To anticipate what developments are appropriate often requires an exceptional sense of the faith. Developments of doctrine always involve a certain continuity; a reversal of course is not a development.

As the reader will easily discover, I do not particularly strive for originality. Very few new ideas, I suspect, are true. If I conceived a theological idea that had never occurred to anyone in the past, I would have every reason to think myself mistaken. The current confusion in theology is in no small part due to a plethora of innovations, which last a few years only to be overtaken by further, and equally ephemeral, theories. The effort to keep up with the latest theological fashions is hardly a profitable investment of time. Far more valuable would it be to insert oneself in the great tradition of the Fathers and Doctors of the Church. I myself try to think and speak within that tradition, while taking due notice of new and deviant opinions.

Without in any way comparing myself to Pope Benedict XVI, I feel that I can make his words my own when he writes:

I have never tried to create a system of my own, an individual theology. What is specific, if you want to call it that, is that I simply want to think in communion with the faith of the Church, and that means above all to think in communion with the great thinkers of the faith. The aim is not an isolated theology that I draw out of myself but one that opens as widely as possible into the common intellectual pathways of the faith. (*Salt of the Earth* [1997], 66)

These words speak very powerfully to me because, as a Jesuit, I am committed to St. Ignatius of Loyola's "Rules for Thinking with the Church."

THE QUEST FOR ETERNAL TRUTH AND WISDOM

The present climate of opinion does not favor tradition and orthodoxy, two terms that have negative connotations for many hearers. Our culture is dominated by experimental science, which works by entirely different methods, leaving its own past behind as it forges into the future. Science, we all know, does not rest on a treasury of revealed knowledge handed down in authoritative tradition. Science has wonderfully increased our powers to make and to destroy, but it does not tell us what we ought to do and why. It does not tell us where the universe came from, or why we exist or what our final destination is. And yet some scientists speak as though their discipline were the only kind of valid knowledge.

This brand of scientism has been around for centuries, but only today is it boasting of its powers to displace philosophical wisdom and religious faith, as I noted in my McGinley lecture "God and Evolution," a year ago. Already as a college undergraduate seventy years ago, I felt the oppressive nature of a culture that had no place for objective moral norms and meaning. I was desperate for enlightenment about whether there was anything worth living and dying for, as I explained in one of my earliest books, *A Testimonial to Grace*. That very desperation set me on the path that led through ancient Greek philosophy to Catholic faith.

All of us today are immersed in a culture that lacks abiding truths and fixed moral norms. But there is no necessity for our culture to have taken this negative turn. Ancient philosophers, like Plato and Aristotle, had refuted the materialism, relativism, subjectivism, and hedonism of their day and had shown the validity of metaphysical knowledge. Western thought followed in the path of cognitive realism for many centuries before the revival of agnosticism in the Renaissance. Catholic believers and indeed all clear thinkers have good reasons not to be engulfed in the superficial trends of the times. In his great encyclical *Faith and Reason* (1998), which forms the topic of one McGinley lecture, John Paul II summoned philosophy to resume its original quest for eternal truth and wisdom.

As mentioned earlier, I entered college in a quagmire of confusion about whether life and the universe could make sense at all. I was conscious of the emptiness of a selfish life based on the pursuit of pleasure. Happiness, I gradually came to see, is the reward given for holding fast to what is truly good and important. To some extent the philosophers of antiquity identified these goals. But Christian revelation brought a tremendous increase of light. God alone, I learned from the New Testament, was good and true in an unqualified sense. And the same God in all his beauty and majesty became one of our human family in Jesus Christ, the truth, the way, and the life. The most important thing about my career, and many of yours, I feel sure, is the discovery of the pearl of great price, the treasure hidden in the field, the Lord Jesus himself.

As I approach the termination of my active life, I gratefully acknowledge that a benign providence has governed my days. The persons I have met, the places I have been, the things I have been asked to do, have all coalesced into a pattern, so that each stage of my life has prepared me for the next. My twenty years on the McGinley Chair have been a kind of climax, at least from my personal point of view. I often feel that there is no one on earth with whom I would want to exchange places. It has been a special privilege to serve in the Society of Jesus, a religious community specially dedicated to the Savior of the world.

The good life does not have to be an easy one, as our blessed Lord and the saints have taught us. Pope John Paul II in his later years used to say, "The pope must suffer." Suffering and diminishment are not the greatest of evils, but are normal ingredients in life, especially in old age. They are to be accepted as elements of a full human existence. Well into my ninetieth year I have been able to work productively. As I become increasingly paralyzed and unable to speak, I can identify with the many paralytics and mute persons in the gospels, grateful for the loving and skillful care I receive and for the hope of everlasting life in Christ. If the Lord now calls me to a period of weakness, I know well that his power can be made perfect in infirmity. "Blessed be the name of the Lord!"

BOOK REVIEWS

30. REVIEW OF
THE COUNCIL, REFORM
AND REUNION
by Hans Küng (trans. by Cecily Hastings)

March 31, 1962

Almost as soon as Pope John XXIII announced his intention
to convoke a general council which would be oriented
toward Christian reunion, Catholic theologians in Europe
began discussing among themselves, and with their Protestant
colleagues, how the coming council could contribute to that goal.
As a result of these discussions, several books have already been
published, embodying not simply the opinions of individuals
but the fruits of cooperative study.

None of these books, in my judgment, is more worthy of
attention than Hans Küng's *The Council, Reform and Reunion*. The
author, a young Swiss priest who teaches at Tübingen in Germany, is thoroughly familiar with the points at issue in the current dialogue with Protestantism. The key to reunion, as he sees
it, lies in a renovation of the Church according to the Gospel.
Such a renewal, he points out, is not simply a matter of good
administration or moral effort; it must be a supernatural work
done in obedience to Christ, the Lord of the Church.

The opening chapters of this book, which treat of the necessity
and possibility of reform, present the author's ideas on worldli-
ness and sin in the Church. In his emphasis on these distress-
ing facts, Küng seems to minimize unduly the effects of grace.
Notwithstanding her constant need for purification, the Church

remains at all times a great and manifest sign of holiness and beneficence.

The later chapters, in which the author discusses concrete measures that might be adopted by the Second Vatican Council, will be the most avidly read. In all probability the council will center its attention on the nature of the episcopal office, thus complementing the work of the First Vatican Council, which concentrated on papal primacy.

But what authority can be given to bishops which they do not presently exercise? As Küng points out, the modern diocese is not and cannot suitably be made an autonomous unit. But he thinks that the authority of national and continental bishops' conferences ought to be strengthened. In this way the Church's proclamation of the Gospel, its liturgy, and its discipline could be adapted to the needs of various peoples. Other reforms, touching on the Mass, the breviary, marriage courts, prohibition of books, and so forth, could be most suitably effected by regional authorities of this kind rather than by the Holy See. Many of Küng's recommendations, such as those regarding the vernacular in the liturgy, the index, and married deacons, have often been voiced before.

Ruthlessly frank, Küng protests sharply against various current practices in the Church: the Vatican bureaucracy, the predominance of Italian bishops (290, as against Germany's 26), "Marian maximalism," and superstition in popular devotions. It is well that such criticisms should be voiced, for they represent the responsible judgment of not only a significant portion of Catholics but also the overwhelming majority of non-Catholics.

Küng's recommendations for decentralization, while deserving serious consideration, are not free from difficulties. Many would fear that the diffusion of power for which the author pleads might result in a multiplication of laws, which he would deplore. Roman centralization, whatever its defects, has at least held in check the tendency of lower authorities to introduce too many local laws and usages. It has also assured that the needs of the universal Church should prevail over any particular interests. In the rapidly shrinking world of our day, centralization is daily becoming more feasible, and perhaps also more imperative.

Küng seems to address himself primarily to the bishops and theologians making plans for the coming council. But he writes with such verve and clarity that his work will reach a far wider audience. Even if it makes little impact on the council, this book will have a great and salutary influence on the way in which many readers, both Catholic and non-Catholic, look on the contemporary situation of the Church and the prospects for reunion.

The translation is accurate and highly idiomatic. But one regrets that the footnotes had to be relegated to the ends of chapters and that a disproportionate number of foreign names and references have been mangled by the printer.

31. REVIEW OF *A QUESTION OF CONSCIENCE*

by Charles Davis

November 11, 1967

M any will buy this book out of curiosity, hoping that it will unveil the intimate details of the author's conflicts with ecclesiastical superiors or of his romance with Florence Henderson. Such readers will be disappointed, since Charles Davis is not particularly interested in his own personal history. He remains what he was before, a theologian absorbed in ideas.

Still a staunch believer, he discourses with meticulous orthodoxy about the triune God, the Incarnation, and the act of faith. He continues to look upon the Church of Christ as a visible and indefectible community, which officially actualizes itself through the seven sacraments. He still defends celibacy as a meaningful vocation, highly appropriate for the clergy. Nearly all the key ideas in this book re-echo those of leading Catholic theologians. While it would be easy to see how an irresponsible radical might leave the Church, it is far more difficult to understand how a theological moderate such as Davis should feel obliged to take this course. *A Question of Conscience* provides the answer.

As a conscientious churchman and a progressive thinker, Charles Davis found himself inwardly torn between two mentalities, both current in Roman Catholicism. The first mentality looks upon truth as an impersonal datum, capable of being captured in immutable formulations. This epistemology leads to a strictly hierarchical ecclesiology, in which a statically conceived "deposit of faith" is mediated by a divinely commissioned class. In an earlier age, when men took it for granted that the cosmos was a system of rigidly graded orders, this objectivist view of truth and of the Church seemed almost self-evident. But today, Davis tells us, the notion that truth can be statically mediated by a divinely instituted hierarchical authority has lost credibility. All reality, man included, is seen in terms of process and historicity. This means that all doctrinal statements, however solemn, are historically conditioned and in this sense relative.

Even on this perspectival view of truth, to which Davis subscribes, official standards of belief may have a certain abiding authority. "A person who dismissed, say, the authority of the Council of Nicaea, would put himself outside the Christian tradition" (100). But the believer's appropriation of ancient doctrines is more personal, free, and responsible than formerly. Theologians must continually seek better understanding and more meaningful formulations of God's Word as it comes to us in Christ.

Thus far Davis is in substantial agreement with the great majority of respected theologians in our day. But he diverges from them in holding that the Roman Church as an institution is irrevocably committed to the "closed" view of truth and its mediation. The hierarchical nature of Catholicism, he maintains, demands that its conceptual formulations should be looked upon as stable, unchanging, and not subject to revision in the light of man's developing intelligence.

The static view of truth, Davis admits, was not that of Thomas Aquinas, nor is it that of Lonergan, Rahner, and Schillebeeckx. Without denying the good faith of progressive theologians, Davis is convinced that it is not allowable to reinterpret the ancient dogmas or temper in any way the absolutism of hierarchical authority. If he were to remain in the Church, he explains, he would feel obliged to submit unconditionally to the teaching of the magisterium taken at face value. The open and dynamic view of truth advocated by the liberals, he believes, could not prevail without undermining the essential structure of Roman Catholicism.

Davis is surely justified in repudiating what he conceives the Roman Church to be: a closed, exclusivist society that can learn nothing from other bodies or even from its own members, and obliged to cling tenaciously to conceptual systems, terms, and practices no longer relevant to our age. But it seems evident that the official Church, especially in the documents of Vatican II, understands itself more liberally than Davis does.

The *Constitution on the Church* emphatically teaches that the Church is a pilgrim people, selflessly dedicated to the promotion of God's cause in the world. The documents on ecumenism and on the non-Christian religions take the view that Catholicism cannot be narrowly complacent or exclusive. The *Constitution on the Church in the Modern World* makes it clear that the Church is not a closed society standing over against the secular world, but an active participant in the world and in its history. The *Decree on the Laity* forbids the Church to regard itself as a "hierocracy," and the *Constitution on Divine Revelation* sets forth the Word of God as a reality too rich to be neatly packaged in timeless formulas. The *Declaration on Religious Freedom*, with its insistence on the primacy of conscience, belies the idea that the Church is a "total institution" of the type that Davis so forcefully rejects.

Davis is of course aware of what the recent council did and said, but he denies that the Church can carry out the task of self-renewal that the council set for it. He seems to think that if the Church were prepared to learn anything from secular society or from other religious groups, or if the hierarchy were to listen to the laity, or if the collegiality of bishops were to become an effective reality, or if there were any appreciable decentralization or cultural pluralism in the Church, such measures would involve the Church in an "essential change" and hence in self-destruction. If the Church should essentially change, he adds, he would have to reconsider his relationship to it.

For his own interpretation of the essence of Roman Catholicism he finds support in the reactionary attitudes of some prelates and curial officials since the council. While no one would wish to excuse all that has happened, even in high places, Davis seems to exceed the bounds of charity and justice in this attack on the present pope's handling of the birth control issue. It is surprising that anyone so sensitive to personal abuse, when directed against himself and his friends (e.g., Herbert McCabe), should characterize Paul VI as a callous liar. Davis has a perfect right to be convinced that the present official stand of the magisterium on contraception is not a matter of divine law, but he should be able to appreciate the motives of others who are no less strongly convinced of the opposite view.

Besides dealing with the question whether the Church can renew itself, Davis's book raises the issue whether, even if it could do so, a renewed Catholicism would be worth having. He seems to feel that it would not. The communion of Christians in the Body of Christ, he holds, does not have to be visibly expressed by membership in a single overarching institution. He would prefer to have smaller, more flexible organizations, corresponding to particular needs.

Davis is right, I believe, in emphasizing the value of such unofficial, limited-purpose organizations, which may be in their way "ecclesial" even when not officially Catholic. But are we faced by an either/or? Can local and provisional organizations perform the total mission of the Church?

On biblical, theological, and practical grounds, it seems clear that there must be, in addition, a universal and abiding structure, although this "structure" would be far more flexible and less totalitarian than Davis thinks the Catholic Church must be. Without institutional permanence and worldwide scope, the Church could not be an effective sign or "sacrament" of the unity that God has given to mankind, in principle, in Christ.

Davis's critique of the institutional Church reflects a current mood, but the mood, I suspect, will pass. In a recent article, John C. Bennett stresses the importance of structures adequate to ensure that the Church can rise above local interests and pressures. He writes:

> The widespread rebellion against all institutions condemns the Church to futility in relation to these larger issues. It also leaves local groups without the support they need from a presbytery or bishop or board. Bureaucracies are necessary to give the Church an independent base in relation to each local situation. I have often noticed that some of the most prophetic churchmanship comes out of bureaucracies, both denominational and ecumenical. . . . Critics of the larger institutional framework tend to kick away the ladder that enabled them to climb to the point where they can see what they see. (*Christianity and Crisis*, December 26, 1966, 296)

In withdrawing from Roman Catholicism, where has Davis gone? His unwillingness to affiliate with any particular denomination leaves him in a tragically isolated situation. He admits the pain of not being able to offer the Eucharist in the communion of any Church. Does God really will that Christians should so situate themselves? Is it possible for any length of time to maintain a vigorous Christian life without joining some definite Christian community? And if it were possible, would it be the best contribution to the work of the Church, the catalyst and harbinger of that unity to which God is calling the human race? While I do not find that Charles Davis makes out his case for the irreformability of the Catholic Church or for "creative disaffiliation," I should not wish to leave a negative impression of this book. In a most compelling way, he calls attention to the dangers of an excessive concentration on the hierarchical and institutional aspects of the Church. He shows beyond doubt that those still championing nonhistorical orthodoxy and clerical paternalism are gravely jeopardizing the Church's mission in the world today. He successfully brings out the value of flexible and provisional structures with limited scope and commitment.

In these and many other respects, this book points out directions in which I hope and expect that the Catholic Church will move. For mature and theologically sophisticated readers, a careful study of this clear and thoughtful work will be amply rewarding.

32. REVIEW OF
THE CHURCH

by Hans Küng

April 20, 1968

O nly Hans Küng could have written this book. It reflects the same combination of painstaking scholarship, lucidity, and reforming zeal that his early works do. It shows the same passionate concern for the renewal of the Church, for Christian unity, and for appropriating the valid insights of the Reformation.

After an introductory chapter on the appearance and the reality of the Church, Küng begins with a careful appraisal of the relationship between the Church and Jesus' own preaching of the kingdom. He then sketches the nature of the Church according to the principal biblical images: people of God, creation of the Spirit, and Body of Christ. Next, Küng discusses the four traditional properties of the Church (he calls them "dimensions"): one, catholic, holy, and apostolic. In an exceptionally rewarding final chapter, he treats of the universal priesthood of Christians and of special ministries in the Church.

As readers of his other books would suspect, Küng makes no effort to conceal difficulties and scandals. In fascinating historical notes he reports the full horror of the persecutions of the Jews, the Inquisition, and other ugly memories. Opposed to any false idealization, he insists that the Church is sinful as well as holy (*simut iusta et peccatrix*). Concretely considered, the nature of the Church is inseparable from an "unnature" that accompanies it through history as the shadow accompanies a man. Evil human instincts find an outlet in the Church, perverting but not totally destroying its true nature.

Throughout this book Küng makes skillful use of polar oppositions. The Church, he says, lives through constant tension between the indicative and the imperative, the present and the future, the word and the spirit, the institutional and the charismatic. Without suppressing either pole, Küng clearly favors freedom rather than law, the prophetic rather than the sacerdotal.

Especially in his last chapter, Küng comes up with numerous surprising facts and draws, or at least suggests, some astonishing conclusions. Thus he asserts that the churches of Antioch, Corinth, and Rome got along quite well in the first generation without bishops, presbyters, or other public functionaries, and that Paul himself knew nothing of the practice of ordination. While Küng is willing to acknowledge a certain "ministerial primacy" in the Roman See, he apparently denies its direct descent, through apostolic succession, from the Petrine ministry. He intimates, moreover, that valid orders are not strictly necessary for administering the sacraments of the Eucharist and penance. The distinction between presbyterate and episcopate, in his estimation, is merely disciplinary, not dogmatic—a position he defends with an appeal to the final text of the *Constitution on the Church* (*Lumen Gentium*)!

If some of these positions are evidently contrary to the canons of Trent on the sacraments, Küng has a ready reply. These canons, he maintains, were based on such abysmal ignorance of the facts of history that they cannot be regarded as binding definitions. In fact, he leaves unsettled the question whether the charism of infallibility ever extends to the guaranteeing of individual utterances of the magisterium. When opinions such as these are espoused by so eminent a scholar, in a book published with full ecclesiastical approval, it is clearly time for the educated reading public to take notice.

No doubt some of the thorny points raised by Küng will eventually bring about revisions of positions previously thought to be unassailable. But one should not panic prematurely. Küng has a way of citing obscure texts as though they were decisive testimonies, and of asking genuinely difficult questions as if they could admit of only one answer. He is no doubt more interested in stirring up discussion than in settling matters apodictically.

A reformer at heart, Küng neglects no opportunity to chide ecclesiastical officials for their pride, hypocrisy, and pomp. Most Americans will sympathize with Küng's leanings toward simplicity and democracy. But at times the preacher in him obtrudes; he nags too much.

This book might have been richer and more positive had fuller use been made of the documents of Vatican II. I missed in these pages any reference to the magnificent idea (fundamental to the council) of the Church as sacrament of the world's salvation. Nor has Küng capitalized on the implications of the collegiality of bishops and of priests. His treatment of the Church's mission is too sparse. While firmly asserting that the Church must preach the Gospel, Küng has little to say about how preaching contributes to the salvation of mankind. Since he insists that men can be saved without hearing the Gospel, one would expect him to discuss whether the salvation of non-Christians is in any sense ecclesial. On points such as this Rahner and Schillebeeckx have offered more helpful suggestions than I have found in these pages.

In spite of certain shortcomings, *The Church* is a very important and valuable book. It brings together an almost unbelievable amount of exegetical and historical information, and effectively shows its bearing on the renewal of the Church today. Like Karl Barth, by whom he has been deeply influenced, Küng is profoundly committed to the renewal of the Church according to the Gospel. This authentic evangelical motif should make his book as appealing to Protestants as it is necessary for Catholics.

33. REVIEW OF
INFALLIBLE? AN INQUIRY
by Hans Küng

April 24, 1971

At the various symposia held last year to mark the centenary of Vatican I, the mood was one of sober self-scrutiny rather than triumphant celebration. In our time the definition of papal infallibility arouses particular misgivings. In an era of ecumenism this dogma seems to erect unnecessary barriers between Catholics and other Christians: in an era of rapid change it seems to tie the Church unnecessarily to the past. Besides, papal infallibility has hardly proved fruitful in terms of concrete results. Only on one occasion in the past hundred years has the pope clearly claimed to speak infallibly, and that was in proclaiming the most notoriously problematical of dogmas—the assumption of the Blessed Virgin. Vatican II, which issued some eight hundred pages of official documents, deliberately refrained from ever invoking its infallible teaching authority. Unquestionably, then, the dogma of infallibility is now ripe for reexamination.

In recent years, the majority of thoughtful Catholic theologians have managed to live with the dogma by restricting infallibility within very narrow limits and by allowing the widest possible latitude for reinterpretation. Hans Küng, in the present volume, takes a very different tack. He repudiates the very ideas of an infallible teaching office and of infallible dogmas. Casting himself in the role of a theological pamphleteer, he attacks the alleged biblical and historical basis of papal infallibility. He writes with bitter antipathy toward Roman theology, the Roman curia, and Pope Paul. In this review I shall try to prescind from the emotional overtones and address myself to the theological issues raised in the more speculative sections of the book.

It is important to clarify at the outset what notion of infallibility Küng is rejecting. The term "infallibility," as he understands it, means not simple truth, but rather propositional truth antecedently guaranteed by virtue of the office from which it emanates. Küng is convinced that the modern Church, especially at Vatican I, adopted an atomistic and Cartesian view of propositional truth and made things worse by compounding this with a highly juridical understanding of the teaching office. Thus infallibility, as Küng presents it, practically amounts to a blank check in the hands of the teaching authorities. He asserts, for example, that infallibility is not restricted to the teaching of revealed truth, nor even to truths evidently and inseparably connected with revelation, but extends to all truths connected with revelation, including the canonizations of saints and so-called dogmatic facts. Few infallibilists today would go so far. At one point Küng even writes: "The teachings of Vatican I really amounts to this, if he wants, the pope can do everything, even without the Church" (105). This interpretation of infallibility gives Küng a wide target to shoot at, but in the end it weakens his case, for moderate infallibilists will say that Küng has not hit the only target they would be interested in defending.

Küng wants to combine his rejection of infallibility with an acceptance of the Church's perpetuity in the truth. He asserts repeatedly that the Church as "the pillar and the ground of truth" (1 Tm 3:15), is protected by the Holy Spirit from ever succumbing to error. But he declares that the Church's "fundamental remaining in the truth" is compatible with "all ever possible errors" (175). Not being God, the Church "can constantly and in a very human way deceive herself and others on every plane and in all spheres" (185). The greatest weakness of the book is perhaps Küng's failure to illuminate these paradoxical statements. While he hints at various biblical and philosophical ideas of truth that might be helpful, his preferred solution is apparently to say that no matter how grievously the Church errs, it still abides in the truth because God intends to bring it back to the truth.

I do not find that this solution does justice to the abiding presence of truth which the Church, with good scriptural warrant, has always understood to be its gift. This claim to abide in the truth does not necessarily imply the static, propositional, atomistic, and juridical conceptions of truth and infallibility against which Küng is in revolt. To the extent that Vatican I, making use of the thought categories of nineteenth-century Catholicism, may have leaned toward a "blank check" theory of infallibility, its decrees demand further refinement and explanation. As theologians reflect further on the meaning of truth in the sphere of revelation, it may prove desirable to relinquish the term "infallibility," which has become so heavily burdened with unfortunate misunderstandings.

Küng's rather "extrinsicist" doctrine of permanence in the truth (seen as an aspect of God's saving will rather than as anything really present in the pilgrim Church) stands in some tension with his respect for dogma, which he defines as "a definitive and obligatory formula for the believing community" (147). Küng accepts without reservation the creeds and dogmatic decisions of the ancient councils. He holds, further, that the modern Church may occasionally find itself in a *status confessionis*, in which it is compelled to utter a clear yes or no. When the Church takes a definite stand in such situations, according to Küng, its statements may be truly binding.

Going somewhat beyond Küng, I should like to suggest that the Church, by reason of the promised assistance of the Holy Spirit, has a guaranteed power to adhere to God's truth in the face of heretical denials. Its infallibility is primarily negative: an assurance that it will not forsake the Gospel. But the Church may on occasion receive the grace to speak positively, giving authoritative expression to what the Gospel means in a particular situation. Such dogmatic declarations are attributable to the promised assistance of the Spirit of truth. When speaking in response to a threat to its existence as the herald of the Gospel, the Church can speak, in a certain sense, infallibly.

Apart from his rejection of the idea that dogmas are infallible, I can agree with much of what Küng says about dogma. I agree that dogma must pertain to the heart of revelation and not to interesting peripheral truths, no matter how many bishops and theologians assent to these. Every alleged dogmatic definition must therefore be examined for its content; the mere juridical formalities are not enough to guarantee its authenticity. Further, Küng is correct in saying that dogma must sometimes be reinterpreted. Since it comes out of some particular sociocultural situation, it cannot be imposed on persons in other situations without regard to the original context.

Is Küng's sweeping rejection of infallibility compatible with the teaching of Vatican I and II? He makes an effort to prove that it is, but I am not wholly persuaded. Admittedly, neither of these councils gave very full attention to the notion of infallibility, but their solemn declarations on the teaching power of popes and bishops would be almost meaningless if one were to reject infallibility. Since Küng apparently does not feel bound by the conciliar teaching, it is not clear why he goes to such pains to reconcile his positions with the true meaning of Vatican I. He here indulges the same kind of hermeneutical sleight of hand that he somewhat unfairly attributes to theologians such as Rahner.

Although concerned to reconcile his views with the two Vatican councils, Küng feels free to dismiss, rather offhandedly, the teaching of Paul VI on contraception. This might be understandable if Küng held, as many theologians do, that *Humanae Vitae* represents reformable doctrine. Küng, however, holds that even before Paul VI spoke the Church had taken a definitive position. The conservative minority of the papal commission, according to Küng, were correct in their judgment that "artificial" contraception was ruled out by the constant and universal teaching of popes, bishops, and all the theological schools in the Church for several centuries. Thus, in Küng's estimation, the teaching of *Humanae Vitae* and the doctrine of infallibility stand or fall together. This is contrary to the opinion that I would accept, namely, that in view of the limits of infallibility and the historically conditioned character of all human apprehensions of the truth, the possibility of doctrinal change cannot be ruled out. In repudiating what he understands to be the universal and definitive teaching of the Church, Küng exhibits how little content he gives to his affirmation that the Church is indefectible in the truth.

In summary, Küng is to be praised for his courage and persistence in raising serious questions about a doctrine that needs to be reexamined. As a result of his book, it will be much harder to defend the rationalistic and juridical views of infallibility that have in the past been prevalent in all but the most sophisticated Catholic theology. By helping to banish such naive misconceptions, Küng's work serves to facilitate a rapprochement among Roman Catholics, Protestants, and Orthodox. But Küng is not fully successful in establishing his own theories. His handling of the biblical and historical data, though erudite, is not fully balanced. He fails too to give an adequate explanation of the promised perpetuity of the Church in the truth. The abiding assistance of the Holy Spirit, I believe, will always preserve the Church from betraying the Gospel. Unlike Küng, therefore, I find the concept of infallibility both credible and meaningful.

34. REVIEW OF
THE REMAKING OF THE
CHURCH: AN AGENDA
FOR REFORM
by Richard P. McBrien

November 10, 1973

F r. Richard McBrien has already established himself as a
progressive theologian with a remarkable gift for popular-
izing some of the best achievements of contemporary ecclesiology. These qualities he shows again in the present work. He
gives a readable summary of the ecclesiological developments
in Vatican II, the more radical reform movements that followed
the council and the resulting polarization in the Church. Then in
the last half of his book he outlines and defends a thirteen-point
"agenda for reform." This reform program is largely but not
exclusively drawn from two main sources: the symposia held
since 1966 by the Canon Law Society of America and the various
bilateral ecumenical consultations that have been meeting in this
country since 1965. A major purpose of the book is to increase
the pressure for constructive ecclesiastical change.

The sketches of preconciliar, conciliar, and postconciliar ecclesiology in the early chapters of the book are drawn with a very
wide brush. While illuminating up to a point, they group together
ideas that hardly fit into a unified picture. For instance, postconciliar ecclesiology (or "Theory C," as it is here called) is made to
include such diverse phenomena as the charismatic renewal, the

dynamics of personal growth, the international bishops' synods, priests' councils, and the protests against *Humanae Vitae*. Underlying the whole comparison of the three synods, priests' councils, and the three ecclesiologies is the bothersome implication that the most recent is presumably the best. I should prefer to say that some preconciliar theology was good, and some postconciliar theology is a disaster.

In his account of the polarization in the Church, McBrien lays the blame on the bishops for failing to give a sufficient theoretical justification for the reforms of Vatican II. While the bishops must bear some responsibility, it would seem that the whole community, including particularly the priests and theologians, must share the guilt. Furthermore, McBrien neglects to indicate the degree to which avant-garde Catholics, purporting to "go beyond" the council, contributed to the polarization. Some of the progressives, after proposing irresponsible innovations, added to the confusion by abandoning the priesthood, the religious life, or even the Church itself.

McBrien's "agenda for reform" comes down to a restructuring of the Church along the lines of contemporary participatory democracy. Senator Mike Gravel's *Citizen Power: A People's Platform* provides one model. In this restructured Church all members are to have clear and constitutionally protected rights. Bishops and popes are to be elected by representative bodies, and to have a limited term of office. Priests are to be free to work in the diocese of their choice, to marry if they so choose and to resign from the ministry at will. Women are to be eligible for priestly and episcopal ordination. Dioceses are to be governed primarily by pastoral councils possessing a deliberative vote. The universal concerns of the Church are to be decided not by the pope alone but by the pope in concert with the Synod of Bishops. Throughout the Church there is to be subsidiarity, decentralization, and separation of powers. In the ecumenical sphere, the Catholic Church is to recognize the ministries and sacraments of Protestant as well as Orthodox Christians, and to permit intercommunion. The

Catholic Church is to join the World Council of Churches and the National Council of Churches, steps "already long overdue."

These suggested reforms are not original with McBrien. In many cases he is paraphrasing almost verbatim the reports and studies referred to in his footnotes. But he brings together into a single program many suggestions that have heretofore been made only in a narrower context, and in this way gives greater scope and coherence to the movement for structural reform.

In general, I am sympathetic with the directions of this book. Many of the reforms McBrien proposes would, in my opinion, help to revitalize the Church by feeding into the ecclesiastical sphere the climate of freedom and participation characteristic of the American secular heritage.

Granted the brevity of this book, it is almost inevitable that there should be lacunae. In his introduction McBrien remarks that his analysis is concerned "not only with the mystery of the Church, but with its remaking." Some would say he is concerned too little with the mystery for his ideas on the remaking to be fully convincing. He gives very little attention to the Church as a place of prayer, worship, and religious experience, and this omission limits the value of his discussion of topics such as conciliarity, ordained ministry, and ecumenism.

Would the parliamentary, democratic Church here envisaged be more Christian and more prophetic than the Church we now have? Probably not, unless the members could be rendered more loyal to Christ and more open to the Spirit. And what would happen to the Church's power to impart a sense of communion with God? I should like some assurance that in McBrien's streamlined Church, with its elections and "public adversary system," there would be room for the folly of the Cross and for that "oddness, transcendence and deviancy" that Harvey Cox so eloquently celebrates in *The Seduction of the Spirit*.

35. REVIEW OF
ON BEING A CHRISTIAN
by Hans Küng

November 20, 1976

Intended as a "relevant and opportune introduction to being a Christian," this work, according to the author's introduction, is in effect a "small 'Summa' of the Christian faith." It aims to clarify what is specific to Christianity and what is common to the separated Christian churches, rather than what is proper to any single Christian tradition. It aims also to rediscover the ancient Gospel as it was originally meant "before it was covered with the dust and debris of two thousand years."

To a great extent, this book includes, in somewhat different order, the materials that one would expect to find in a survey of Christian doctrine: the existence and attributes of God, the Trinity, Christology, soteriology, ecclesiology, and eschatology. The emphasis, however, is more apologetical than dogmatic. Using a historicocritical approach to the New Testament, Hans Küng seeks to set forth the essentials of Christianity and to show reasons why this faith might be chosen today in preference to the various secular humanisms and the non-Christian religions. In the final section, Küng touches on several basic problems of moral theology: the existence of moral absolutes, the question of what is specific to Christian ethics, and the role of the Church in sociopolitical questions.

In view of the rich fare that is offered, it may not be appropriate to speak of lacunae in this work. But a comparison with other dogmatic manuals and "catechisms" would reveal the absence of any thematic discussion of grace (in the sense of actual and sanctifying grace, rather than God's merciful pardon) and of sacraments (aside from some rather negative remarks on the Mass as a sacrifice). In a footnote at the end, Küng remarks that he had planned to write a section on prayer, meditation, and Christian worship but was impeded by other tasks.

The center of attention in this book is clearly Christology. About half the pages are taken up with the person, career, and theological interpretation of Jesus. In his treatment of these questions, Küng uses a modern historicocritical approach to the New Testament. For authentic testimony concerning Jesus, he relies chiefly on Mark's gospel, on the so-called Q passages common to Matthew and Luke, and on the early Pauline epistles. He makes little use of the fourth gospel and is sharply critical of the reliability of the infancy narratives and of Luke and Acts. Generally speaking, he depreciates what are thought to be the later New Testament writings. His evaluation and interpretation of the New Testament reflect the views of his Protestant Tubingen colleague, Ernst Käsemann, a New Testament scholar.

The obvious strength of this book consists in its fundamental theology. Küng gives a highly effective apologia for basic Christianity. The opening sections on the existence of God, on the other religions, and on modern humanism (especially the neo-Marxism of the Frankfurt school) are relatively strong. The high point of the book, in my estimation, is the central section on the life and teaching of Jesus. Küng splendidly illuminates the significance of Jesus' miracles, the originality of Jesus' doctrine of God, and the reasons why he came into conflict with the religious leadership of contemporary Judaism. His description of Jesus' final abandonment on the Cross is rhetorically powerful, and his account of the rise of the Easter faith is, in my judgment, both persuasive and inspiring. Küng makes it quite clear why the Christian cannot be content with psychological and mythical explanations of the Resurrection but will insist on the reality of Jesus' new life with God. Better than most other theologians of our day, Küng shows why the Christian exegete will not be satisfied with an analysis of the New Testament according to the canons of literary criticism. The primary focus of interest for the believer, as Küng contends, is not the text and its literary quality but the reality itself—that is to say, the person depicted in the literary form, and the relevance of that personal reality for the individual and society today.

Likewise valuable in this book, in my opinion, are the concluding sections on ethics. Küng deals capably, so far as I am competent to judge, with the complex question of reconciling the absolute character of moral obligations with the merely relative validity of particular norms. In discussing what, if anything, is specific to Christian ethics, he points out that the distinguishing feature is not to be found in particular precepts or prohibitions but in an attitude of faith that subordinates all individual precepts and prohibitions to Jesus Christ and his rule. In his treatment of political theology and liberation theology, Küng successfully safeguards the sociopolitical relevance of the Christian message while prudently warning against an excessive identification between Christianity and any particular political or social doctrine. He makes it abundantly clear why the Christian cannot find the total meaning of faith in the transformation of the sociopolitical order.

The most controversial and, in my view, the least satisfactory sections of this book are those dealing with dogmatic questions. Küng's methodology almost guarantees that he will come into conflict with the dogmatic tradition both of Roman Catholicism and of other Christian churches. As mentioned above, he adopts a strictly historicocritical approach to the New Testament. On the basis of his exegetical options, he attaches small value to many of the passages that have been most used for dogmatic purposes— the fourth gospel, the Pauline captivity epistles, and, of course, the infancy narratives—all of which are highly important for the traditional understanding of the Trinity, the Incarnation, Mariology, and ecclesiology. Furthermore, adhering to his own previous rejection of infallibility, Küng takes a sharply critical attitude toward all Church councils, not excluding Nicaea and Chalcedon. He is particularly hostile to the Council of Ephesus and to Cyril of Alexandria, the dominant voice at that council. Church councils subsequent to the first five centuries hardly come up for mention except where Küng wishes to differ from them.

In a qualified way, Küng distances himself from traditional Christology, with its doctrines of the Incarnation and of the divinity of Christ. Conceding that Jesus is the full revelation of God in the flesh—and in that sense, the Incarnate Word—Küng in effect affirms Christ's divinity in functional terms. He is unwilling, however, to translate this affirmation into ontological or essential terms, and therefore stops short of saying that Jesus is truly God. He sides with Harnack and others who have accused the Greek Fathers of unduly hellenizing the Gospel. Küng might be able to defend this stand as biblical, but in my view it is inadequate for any dogmatic theology written since the fourth century. Once certain questions have been asked, and have come into common currency, one cannot speak as though they had not. The ontological implications of Jesus' "functional" identity with God must be discussed. If Jesus is in a singular way God's revelation in the flesh, there must be something special about Jesus that makes him, rather than anyone else, such a revelation.

Although Küng finds biblical justification for regarding Mary as "the example and model of Christian faith," he opposes many of the Marian developments of the dogmatic tradition. Contrary to the Council of Ephesus, he asserts that Mary is not Mother of God. Küng's position on this point is of course consistent with his interpretation of the Incarnation, but he does not seem to acknowledge that if Jesus, in his divine nature, is God, then he who is God does in fact have a human mother. In that sense, Mary is Mother of God.

Küng's discussion of the other Marian doctrines is rather polemical. I do not find that his treatment of the virginal conception of Jesus and of Mary's perpetual virginity does full justice to the complexity of the biblical evidence, let alone the tradition of the ancient Church.

The treatment of the Church in this work suffers by comparison with some of Küng's own previous writings. As an integral part of his text, he reproduces verbatim the collective manifesto "Against Discouragement in the Church," published in 1972. (The English translation refers to the *National Catholic Review* where the *Reporter* is evidently intended.) Küng incorporates also, without change, his own article "Why I Am Staying in the Church." These inserts do not fit very harmoniously into the present volume, which is presumably addressed as much to Protestants as to Catholics. As in his book *Why Priests?* Küng advocates once again in this volume a Church dominated by the ideals of "liberty, equality and fraternity"—a Church with ministry but without office, with pastors but without priests. On these points, Küng does not here advance the discussion beyond where he left it in his previous books.

I have some difficulty with the notion of ecumenism that seems to underlie much of the present volume. Küng apparently holds that, for the sake of Christian unity, all churches must be prepared to renounce what is specific to their own traditions and to build anew from the New Testament as studied by a theologically neutral historicocritical approach. This program might appeal to some liberal Protestants, but it will not be attractive, in my opinion, to the majority of Protestants, to say nothing of Anglicans, Orthodox, and Roman Catholics. I would personally feel that it is more helpful to try to work positively with the various traditions, bringing them into dialogue with one another. In this dialogue, the Bible will play an important role, but the exegete will not necessarily have the last word.

To summarize, I might say that Küng's "small 'Summa'" is successful as apologetics, but somewhat less than successful as dogmatics. In his effort to present a meaningful, credible, and challenging statement of why one might wish to be a Christian in our time, Küng performs brilliantly. He writes with verve and eloquence, and conveys a mass of solid learning without ever becoming dull or obscure. I understand that many readers of the German edition have gained from these pages a fresh appreciation of the meaning of Jesus for their lives, and I have no doubt but that the translation—which seems to me both faithful and graceful—will extend the same benefits to many English-speaking readers.

My difficulties with certain of Küng's doctrinal positions are not peculiarly my own. They have already been voiced by other Catholic theologians in Europe. But let the prospective reader not be deterred. Küng has every right to a fair hearing. His positions are consistent, are forcefully argued, and merit serious consideration. Perhaps in the course of time, these positions will win an acknowledged right of existence within the Catholic community. If so, Küng himself will deserve a large share of the credit.

36. REVIEW OF CATHOLICISM

by Richard P. McBrien

June 14, 1980

Notwithstanding the spate of recent catechisms, Catholics have lacked any theological textbook that attempts to incorporate the dramatic developments since Vatican II. This formidable task is here undertaken in a work that will not soon be surpassed in scope and quality. The author, a distinguished ecclesiologist, with fifteen years of teaching in Boston, has just been named chairman of Notre Dame's theology department.

Part I of this work, on theological anthropology, deals with the human situation, human nature, grace, and original sin. Part II discusses revelation, religion, and the doctrine of God, including the Trinity. Part III treats of Christology; Part IV, of Church, ministry, and sacraments. Part V presents some elements of moral theology, spirituality, and eschatology. The book closes with a chapter on the distinctive traits of Catholicism (sacramentality, mediation, and communion).

Within these parts, Richard McBrien takes up selected questions, on each of which he surveys the biblical data, the history of the question, the official Church pronouncements, and modern theological views. In many cases he adds some theological reflections or criteria for Catholic thinking. At the end of each section he summarizes (perhaps unnecessarily) what he has already said and lists some suggested readings in English.

On controverted questions, especially in moral theology, McBrien tends to report the various positions and arguments without taking a definite position of his own. Given the purposes of the book, the author's reticence must be respected. He is presumably more interested in getting the reader to see the force of the arguments on either side than in advocating any one position. Even when the arguments on one side are notably stronger than on the other, McBrien seems intent on presenting both sides in a favorable light.

Although McBrien does not rely implicitly on any theory, author, or theological system, he leans toward Karl Rahner's positions on most central questions. But he takes pains to cite a wide spectrum of authors who are acknowledged as specialists on the question under examination. Without trying to construct a tight system with clear philosophical presuppositions, McBrien operates more on the basis of common sense and displays an openness to all views he deems consistent with a modern understanding of the Catholic faith.

Among the merits of this book I would call attention, first of all, to the clarity of thought and style. Simply and lucidly, McBrien highlights what is distinctive to various authors and schools. He shows wide familiarity with the history and sources, and gives well-chosen references to current literature.

Part IV, dealing with Church, ministry, sacraments, and Mariology, is particularly successful. On these questions McBrien is, as one might expect, in full control of his materials; yet he avoids idiosyncratic positions. In the sections on ministry and sacraments, he makes excellent use of the recent ecumenical dialogues. As background for the modern Marian dogmas (Immaculate Conception, assumption), he gives an instructive historical overview of Mariology.

Like any lengthy work, this book is stronger in some sections than in others. I would hope that in future editions McBrien might give a fuller discussion of theological method, with attention to philosophical hermeneutics and the problems of religious language, including analogy and doxology. The section on God, in my judgment, could advantageously contain a fuller discussion of the divine attributes, thus clarifying the specific characteristics of Christian theism. In the light of a fuller doctrine of God, the author might find it possible to achieve a more positive evaluation of petitionary prayer.

In speaking of future editions, I mean to make a serious proposal. Too rarely are American theological works revised to keep them abreast of the author's thinking and the state of the literature. This is too valuable a book to be allowed to go out of date. Excellent in its present form, it could be improved in subsequent editions. The publisher is to be congratulated for having produced at a relatively moderate price two handsome boxed volumes, with good printing, paper, and binding.

APPRECIATIONS

37. HENRI DE LUBAC

September 28, 1991

Together with Rahner, Lonergan, Murray, von Balthasar, Chenu, and Congar, Henri de Lubac stood among the giants of the great theological revival that culminated in Vatican II (1962–65). His death on September 4, 1991, leaves Yves Congar, O.P., ill and hospitalized, as the only surviving member of this brilliant *Pleiade*.

Born in 1896, de Lubac entered the Society of Jesus in 1913. After serving in the army and being severely wounded in World War I, he studied for the Jesuit priesthood under excellent masters. During his studies he gained an enthusiasm for Thomas Aquinas, interpreted along the lines suggested by Blondel, Rousselot, and Maréchal. Without any specialized training or doctoral degree, he was assigned to teach theology in the Catholic faculty at Lyons, where he taught, with some interruptions, from 1929 to 1961. There, and in his occasional courses at the neighboring Jesuit theologate at Fourviere (1935–40), de Lubac quickly began to forge new directions in fundamental theology and in comparative religion.

De Lubac's first book, *Catholicism* (1938), was intended to bring out the singular unitive power of Catholic Christianity and its capacity to transcend all human divisions. Developing his interest in the Fathers of the Church, he founded in 1940, with his friend Jean Danielou, S.J., a remarkable collection of patristic texts and translations, *Sources chretiénnes*, which by now includes more than three hundred volumes. During the Nazi occupation of France, he became coeditor of a series of *Cahiers du Témoignage chrétien*. In these papers and in his lectures, de Lubac strove particularly to exhibit the incompatibility between Christianity and the anti-Semitism that the Nazis were seeking to dissemi-nate among French Catholics. On several occasions his friends had to spirit him away into hiding to prevent him from being captured and executed by the Gestapo, as happened to his close friend and colleague, Yves de Montcheuil, S.J.

After the war, de Lubac developed his theology in several directions. In an important study of medieval ecclesiology, *Corpus mysticum* (completed in 1938 but not published until 1944), he demonstrated the inner bonds between the Church and the Eucharist. To his mind, the individualism of modern eucharistic piety was a step backward from the great tradition, which linked the Eucharist with the unity of the Body of Christ. Seeking to stem the spread of Marxian atheism, he wrote on the intellectual roots of French and German atheistic socialism. He also com-posed several shorter works on the knowability of God and the problems of belief.

De Lubac's most famous work, *Surnaturel* (1946), maintains that the debate between the Baianists and the scholastics in the seventeenth century rested on misinterpretations both of Augus-tine and of Thomas Aquinas. Both parties to the debate, it main-tains, were operating with philosophical and juridical categories foreign to ancient theology. Contemporary neoscholastics, espe-cially in southern France and Rome, taking offense at de Lubac's attack on their methodology and their doctrine, interceded with the Holy See for a condemnation. When Pius XII published the encyclical *Humani Generis* (1950), many believed that it contained a condemnation of de Lubac's position, but de Lubac was relieved to find that the only sentence in the encyclical referring to the supernatural reproduced exactly what he himself had said in an article published two years before.

Seeking to deflect accusations against the Society of Jesus in France, which was being accused of promoting a suppos-edly modernistic "new theology," the Jesuit general, John Baptist Janssens, removed de Lubac and several colleagues from their teaching positions and required them to submit their writings to a special process of censorship. These regulations did not affect de Lubac's work on Origen's interpretation of scripture, *Histoire et Esprit*, which came off the press in 1950, just as the storm was breaking. Because of the restrictions placed on his theological research, de Lubac in this period turned toward the study of non-Christian religions. He published three books on Buddhism, which interested him as an example of religion without God.

In 1953, during his "exile" in Paris, de Lubac published a popular work on the Church constructed out of talks given at days of recollection before the war. (He was embarrassed by the triumphal sound of the title given to the English translation, *The Splendor of the Church*, as well as by suspicions in some quarters that his expressions of love and fidelity toward the Church in this book were intended to atone for the offense given by his previous works.) Pained though he was by the widespread doubts about his own orthodoxy, de Lubac was even more distressed that some disaffected Catholics used his troubles as an occasion for mounting bitter attacks on the magisterium and the papacy.

The clouds over de Lubac began to dissipate in the late 1950s. In 1956 he was permitted to return to Lyons, where he began research for his major study of medieval exegesis, which was to appear in four large volumes between 1959 and 1964. In 1960 Jesuit superiors, fearing that the works of Teilhard de Chardin were about to be condemned by Roman authorities, asked de Lubac to write in defense of his old friend, who had died in 1955. Beginning in 1962, de Lubac published a series of theological works on Teilhard and edited several volumes of Teilhard's correspondence. Probably more than any other individual, de Lubac was responsible for warding off the impending condemnation.

In 1960 Pope John XXIII, who, as papal nuncio in France, had gained an admiration for de Lubac, appointed him a consultant for the preparatory phase of Vatican II. As a consultant, he found much to criticize in the schemas prepared by the neoscholastic Roman theologians. These schemas, which contained statements intended to condemn both him and Teilhard de Chardin, were rejected when the Council Fathers assembled. De Lubac continued to serve as an expert (*peritus*) at the council, making his influence felt on many documents such as the *Constitution on Divine Revelation* and the *Pastoral Constitution on the Church in the Modern World*. Some of his ideas are reflected also in the *Decree on the Church's Missionary Activity* and in the *Declaration on the Non-Christian Religions*.

Greatly esteemed by Pope Paul VI, de Lubac was one of the eleven council theologians chosen to concelebrate with him at the Eucharist preceding the solemn promulgation of the *Constitution on Revelation* in November 1965. (During the council, de Lubac established a close working relationship with Cardinal Karol Wojtyla, who as John Paul II, was to elevate him to the rank of cardinal in 1983.) For several years after 1965, de Lubac traveled widely to explain the achievements of the council. He visited the United States and Latin America, as well as many parts of Europe. He published an important commentary on the *Constitution on Revelation*, and in other writings sought to clarify the relationships between primacy and collegiality, and between the universal and the particular Church. Perceiving the advent of a new crisis of faith, he wrote *La foi chrétienne* and *L'Eglise dans la crise actuelle* (both 1969). His preoccupations with the present state of the Church, however, did not prevent him from continuing his studies in the history of theology, such as his work on Pico della Mirandola (1974) and on the spiritual posterity of Joachim of Fiore (2 volumes, 1979, 1981).

By his own admission, de Lubac was not a systematic thinker. He never tried to articulate any set of first principles on which to base his philosophical or theological findings. Many of his books are composed of historical studies loosely linked together. Although he made forays into many areas, he never composed a treatise on any of the standard theological disciplines. In his last work, an autobiographical reflection published in 1989, he chided himself for having failed to undertake the major work on Christology that he had once projected.

For all that, de Lubac's work possesses a remarkable inner coherence. As his friend and disciple Hans Urs von Balthasar pointed out, de Lubac's first book, Catholicism, is programmatic for his entire career. The various chapters are like limbs that would later grow in different directions from the same trunk. The title of this youthful work expresses the overarching intuition. To be Catholic, for de Lubac, is to exclude nothing; it is to be complete and comprehensive. He sees God's creative and redemptive plan as including all humanity and indeed the entire cosmos. For this reason the plan demands a unified center and a goal.

That center is the mystery of Christ, which will be complete and plainly visible at the end of time. The universal outreach of the Church rests on its inner plenitude as the Body of Christ. Catholicity is thus intensive as well as extensive. The Church, even though small, was already Catholic at Pentecost. Its task is to achieve, in fact, the universality that it has always had in principle. Embodying unity in diversity, Catholicism seeks to purify and elevate all that is good and human.

In the patristic and early medieval writers de Lubac found an authentic sense of Catholicism. He labored to retrieve for our day the insights of Irenaeus and Origen, Augustine and Anselm, Bernard and Bonaventure. He remained a devoted disciple of Thomas Aquinas, whom he preferred to contemplate in continuity with his predecessors rather than as interpreted by his successors.

In de Lubac's eyes, a serious failure occurred in early modern times, and indeed to some extent in the late middle ages. This was the breakdown of the Catholic whole into separate parts and supposedly autonomous disciplines. Exegesis became separated from dogmatic theology, dogmatic theology from moral, and moral from mystical. Worse yet, reason was separated from faith, with the disastrous result that faith came to be considered a matter of feeling rather than intelligence.

One step in this process of fragmentation, for de Lubac, was the erection of an order of "pure nature" in the scholasticism of the Counter-Reformation. The most controversial act of de Lubac's career may have been his attack on Cajetan and Suarez for their view that human nature could exist with a purely natural finality. For de Lubac, the paradox of a natural desire for the supernatural was built into the very concept of the human.

De Lubac was convinced that the newness of Christ was both a fulfillment and a gift. Somewhat as nature was a preparation for grace, while grace remained an unmerited gift, so the Old Testament foreshadowed the New, without however necessitating the Incarnation. In his exegesis, de Lubac sought to show how the New Testament gave the key to the right interpretation of the Old Testament, which it fulfilled in a surpassing manner.

De Lubac's exegesis has often been depicted as anticritical or precritical, but it was neither. It might with greater justice be called, in Michael Polanyi's terminology, postcritical. De Lubac practiced what Paul Ricoeur was to call a "second naiveté." After having studied the literal sense of scripture with the tools of modern scholarship, he returned to the symbolic depths of meaning with full awareness that these depths go beyond the literal. The "spiritual" meaning transcends, but does not negate, the "historical."

At the root of de Lubac's theology stands an epistemology that accepts paradox and mystery. Influenced by Newman and Blondel, Rousselot and Maréchal, he interpreted human knowing as an aspect of the dynamism of the human spirit in its limitless quest for being. Without this antecedent dynamism toward the transcendent, the mind could form no concepts and arguments. Concepts and arguments, however, arise at a second stage of human knowing and are never adequate to the understanding they attempt to articulate. In every affirmation we necessarily use concepts, but our meaning goes beyond them.

De Lubac was satisfied that Vatican II had overcome the narrowness of modern scholasticism, with its rationalistic tendencies. The council, he believed, had opened the way for a recovery of the true and ancient tradition in all its plenitude and variety. But Catholics in France, and indeed in many parts of the world, having imbibed too narrow a concept of tradition, took the demise of neoscholasticism as the collapse of tradition itself. In postconciliar Catholicism, de Lubac perceived a self-destructive tendency to separate the spirit of the council from its letter and to "go beyond" the council without having first assimilated its teaching. The turmoil of the postconciliar period seemed to de Lubac to emanate from a spirit of worldly contention quite opposed to the Gospel.

For his part, de Lubac had no desire to innovate. He considered that the fullness was already given in Christ and that the riches of scripture and tradition had only to be actualized for our own day. In a reflection on his own achievement, he wrote: "Without pretending to open up new avenues of thought, I have rather sought, without any archaism, to make known some of the great common sources of Catholic tradition. I wanted to make it loved and to show its ever-abiding fruitfulness. Any such task required a process of reading across the centuries rather than critical application at definite points. It excluded too privileged an attachment to any particular school, system or period" (*Mémoire sur l'occasion de mes écrits*).

Terms such as "liberal" and "conservative" are ill suited to describe theologians such as de Lubac. If such terminology must be used, one would have to say that he embraced both alternatives. He was liberal because he opposed any narrowing of the Catholic tradition, even at the hands of the disciples of St. Thomas. He sought to rehabilitate marginal thinkers, such as Origen, Pico della Mirandola, and Blondel, in whom he found kindred spirits animated by an adventurous Catholicity of the mind. He reached out to the atheist Proudhon and sought to build bridges to Amida Buddhism.

But in all of these ventures he remained staunchly committed to the Catholic tradition in its purity and plenitude. He humbly and gratefully accepted what the tradition had to offer and made it come alive through his eloquent prose and his keen sense of contemporary actualities. His eminent success in enkindling love for Christ and the Church in the hearts of his readers stemmed, no doubt, from his own devotion, humility, and selfless desire to serve. The suffering of his long years of adversity, including two world wars and decades of great tension in the Church, are still bearing fruit. In the last few years, as his earthly life drew to a close, his disciples and admirers became more numerous and influential. De Lubac's creative reappropriation of the ancient tradition has earned him a place of honor in a generation of theological giants.

38. YVES CONGAR

July 15, 1995

T he death of Yves Congar, O.P., on June 22, 1995, at the age of ninety-one, marks the end of an era. Born in the same year as Karl Rahner, Bernard J. E. Lonergan, and John Courtney Murray, he was the last of these great giants to die. With M. D. Chenu, Henri de Lubac, and Jean Daniélou, he contributed mightily to the theological renewal in France after World War II.

Vatican II could almost be called Congar's council. In his days as nuncio at Paris, John XXIII may have gotten from him the idea, fundamental to the council, that inner-Catholic renewal and ecumenism were intrinsically connected. As a theological adviser at the council, Congar made direct or indirect contributions to most of the major documents, which reflect his ideas on revelation, ecclesiology, priesthood, laity, missionary activity, and ecumenism.

From his youth Congar felt strongly called to the ecumenical apostolate. In 1929, on the eve of his priestly ordination, he made a retreat centered on the theme of Christian unity as expressed in Christ's high-priestly prayer (Jn 17). In 1937, on the basis of a series of sermons preached a year earlier, he published his *Chrétiens Désunis*, which in many ways reads like a commentary on Vatican II's *Decree on Ecumenism* produced twenty-five years later. It was the first volume of a new series, *Unam Sanctam*, which he was to edit.

Congar's scholarly labors were interrupted during the Second World War when he served in the army and spent five years as a prisoner of the Germans. Returning to Paris after the war, he resumed teaching at the Dominican scholasticate there and played a major part in various new initiatives, including the ill-fated worker-priest experiment.

Like several other major precursors of Vatican II, Congar fell under suspicion during the 1950s. He was suspended from teaching and at one point exiled from his native France. Some of his books were forced out of print and prevented from being reprinted or translated. Convinced that "the cross is the condition for every holy work," Congar took these setbacks without complaint. He was a deeply spiritual man, content to wait for the time to be ripe. Those who labor for the reform and renewal of the Church, he said, must cultivate the virtue of "active patience."

In 1952 Congar became a founding member of the Catholic Conference for Ecumenical Questions, directed by the future Cardinal Jan Willebrands. That organization collaborated informally with the World Council of Churches and later provided much of the leadership and the agenda of the Papal Secretariat for Promoting Christian Unity, established under Cardinal Augustin Bea in 1960.

Congar's ecumenical work took him into a profound study of the relations between scripture and tradition. His dynamic understanding of tradition, set forth in several substantial volumes, found its way into Vatican II's *Constitution on Divine Revelation*. Early in the 1950s he pioneered Catholic thinking on the role of the laity in the Church—a subject later taken up by Vatican II in its *Decree on the Apostolate of the Laity*. He demonstrated that the supposedly Protestant concept of the priesthood of all believers had authentic biblical and Catholic roots.

In ecclesiology Congar tried to overcome the excessive concentration on the papacy, the hierarchy, and jurisdiction that he regarded as characteristic of the second millennium. He cherished the writers of the early Church for their intense spirituality, their prayerful listening to the voice of the Lord, and their openness to conversion and reform. The Church, for Congar, was essentially communal and conciliar. Influenced by Russian Orthodox theologians, he sought to find an equivalent for their term "sobornost," and settled on "collegiality." His positions (and those of his friend, the Rev. Joseph Lécuyer) regarding the collegiality of bishops became official Catholic teaching at Vatican II.

After the council Congar suffered from a progressive paralysis that made him depend first on a cane, then on crutches, then on a wheelchair, and finally, in 1984, required his confinement to a hospital. But notwithstanding these ailments, he continued to attend conferences through the early 1980s and produced an avalanche of literature in the fields of his specialization. Through in-depth historical studies he helped to clarify the concept of the magisterium and the allowable limits of dissent in the Church. He also called attention to the importance of "reception" as a response to authoritative teaching.

Congar's last major work was a three-volume study on the Holy Spirit. Seeking to overcome the division between Eastern and Western Christianity, he drew extensively on the Eastern Fathers. While personally accepting the "Western" doctrine that the Holy Spirit proceeds from the Father and the Son (*Filioque*), he strove to find formulations that would make it possible for Orthodox and Catholics to speak in harmony on this controverted point.

Congar expressed himself so carefully that his critics were never able to convict him of error. With his mastery of the tradition, he was always able to find support for his positions from venerable sources. Many of his most creative ideas were presented in indirect discourse, through citations from Church Fathers and medieval theologians, including his beloved Thomas Aquinas. Although he disguised his own originality, knowledgeable readers were able to appreciate the creativity that enabled him to concoct new and contemporary syntheses out of fragments gathered from ancient and forgotten texts.

An incessant worker, Congar could be brusque in dealing with others, but he developed a broad circle of friends and colleagues of different nationalities and religious persuasions. He was humble and self-deprecating about his own achievements.

As a Dominican priest, he was scrupulously faithful in observing his religious duties.

Congar won the esteem of several popes. John XXIII personally designated him to be a member of the preparatory commission for Vatican II. Paul VI nearly named him a cardinal but was dissuaded from doing so because Congar had recently signed a statement critical of the Holy See. John Paul II, who had come to admire him at the council, raised him to the cardinalate in 1994. Congar welcomed this recognition, even though he was unable to travel to Rome for the consistory.

Yves Congar was not only a great scholar but a churchman deeply devoted to the renewal and unity of God's people. In his impact on official Catholic teaching and on interchurch relationships, he perhaps surpasses every other theologian of our century.

AN INTERVIEW

39. REASON, FAITH, AND THEOLOGY: AN INTERVIEW WITH JAMES MARTIN, S.J.

March 5, 2001

Widely regarded as the dean of American Catholic theologians, Avery Dulles, S.J., was created a cardinal by Pope John Paul II at a consistory in Rome on February 21 [2001]. He is the first US theologian to be named to the College of Cardinals, as well as the first American Jesuit to receive this honor. The son of former US secretary of state John Foster Dulles, Cardinal Dulles has been teaching theology since he completed his doctoral degree at the Pontifical Gregorian University in Rome in 1960. From 1960 to 1974, he taught at the Jesuit house of studies at Woodstock College in Maryland, and then began a career at the Catholic University of America, in Washington, D.C., which lasted until 1988. Since that year he has been on the faculty at Fordham University in New York, where he is today, at age eighty-two, the Laurence J. McGinley Professor of Religion and Society.

Avery Dulles is perhaps best known for *Models of the Church* (1974), his highly influential treatment of ecclesiology. But he is also the author of twenty other books and more than 650 articles, many of which have appeared in the pages of *America*. His career, by all accounts, has been nothing short of remarkable. In this interview, conducted on February 3, Cardinal Dulles discusses his early years as a Catholic, his initial experience of teaching theology, the role of the theologian in a secular culture, the current polarization in the American Church, the question of dissent, and the place of prayer in his own life.

In A Testimonial to Grace, *the story of your conversion, you described your early attraction to philosophy. How did God work to move you from an appreciation of philosophical texts to embracing Catholicism?*

The move toward philosophy was for me the presupposition of religious faith. I don't know that it always has to go that way, but that is the way it went with me.

The first stage was Aristotle convincing me that the mind was a faculty that penetrated reality, so that when one was thinking correctly one was entering more deeply into reality itself. He helped me see that our ideas are not merely subjective but that they reflect the structure of the world and the universe. The so-called metaphysical realism of Aristotle was a first stage for me, and it gave me a confidence in human reason.

The second stage was Plato, who basically said that there was a transcendent order of what is morally right and wrong and that one has an unconditional obligation to do that which is right, even when it seems to be against one's self-interest. That set me thinking about where that obligation comes from. It seemed to come from something higher than humanity. We don't impose it on ourselves. And no other human being can impose it on us or exempt us from it. So there is an absolute order to which we are subject. This seemed to imply an absolute Being—and a personal being to whom we are accountable. And this set me thinking that there is a God who is a law-giver and a judge, who knows everything that we do and who will punish or reward us duly. In this way I found a basis in natural theology.

Then after that I read the gospels, and it seemed to me that they taught all of this, and more. The revelation given in Jesus Christ was a reaffirmation of all these principles I had learned in Greek philosophy—but the gospels added the idea that God was loving and merciful and had redeemed us in Christ, offering us an opportunity to get back on board when we had slipped and fallen overboard. That's a very brief sketch of what I tried to lay out in greater detail in my *Testimonial to Grace*.

How did you move from those general Christian beliefs to Catholicism more specifically?

I studied quite a lot of history in connection with my work in early Renaissance studies, which was my special field. But since I had to do the patristic and medieval background for the Renaissance, I had to read something of the Greek Fathers and a good deal of Augustine and the medieval tradition, especially Bernard, Thomas Aquinas, and Dante. And, in particular, for my dissertation I worked on the Renaissance philosopher Pico della Mirandola, who had his roots deep in medieval scholasticism. So I got to know the medieval Church quite well and was strongly attracted to it, particularly Thomas Aquinas. Also I studied the Reformation and so learned about the Reformers: I read Luther, Calvin, and the decrees of the Council of Trent. I found my sympathies were always on the Catholic side and felt that was where I belonged.

Also, I ran into contemporary Catholicism through the books of writers such as Jacques Maritain and Etienne Gilson, both of whom enjoyed very high prestige at Harvard when I was studying there. My professors had great esteem for them, and I myself found them extremely helpful in applying Christian principles to the modern world in many spheres, from aesthetics all the way to politics and international affairs. I found them full of light.

Finally, I was living in Cambridge, Massachusetts, which at that time, and perhaps still today, is a very Catholic city. The Catholic Church had a hold on its people that no Protestant church seemed to have. The people were attending church services in huge numbers and going to confession, communion, benediction, and Holy Week services and things like that. And I was attracted in many ways to the liturgy too. So it was a combination of all those factors, without much personal contact with any individual Catholics—I didn't really have any close friends who were practicing Catholics. It was a kind of a solitary journey, and then I later discovered that others were making the same journey, though I did not realize it at the time.   .

How did your family respond to your conversion to Catholicism?

I thought that I had prepared them quite well, intimating what I was reading and working on. But it came as something of a shock to them when I wrote to them that I planned to become a Catholic. They said, "Well, come down, let's discuss this matter." So I did. I made a trip from Cambridge to New York and discussed it with my father. I think he saw that I had thought the thing through: that it was not just a rash, momentary infatuation, that it was something for which I had some solid reasons. So finally he said, "Well, you're an adult, you can make your own decisions. They're not the decisions we think are right, but you are entitled to follow your own judgment in these matters." And I said that for me it was a matter of conscience.

As a Jesuit scholastic, you taught philosophy at Fordham University. What drew you to consider a career in teaching theology?

Like most other things, I did it because I was asked to! When I was in my second or third year of theology studies at Woodstock College, I think it was Fr. Gustave Weigel who came to me and said, "Now don't respond immediately—you will have to think this over—but we of the Woodstock faculty are going to recommend you to the provincial to study theology and teach theology later, probably at Woodstock. But we know you're assigned to philosophy at the present. So think it over." I said, I don't have to think it over, I'd be delighted to go into theology—it's really my first interest anyway. So they did recommend that to the provincial, and the provincial accepted it. Then I knew I was going to be sent to theology studies after I finished my regular degree.

Perhaps the work you are best known for is your book Models of the Church. *If you were writing the book today, how might it be different?*

Having recently had a chance to look it over, I would pretty much reaffirm everything in the book. It may reflect slightly the late sixties and early seventies, when I did most of my work on that subject. There was a good deal of unsettlement in the Church after Vatican II, and we didn't know just how far the reforms were going to go and how much historical change there would be. So it reflects a kind of openness perhaps to more radical changes than in fact have occurred or that I think should occur. Aside from that, perhaps it reflects a little of the anti-institutionalism of that time—although not a really radical anti-institutionalism. In my chapter "The Church as Institution," I do emphasize that the Church is and must be an institution. It has an institutional structure that it needs to maintain. But I did insist that the institution is not primary, and I still would affirm that. The institution is for the sake of the spiritual life and for the sake of holiness, and is not an end in itself.

How would you characterize the role of the theologian in today's very secular society?

The theologian is always trying to see how the tradition of the Church can be adapted to speak to contemporary culture. But speaking to the culture does not necessarily mean embracing the dominant presumptions of the culture. These presumptions have to be scrutinized, accepting what is good and rejecting what is bad.

From my own knowledge of Church history, I would judge that the principal errors occurred when the Church has adapted too much to the culture, reflecting the prevailing values of the culture and tending to obscure the distinctiveness of the Gospel. So the task of the theologian is to be very critical, to use in some cases what St. Ignatius would call *agere contra*. Where one sees a tendency to move in a certain direction that is contrary to the Gospel, Ignatius would say, move in the opposite direction. Throughout my career I have tended to be critical of what I saw as the principal dangers of the day. Sometimes the danger was to be insufficiently open and to adhere too strongly to past traditions, forms, and ways of behaving. The opposite danger confronts us today in thinking that everything is up for grabs. We have to be careful to insist on what is permanently and universally true. That is what I have been trying to accent in my recent work.

Upon being named a cardinal, you stated that you felt that the honor was also one for American theology in general. What would you say characterizes a typically "American" theology?

It would be hard to summarize, but I think that American theology has done a number of excellent things. Certainly in the fields of positive historical scholarship, like biblical studies, America has made enormous contributions through the work of people like Joseph Fitzmyer and Raymond E. Brown. In systematic theology, we have generally not been as strong, but there have certainly been significant developments.

Some of the American contribution was at Vatican II. Maybe our chief contribution as a country was to put the influence of the bishops from the United States behind the *Declaration on Religious Freedom*. But we also made a very significant impact in ecumenism, through the work of people like Gustave Weigel. In fact, my two mentors, Gustave Weigel and John Courtney Murray, both of Woodstock, helped to get me interested in the areas of ecumenism and religious freedom. These were two of the areas where American theology has moved ahead. Catholic ecumenism got started first in Europe—especially in France, Germany, Belgium, and Holland. But we picked it up in the United States, and in some ways it moved more quickly ahead because there was less traditional hostility among the churches. We got along personally with people who were not of our own particular communion. We have very close friends across denominational barriers, and this has facilitated ecumenical agreements that have not come forth as readily in Europe.

Perhaps a third area, besides ecumenism and religious freedom, would be the work on the economy. Our own experience of the free-market system is rather different from the kind of capitalism that was denounced in some nineteenth-century documents. The so-called Manchester liberalism, for example, was accused of allowing everything to be dictated by desire for profits. What Michael Novak calls "the spirit of democratic capitalism" has to be taken quite seriously as an element in the development of the economy, as opposed to a kind of welfare state. In some of his documents, John Paul II has reflected that kind of understanding and perhaps was influenced somewhat by the relative success of the American economy.

In what area do you see Catholic theologians in this country most polarized?

The polarization primarily occurs regarding the degree of change that can take place in adaptation to the culture. The more conservative types insist more on the maintenance of the venerable traditions of the Church—those that go back centuries, or even millennia—as being something sacred and immutable. The American mentality, on the other hand, tends to favor the idea that we can change almost anything we want to change. Here you might say there is a question of the sacred and the secular. How many of the traditions are really sacred and inviolable? How many of the them depend upon revelation itself, divine law, divine revelation? And how many of the traditions are things that God has placed in our own hands to adapt as we see fit? The problem, which cuts across the divisions between dogmatic theology, moral theology, and liturgical theology, is the main source of polarization in the American Church today.

Do you see a way out of this polarization?

First of all, we have to listen to one another and sit down and talk together in a civil spirit. I regret the way in which some go off in a sectarian way within the Church and make their own little home in one wing or the other and become either liberal Catholic reformist types or truly adamant conservatives. Then they just tend to shoot across at one another from their trenches. This is not a healthy thing within the Church. We have to cultivate the spirit of unity among Catholics and to try to understand one another's point of view and learn from one another. This would be my hope.

Along those lines, what do you feel is the role of dissent in the Church today?

There is a role for dissent, but it's a marginal role and shouldn't be the first thing one thinks about.

When we hear the word "authority" today, it is all too easy to make "abuse" the first word that comes to our mind. We often think of authority generally as abusive, which is not true, at least not in a church where authority has particular graces and charisms given by God. It should be trusted, generally speaking. To be a Catholic is to trust in the leadership of the pope and bishops.

Now in individual cases, it may be that they say something that we find very hard to accept because of our own earnest convictions. Here we must rethink our own positions in the light of what authority has said and, if possible, try to see the reasons why authority has spoken as it did—the presumption being that they had good reasons to do it. However, it may be that with the best will in the world we cannot really convince ourselves that this is right. And if so, we are inevitably thrown into a position of dissent. But I think we must be modest about it and realize that our own opinion is not necessarily the last word. Maybe somebody is wiser than we are. And maybe the Church has a wisdom from which we have to learn. So we shouldn't constitute ourselves as a kind of alternate magisterium.

I also think it is not appropriate in the Church to organize politically against the pope, the bishops, or other authorities and to try to bring pressure to bear upon them by, for example, cutting off funds, taking out full-page ads in newspapers, or calling press conferences in order to propose an alternate opinion that is one's own—saying that this can safely be followed even though the magisterium teaches otherwise. One's approach should be more through pointing out to authorities reasons why one disagrees and perhaps sharing one's reasons with fellow theologians, but not making public statements or a public display of one's own dissenting decision as though one were condemning the Church authority.

You feel that public statements like these are counterproductive?

They're counterproductive, and also not compatible with Christian humility. I really do think that Christ has given the charge of the Church to pastors, and it makes it very difficult for them to lead the Church if they can say only what people agree with. They have to be able to teach, and that teaching authority has to be respected. And this is part of what it means to be a Christian and a Catholic, as far as I am concerned.

On a more personal note, how does your prayer influence your study of theology?

I think one has to pray about what one thinks as a theologian. It is interesting to me that to be a Doctor of the Church or a Father of the Church one has to have a kind of sanctity. Only saints are made Doctors and Fathers of the Church because they have a close existential affinity with the things of God. And that must be cultivated through an intense life of prayer. The *lex orandi* is considered to be a source for the *lex credendi*: the law of prayer establishes the law of belief, according to a famous saying of Prosper of Aquitaine. That goes to some extent for private prayer and certainly goes for the public prayer of the Church. So the theologian must participate in the prayer life of the Church and be a praying person himself or herself in order to think the thoughts of God, as we theologians try to do. A theologian who does not pray could hardly be a good theologian.

Finally, how do you think that being named a cardinal will change your life?

I really have to see what responsibilities are placed upon me. Considering my age, which is eighty-two, it seems likely that the appointment to the rank of cardinal is largely an honorary one, which recognizes that my achievement has been appreciated by the universal Church and by Rome in particular. It might perhaps give a little more authority to the writing I have done. But I don't know whether I will be particularly involved in new responsibilities, whether I will have to go to Rome for meetings. I guess it remains an open question at this point. I would like to continue to teach and lecture and write as I have in the past decades. So I might be left alone to continue in this kind of work, as some other cardinals who have been theologians have been allowed to do.

Avery Cardinal Dulles, S.J. (1918–2008), was a Jesuit priest who was appointed a cardinal by Pope John Paul II in 2001—the first American-born theologian who was not a bishop to receive the honor. At the time of his death, Dulles was the Laurence J. McGinley Professor of Religion and Society at Fordham University, where he served for twenty years.

Dulles was a veteran of the United States Navy. An internationally known author and lecturer, he served on the faculty of Woodstock College from 1960 to 1974 and at The Catholic University of America from 1974 to 1988. He had been a visiting professor at a number of colleges, universities, and seminaries throughout his career.

Dulles was the author of more than 750 articles and twenty-three books, including *Models of the Church* (1974), *Models of Revelation* (1983), *The Splendor of Faith: The Theological Vision of Pope John Paul II* (1999, revised in 2003), *Newman* (2002), and *Magisterium* (2007).

He served as president of the Catholic Theological Society of America and the American Theological Society. Dulles also served on the International Theological Commission and as a member of the United States Lutheran/Roman Catholic Dialogue.

Americamagazine.org
Facebook: America Magazine–The Jesuit Review
Twitter: @americamag
Instagram: @americamedia

James T. Keane is a senior editor at *America* magazine.

Rev. James Martin, S.J., is a Jesuit priest, author, and editor-at-large at *America* magazine.

AVE

AVE MARIA PRESS

Founded in 1865, Ave Maria Press,
a ministry of the Congregation of
Holy Cross, is a Catholic publishing
company that serves the spiritual and
formative needs of the Church and its
schools, institutions, and ministers;
Christian individuals and families; and
others seeking spiritual nourishment.

For a complete listing of titles from

Ave Maria Press

Sorin Books

Forest of Peace

Christian Classics

visit www.avemariapress.com

AVE MARIA PRESS
Notre Dame, IN
A Ministry of the United States Province of Holy Cross